ZOOMIES, SUBS AND ZEROES

ZOOMIES, SUBS AND ZEROES

BY

CHARLES A. LOCKWOOD

AND

HANS CHRISTIAN ADAMSON

Zoomies, Subs and Zeros by Charles A. Lockwood and Hans Christian Adamson. First published in 1956.

Annotated edition with footnotes and images published 2019 by Merlin Books.

Annotations copyright 2019 by Merlin Books. All rights reserved.

FIRST PRINTING, 2019.

ISBN: 9781095058077.

CONTENTS

1 – "Hot Irons in the Fire"..7
2 - The Lifeguard League Is Born............................12
3 - The Skate Wins Her Zoomie Star......................20
4 - Westward Ho with Spruance and Mitscher........32
5 - Harder Stages Surf Rescue................................36
6 - Tang Gets a Steel Umbrella...............................52
7 - Stingray Gives First 'Scope Ride'......................60
8 - Finback Also 'Scopes Zoomie'............................75
9 - Haddo and Mingo as Angels..............................84
10 - Sailfish Lays Ghost of Squalus.......................92
11 - Archerfish in Big League................................98
12 - Pomfret Braves Tokyo's Defenses..................103
13 - Chub Defies Attacking Zeros.........................116
14 - The Bullhead Finds a Way.............................125
15 - Gato's Zoomie Was Weighed and 134
16 - Scabbardfish Converts B-29ers.....................142
17 - POW's—Unwanted Guests............................154
18 - Tigrone, Trutta Beat 'Ole Debbil Sea'............162
19 - AAF Pays a Tribute..171
20 - Gabilan Target of U.S. Guns.........................181
21 - Whale Provides Curb Service.......................188
22 - RAF Fliers Take Sub Ride.............................200

23 - Aspro in Hirohito's front yard........................ 207
24 - A-bomb Changes War Plans........................... 223
25 - Lifeguard Earns Hearty Well Done!".............. 232

1 – "Hot Irons in the Fire"

"Down wheels; down flaps."

The Army B-24, packed to the limit with passengers from Australia, Guadalcanal, and New Caledonia, circled for a landing at Hickam Field, the Army Air Base just outside the gates of the U.S. Naval Station at Pearl Harbor.

I stood silently behind the pilots, thrilled anew by the incomparable beauty of Oahu with its blue-green hills in the distance and its vivid checkerboard of cane, pineapple, and taro fields. Dozens of ships lay motionless at the docks in Pearl Harbor. How peaceful it all looked in the clear air of that Sunday morning, February 14, 1943.

Just so peaceful, I thought, it must have looked that Sunday morning in December 1941, before Japanese bombers and torpedo planes rained death and destruction upon it.

I viewed the scene with conflicting emotions: pleasure at being back at the real headquarters of the Pacific war theater and with my own people after ten months down under; distress at leaving West Australia, thousands of miles closer to the fighting and under constant threat of invasion from the Malay Barrier. I felt almost as though I had deserted in the face of the enemy.

I had put thousands of man hours into the job of operating my Submarines Southwest Pacific against advancing enemy forces. Disappointments, progress, tragedy, and triumph had all played their parts, and the going had been tough, but I was loath to leave my hard-fighting submarines while enemy shipping still plied the waters of the East Indian and Philippine seas.

Dispatch orders from Cominch (Commander in Chief U.S. Fleet, Admiral Ernest J. King), directing me to take over the job of Commander Submarines Pacific, had left me no choice. My predecessor in that command, Rear Admiral R. H. "Bob" English, had been killed on January 21, 1943, with three members of his staff, in a tragic plane crash in the mountains of northern California while en route to a top-level conference of submarine builders and representatives of the Bureaus of the Navy Department.

The wheels of the big plane kissed the concrete, brakes screeched, and we taxied to the disembarkation area. The long two-day flight from Brisbane, Australia, had ended. It was good to feel solid ground once more beneath my feet and to have a respite from the constant roar of the plane's powerful engines.

As I arrived at the foot of the gangway, the ringing in my ears still made it difficult for me to hear the greetings of Captain John H. "Babe" Brown, all-American guard and hero of several pre-World War I football games, when beating the Army was one of the most serious problems with which the Navy had to contend.

As the senior submarine officer at Pearl Harbor, John had assumed temporary command upon the death of Bob English.

Accompanying him were the Submarine Force Chief of Staff, Captain John Griggs, and the Flag Lieutenant, J. A. "Sparky" Woodruff. Their grave faces and hushed voices reflected the sorrow and shock which the loss of three messmates and their Force Commander had inflicted. Bob English had fought in submarines in World War I and was admired and respected throughout the Service. The three staff members lost with him, Captain Robert H. Smith and Commanders John Crane and Reilly Coll, were old friends of mine and skilled specialists whom we could ill afford to lose.

I felt the weight of the duties I was about to assume as well as deep sorrow for the fine lads so suddenly taken from us.

"Boys," I said, looking from one to another of our little group, "Bob English's shoes will take a lot of filling and I shall need all of your help even to attempt the job... Let's get going."

I reported at once to Cincpac (the Commander-in-Chief Pacific Fleet), Admiral Chester W. Nimitz, in Aiea Naval Hospital, where he was recovering from an attack of malaria evidently contracted in a recent inspection trip to Guadalcanal and the South Pacific. I had never served with the Big Boss before, but I knew his reputation for running a "taut ship;" the type of ship wherein the captain tolerates no slackness, the type of ship most sailormen prefer.

You always know just where you stand and just what to expect with a taut skipper; the type known as a "popularity Jack" is too likely to be unpredictable in his favors and judgments. It required only one glance at the cut of Admiral Nimitz' jaw and the steel blue of his eyes to confirm what others had told me, but the geniality of his smile also told me of his sense of humor.

Here was the ideal leader—one who could lighten the gravity of a tense situation with a witticism; one who could temper justice with mercy and the wind to the shorn lamb. I have yet to find it necessary to revise the opinion I formed that morning.

I delivered a secret personal message to him from General MacArthur, gave him a brief rundown of the situation in Western Australia, and then retired to dig myself into my new job.

"Admiral," said John Brown, when he and the Chief of Staff had rejoined me in my new office, "we've got a hell of a lot of irons in the fire and some quick decisions to make. I've held off the top-level stuff until you could get here."

When Babe was being official, I was "Admiral" to him; otherwise I was "Charlie," a brother skipper who had grown up as he had, in subs, and shared the heritage of all early submariners: the struggle for better torpedoes, better engines, better boats.

Then followed twenty-four hours in which we hardly left my office. Quarts of hot coffee kept us awake and meals on trays came down from our mess.

The time passed all too quickly, for there were king-sized hot irons in the fire and too few asbestos gloves with which to handle them. Time was of the essence.

In spite of titanic efforts in the United States to repair and enlarge our battered fleet, submarines were still the only men-of-war which could carry the battle into enemy waters. Thus, on that small force rested the whole responsibility of stopping the flow of munitions and aircraft to the far-flung Japanese perimeter. On the submarines rested also the equally crushing burden of stopping the flow of oil and strategic materials from the Japanese Co-Prosperity Sphere into the factories and shipyards of the Empire.

That was Hot Iron Number One, and pulling it out of the fire required intestinal fortitude—guts—on the part of our submarine skippers and crews, plus foolproof, dependable torpedoes to do the execution.

The first item we had in abundance; in the second we were deplorably lacking.

The defects in our Mark XIV torpedoes were serious, but they were corrected in a few months and in a manner which reflected great credit upon the clever, determined youngsters who sweated out the answers.

The second hot iron concerned the development of Midway Islands into a full-scale base where submarines could be completely refitted at the end of their patrols, thus lopping 2,400 miles off the round trip to Empire home waters.

That problem we also solved with the approval of the Big Boss and the assistance of Admiral Ben Moreel's miracle-working Sea Bees [Construction Battalions, i.e. 'C.B.'s.]

The third hot iron involved operations which were still in the planning stage in my office and in the great, mud-colored, bomb-proof headquarters which flew Admiral Nimitz' flag and seethed with the activities of the members of Cincpac's joint Army, Navy, and Marine Staff. Every conceivable phase of naval warfare was represented therein by its paper-working brain-trusters. Operations, Logistics, Intelligence, Planning, Code Breaking—all were housed in close contact and all were working toward a single goal: the winning of World War II.

We did not know it then, but that Iron Number Three contained the germ from which grew our Lifeguard League—a submarine organization dedicated to saving Army, Navy, Marine, and Allied fliers shot down or otherwise forced down at sea. The lives of hundreds of American fighting men, our brothers of the air forces, were destined to be saved by the Lifeguard League.

Fleet Admiral Chester William Nimitz, Sr. pins the Navy Cross on Doris "Dorie" Miller at ceremony on board USS Enterprise, Pearl Harbor, May 27, 1942.

2 - The Lifeguard League Is Born

In February-March 1943, our naval surface forces in the Central Pacific were at a low ebb. Four carriers—Lexington, Yorktown, Wasp, and Hornet—had been lost to Japanese bombs and torpedoes, three in the South Pacific and one at Midway.

The bulk of our available battleships and carriers, under Admiral Halsey, supported Army and Marine forces in the Solomons' area. The Central Pacific Force, later to become the Fifth Fleet, consisted of several old battleships, two carriers, and a few cruisers and lighter craft. At that time our initial strategy in the reconquest of the Pacific was not even fairly well crystallized.

It had been decided that two roads were to be pushed through toward Tokyo—though just where their junction would be was still under discussion in the top-level councils. As it turned out, several unforeseen and important detours and bypasses, dictated by the turn of events, were to be thrown onto the trestle-boards of the master draftsmen.

Nevertheless, the Joint Chiefs of Staff had decreed that the construction gang led by General MacArthur, Admiral Halsey, and Admiral Kinkaid should hew its way up the New Guinea coast and through the Bismarck Barrier with Mindanao as its immediate objective.

The bridge builders and island hoppers commanded by Admiral Nimitz and General Holland Smith of the Marines were to push their freeway through the Marshall and Caroline Islands. Their westward goal might be Singapore and it might be Hong Kong.

The objectives contemplated by these early plans were radically altered to northward as our attack gained momentum and the weight of our offensive made itself felt upon the enemy. It was foreseen, in our Navy Planning Sections, that this latter line of advance—westward across the wide, tumbled spaces of the Pacific—would require plenty of air offensives to hunt down and destroy enemy aircraft and air bases which had sprung up like mushrooms upon the islands that dotted the chosen route.

Furthermore, our advancing fleet, while shepherding the amphibious forces, must be prepared at any moment to join battle with the Japanese fleets.

These fleets were built around battleship-carrier task forces and which could be expected to vigorously dispute our advance.

The problem of providing adequate air support in the far reaches of the Pacific, beyond the radius of the scant supply of land-based planes then available, could be solved only by pouring aircraft carriers and yet more aircraft carriers into the Pacific Theater.

The resultant flood of CV's [aircraft carriers], CVL's [light aircraft carriers], and CVE's [escort aircraft carriers, or "jeep" carriers] produced a naval air arm the like of which had never before been seen in the history of the world. In the ensuing operations, the splendid performance of these forces saved the lives of thousands of American fighting men who stormed the beaches.

Just how my new command, Task Force 7 (later changed to Task Force 17) Submarines Pacific Fleet, was to pioneer, assist, and cooperate with this westward and northward advance was my Hot Iron Number Three—and it was plenty hot.

A big game hunter once said to me, while patting his favorite rifle: "She has taken me into many places where I wished I hadn't gone."

I might say the same of that Iron Number Three—and with the same tone of pride—for supporting fleet, air, and amphibious operations introduced to us phases of submarine adaptability and flexibility as yet unexplored; phases fraught with extreme hazard of sudden extinction; phases in which the natural weapon of the submarine, its torpedo, was of no avail; and, last but not least, phases in which the greatest natural defense of the submarine, its ability to disappear beneath the surface, could not be resorted to.

Extracurricular jobs were not new to the submarine forces. Our primary mission was, of course, to patrol the waters of the Pacific Ocean and its subjoined seas—some eight million square miles of water—and to sink everything which floated and flew an enemy flag.

However, since the beginning of the war, submarines had demonstrated their versatility by doing, as Kipling might have said, "all sorts and all manner of things."

The Trout, under Commander Mike Fenno, ran medical supplies and antiaircraft ammunition into beleaguered Corregidor and brought out the currency reserve of the Philippines—twenty tons of bullion, coin, and securities—funds that never fell into enemy hands.

The Searaven, under the redoubtable Commander Hiram Cassedy, working out of Perth, West Australia, in early 1942 had rescued thirty-three Australian fliers from the enemy-held island of Timor and thereby won the hearts of our sturdy allies.

So dangerous had been this mission that I made my first recommendation of World War II for a personal award—a Navy Cross—for Ensign G. C. Cook, USNR, the Searaven's boat officer who made the actual landings and rescue.

A dozen or more other submarines—among them the Seawolf, Seadragon, Sorgo, Swordfish, Permit, Snapper, Spearfish, Porpoise, Nautilus, Grayback, Gudgeon, and Gato—had won their spurs and had hair-raising adventures in removing refugees from enemy-held territory all the way from the Philippines to the Solomons. Their passengers ranged from service personnel, civilians, nurses, missionaries, and nuns to the U.S. High Commissioner of the Philippines and President Manuel Quezon.

The submarines boasted a record of never having lost a passenger but evidently the creature comforts accorded were not of the highest order. At any rate, it was rumored that some passengers stated they would rather endure the hazards of dodging the enemy ashore than live in a depth-charge-battered sardine can.

Out of these experiences grew a fund of information which served us well when the need arose to land and retrieve coast watchers and liaison personnel, to supply the guerrillas fighting in the Philippines, and to reconnoiter and photograph islands marked for invasion.

By the summer of 1943, our rapidly increasing fleet of splendid aircraft carriers was beginning to crowd the none-too-spacious harbors available; Guadalcanal and the Solomons in the South Pacific had been secured and forces were being trained and massed for the mighty roll-up of Japanese-held islands which was to begin with bloody Tarawa and end with even bloodier Okinawa.

In order to keep the enemy guessing as to the direction from which these island-hopping attacks might be expected and at the same time give Task Force 58, the carrier force of the Fifth Fleet, valuable dress rehearsals and perfect their tactical dispositions, Rear Admiral Charles A. "Baldy" Pownall planned three elementary operations.

The first of these was to strike tiny Marcus Island, a mere dot in the Western Pacific some 1,000 miles southeast of Tokyo. The second was aimed at the Gilbert Islands of which Tarawa is one—some 1,700 miles to the southeast of Marcus. The third would be in the center of the line at Wake Island, scene of a heroic though hopeless Marine defense against overwhelming odds in December 1941.

One morning early in August 1943, my telephone at Sub Base Pearl Harbor rang. At the other end was Rear Admiral Pownall, two years my senior and a valued friend ever since service together in the Asiatic station in the early 1920's.

"Charlie," said he, "I've got a project which concerns you considerably and vitally concerns me. It may save a lot of lives. Could you drop in at my office sometime soon and look it over?"

"Charles," I replied, reaching for my battered seagoing hat, "I'm on my way."

A call on the squawk box brought my Force Operations Officer, Captain Richard G. "Dick" Voge. A man of many parts was Dick Voge, a strategist and tactician constantly poring over charts and devising more effective ways and means of destroying the enemy; a humorist and poet whose refreshing humor and poetic ability frequently produced masterpieces of rhymed cheer for our nightly communiques to the lads far out in enemy waters.

We found Admiral Pownall surrounded by a group of eager-faced aviators. His usual broad smile and florid, cheery face were somewhat sobered by the weight of his responsibilities in the impending mission. To him, as Task Group Commander of the big carriers Yorktown, Essex, and Independence, had fallen the honor of starting our long-awaited offensive to westward.

Marcus Island, some 2,500 miles from Pearl Harbor and less than 1,000 miles from Tokyo, was to be his first bombing target in a rehearsal intended to destroy enemy planes and air facilities as well as to develop techniques and procedures for future raids and invasions. Marcus might be caught with its planes down.

On the other hand, our zoomies—a name bestowed upon fliers by submariners—might catch a Tartar. Losses might be nil, or they might be considerable.

Admiral Pownall's proposal was that I should station surfaced submarines during the forthcoming strikes at points close to the target area where they might rescue aviators shot down or forced to ditch or hit the silk [parachute].

"If you can do that," explained Pownall, "it will give a much needed and comforting sense of security to my fighter and bomber crews and save a lot of boys from drowning or becoming shark bait."

I could readily see that such an operation was not going to be all beer and skittles for the submarines that might undertake it. Enemy shell fire from the beach had to be anticipated, as well as attacks by enemy fighters and bombers. The chance of picking up a few downed aviators had to be balanced against the risk of losing a highly valuable submarine with her entire crew.

On the other hand, an aviator's knowledge that, if shot down, he would still have a submarine in which to take refuge from sharks and strafing Jap planes would certainly increase his morale, add daring to his attacks, and multiply damage inflicted on enemy installations. Also, such assurance would combat the idea held by some aviators that they were expendable.

Dick Voge was strong for the project, which was all the additional support I needed.

Suicide attacks are not a part of American psychology. Everyone wants a chance for survival—even a chance as slim as that of a submarine being on hand to pick a very small human being out of a very large ocean. This is in line with the general feeling of the average individual to the effect that he is prepared enough, lucky enough, and smart enough to knock the other fellow out and still come home with a whole skin.

In this factor of safety—an important morale factor—it was up to us, the submarines, to provide that feeling of security, however tenuous—that chance for survival after all else seemed lost. No one else could do the job. Only a submarine could underwrite that kind of a last-chance insurance policy.

"It's a deal, Charles," I said after thinking over the pros and cons. "I'll explain the plan to Admiral Nimitz. I'm sure he will give it his blessing. This last chance is something your lads need and deserve, and I feel absolutely certain that we can provide it for you!"

Thus in 1943—in hardly more time than it takes to tell it here—the Lifeguard League was born. Over the next two years it was to pay dividends in low-level attacks of unequalled abandon and in devastation to enemy units and installations. Without that last-chance saving clause, those attacks would have lost much of their ferocity, flash, and fire.

Moreover, it paid extra dividends to the tune of 504 fliers of all branches of our armed services, including some Britishers and Australians, who were saved from death by thirst, by man-eating fish, or by murderous enemy planes, through the almost magical presence of lifesaving submarine crews.

The work of planning coordination between Lifeguard submarines and our fliers was begun immediately, and training was outlined to division and squadron commanders. Communication with and recognition by the planes in the air was the chief difficulty to be overcome. Our submarines had not yet been equipped with radio phones which were the only practicable communication media for planes in combat areas.

It appeared, therefore, that information would have to be passed from sub to plane, and vice versa, via the aircraft carriers. However, before long, our smart submarine radiomen discovered that the chatter between the planes, with which they were training, could be picked up on the ordinary commercial radios in the wardroom and in the crew's mess.

Thereafter, instructions regarding location of downed aviators were passed direct by the planes to the Lifeguards. Replies, if any were required, were sent back by Morse code via the carrier flagship.

The geographical points at which our Lifeguard submarines would be stationed were given secretly to the carriers before each strike. These points were laid down, whenever possible, on a definite bearing from and at a stated distance from an easily recognizable landmark. Lifeguards were each given a code name—a name well sprinkled with the letter "L" so as to trap the tongue of any enterprising Japanese aviator who tried to trick our submariners. As experience was gained, numerous clever procedures were added. Recognition signals between planes and submarines were always a serious problem. As a result of this difficulty, twenty-eight subs were bombed or strafed by "friendly" planes flown by "trigger-happy" zoomies.

The loss of the Dorado in the Caribbean Sea and of the Seawolf north of New Guinea were grim reminders that death was always close to a submarine at sea. The Dorado was undoubtedly lost [off Panama on 12 October 1943] with all hands because of a tragic failure of our recognition procedures. The Seawolf also was [most likely] undoubtedly lost in a similar manner [friendly fire] from after a combined attack by planes and a destroyer escort [USS Richard M. Rowell off Morotai on 3 October 1944].

Neither of these submarines was on Lifeguard duty at the time but, as we shall see, several Lifeguards were attacked while on station in locations of which our air and surface forces had been advised.

USS Dorado (SS-248) in construction, 1943.

3 - The Skate Wins Her Zoomie Star

The first two Lifeguarding missions were dry runs.

The Snook at Marcus on Sept. 1, 1943 did not have any fliers to pick up, nor did the Steelhead have any rescues to make when the Gilberts were hit on September 18-19. The next training strike was planned for October 6-7, 1943, when six big carriers, seven cruisers, and twenty-four destroyers under Rear Admiral A. E. Montgomery were to give Wake Island a working-over.

For the Lifeguard job on this occasion we selected the Skate. She was a brand-new submarine built at Mare Island and had just completed training and target practice for her first war patrol.

Her captain was Commander E. B. "Gene" McKinney of Eugene, Oregon. Her Executive, Lieutenant Commander Marion Frederic Ramirez de Arellano of Puerto Rico, was called Freddy for short and later was to become renowned as the Officer in Charge (dubbed "The Sheriff") of our Camp Dealey Recuperation Center in Guam.

They faced quite a problem in getting ready for her first war patrol a ship which had only twenty qualified submarine men among her seventy-two enlisted personnel. However, their determination and drive had accomplished wonders, and her last "readiness" inspection before leaving Pearl Harbor had proved that she was in an excellent state of training.

My attention had first been attracted to the Skate when she arrived from Mare Island with a stowaway on board. The culprit was a fifty-year-old World War I reserve quartermaster named Minton, whom the skipper had decided to leave behind as being too old for the rugged life of a submarine sailor.

The quartermaster thought otherwise, and with the aid of the quartermaster of the watch, whose name I shall withhold, Minton smuggled himself aboard the Skate during the early morning hours of her sailing day. He managed to remain hidden from the eyes of the ship's officers for three days. The cooks knew he was aboard and supplied him with rations. Finally, he surrendered and pleaded to be kept aboard.

The skipper, however, was adamant, but after a conference with me, he decided that no disciplinary action should be taken. As a matter of fact, I felt quite proud of the incident. Men don't stow away aboard unhappy ships, often called "hell ships," and few men ever stow away to go to war. We had one other such case and I'm proud of that, too.

Minton, with tears in his eyes, saw the Skate off from the dock and sadly went back to his job with the repair crews. He had my sympathy. I, too, had been refused permission to go on war patrols. I went back to a mountain of paperwork.

After a high-speed run to Midway Islands where she topped off her fuel tanks, the Skate headed for Wake Island. Her days and nights were filled with surprise dives and casualty drills.

Gene McKinney and Freddy de Arellano were fighting to cut off those extra seconds in diving time which they knew might spell the difference between life and death in this Lifeguard game—a game played on the surface under the shadow of Japanese Zeros, the fastest fighters the enemy possessed.

She arrived early on station and on October 4-5 reconnoitered the islands and made weather reports for the benefit of the fliers. She recorded sighting many buildings and installations and that the enemy appeared well dug in. Perhaps they believed Wake was going to be a permanent unit of the Asiatic Co-Prosperity Sphere. If so, the Japs got a rude awakening in the early morning of October 6 when hundreds of bombers and fighters from the six big carriers of Admiral Montgomery's task force hit them at 0448.

Twelve years later, Gunner's Mate William A. "Bill" Shelton in his comfortable home in Santa Clara, California, told me of the awe-inspiring and tragic happenings of that first morning, the Skate's baptism of fire and initiation into the Lifeguard League. Shelton had the morning watch (0400 to 0800) as the starboard lookout high on the periscope shears. Lieutenant Ralph Stroup was the Officer of the Deck and Lieutenant (jg) Willis E. Maxson III was the Junior OOD.

"The night was still black," said Shelton, "when the first heavy bombers swept over at high altitude. The flares they dropped looked like falling buckets of fire and the crruump, crruump, crruump of their bombs was terrific. All hell broke loose as the Japs opened up with AA and automatic weapons. Tracer bullets streaked through the night. As they came in, the strafing planes reminded me—with just a bit of what might have been called homesickness—of the summer night fire-falls from the canyon rim at Yosemite National Park.

"Fires broke out ashore and they were fine beacons for the bombers which came from our carriers in great swarms. Everybody in the Skate wanted to come on the bridge. That, of course, couldn't be allowed. But even with the Old Man's frequent refusal of the customary request: 'Permission to come on the bridge, sir?' as daylight broke, I could count nine or ten people on the bridge and cigarette deck.

By means of a throat mike, the Executive kept up a running description to the crew. As a newscaster, he was a wow. A small radio set had been brought to the conning tower and set on the same wavelength as the zoomies used for their radio phones. That way we could hear the flight and squadron commanders telling off targets or getting word to us of plane crashes.

"There were thrills and chills by the carload. For instance, just as one group of fighters approached us, we heard some zoomie holler: 'There's a sub. Let's get 'em!' But, thank God, his squadron leader came right back with a quick: 'Lay off—he's for us.'"

Terrific mushrooms of dust, debris, and smoke arose as explosions rocked the three tiny islets that compose the atoll. Despite this heavy pounding, enemy planes rose to meet the invaders. The Skate had a ringside seat for the show. With many of her crew hearing their first shots fired in earnest, Commander Gene McKinney had a hard time keeping the eyes of his lookouts on their assigned sectors.

Dogfights were everywhere and fighting commands babbled endlessly over the radio loudspeakers. Eight or ten planes, trailing long streamers of sooty black smoke, spun to their deaths in the sand or, with terrific geysers of water and flame, into the glassy sea. In less than half an hour, our carrier planes, it appeared, had command of the air and were forming up for more bombing runs.

Meanwhile the Skate, at flank speed of 19-20 knots, with spray flying from her onrushing bow, was heading for the nearest crash.

Suddenly came the excited shout of the after lookout, Seaman Van Horn: "Plane coming in on starboard quarter!"

Both the Captain and the Executive swung around. "It's one of ours!"

From head-on to almost three-quarter profile, the Jap Zero [Mitsubishi A6M] did closely resemble the Navy Hellcat [Grumman F6F Hellcat].

"No, sir," yelled the lookout, "it's got a meatball [the big red dot of Japan] on its side!"

"Lookouts below!" yelled the Skipper. "Clear the bridge! Take her down! Flood negative!" Commands to be echoed by hundreds of submarine skippers in the same dire situation across the wide Pacific in many months to come.

"The men tumbled down the hatch two or three at a time, trampling on each other's shoulders," related Shelton. "When I got into the conning tower, I grabbed the wheel from the relief man who had it and rang up 'Ahead, Frantic' (Ahead, Flank Speed). The Captain could have been proud of that dive. We made it to ninety feet faster than we had ever made it to periscope depth."

Periscope depth of our subs is classified information, but I may say it is considerably less than ninety feet.

Machine-guns spitting death from its wings, on came the Zero. Its bullets screamed off the hull as the Skate's bow slanted down and the waters rose over her deck. Even in this tight corner, Captain McKinney counted heads as the men dashed past him. He wanted no one left on deck. As the count reached eleven, the Skipper scrambled down the hatch himself and slammed the cover shut. Twelve men had been on the bridge. Twelve came down.

"Thank God!" murmured Gene. "Nobody hit!"

The tragic truth, however, was that young Willis E. Maxson, Lieutenant, Junior Grade and Junior Officer-of-the-Deck, had been hit. He managed to reach the control room. There he collapsed, his hands clutching his stomach, his face contorted with agony.

"I guess he got me, sir," he gasped, as McKinney knelt beside him. Then he lapsed into unconsciousness.

They took him into the wardroom. There swift hands of shipmates and Florshinger, the Pharmacist's Mate, found a bullet wound in the right side of Maxson's back between the shoulder and the hip.

A syrette of morphine was administered immediately and the wound dressed. The bullet had evidently lodged in the region of the stomach. Maxson had been hit by a ricochet while crouching behind the periscope shears as the plane bored in. Shelton was crouching right behind Lieutenant Maxson when he was hit.

"I heard the thud of the bullet," Shelton told me. "It's a hell of a horrible sound—a bullet hitting flesh—but you can't mistake what it is."

The crashing of three bombs, as she passed ninety feet, hastened the Skate's descent but did no great damage. The bathythermograph, a thermometer for recording automatically the sea water temperatures, was the only other casualty. Its outside element was hit by a bullet.

The wounding of Willis Maxson cast a pall of gloom over the ship. He was a splendid lad, an officer of great promise and a general favorite throughout the vessel. His wound obviously could be a serious one and, short of major surgery, no help could be envisioned.

This was the sort of tragedy to which a submarine is wide open when it operates on the surface in the presence of planes that can attack quicker than a sub can clear the bridge and dive.

As talk about the incident sped throughout the ship, dark doubts assailed even the most stout-hearted veterans. Was Lifeguarding too great a hazard? Would subs lose more lives than they saved? Certainly, this was a bad start. So ran the whispers from forward to after-battery aboard the Skate.

Hence it was with sober thoughts and aching hearts that McKinney and his men brought the Skate to the surface at 0617 to continue the search for downed aviators.

Previous conclusions that the carrier forces had obtained command of the air were proven premature. Twice during the day, the Skate was forced into quick dives by enemy Zeros. She found no downed aviators but while submerged heard numerous heavy explosions. Some of them were fairly close. They might have been depth bombs dropped by planes.

During the afternoon the cruisers and destroyers moved in and bombarded the island to silence its guns. Although they did a fine job, they failed to knock out all of the Japs' six- or eight-inch guns.

The night of October 6-7 passed quietly, but McKinney was sick with worry about Lieutenant Maxson. The latter was conscious most of the time. Although in great pain, he bore it bravely and in silence. The youngster repeatedly requested that the show go on and that the Skate carry out her mission without regard for him.

Naturally, the Captain sent a dispatch to me reporting Maxson's serious condition. I immediately asked Admiral Montgomery to send a destroyer to rendezvous with the Skate and remove the wounded officer. I further directed the Commanding Officer of the Skate to proceed at full speed to Midway at the end of the second day's strike if Maxson had not yet been transferred.

Reviewing those nightmarish days of strain and anxiety a decade later, Captain McKinney said: "I received instructions to rendezvous with a destroyer that night about twenty miles north of Wake.

"We were there at the prescribed time, but the destroyer just wasn't there or anywhere near the designated spot. After trying most of the night to affect a rendezvous without success, we returned to our new station ten miles southwest of Wake, in preparation for the second day of attacks, October 7."

The morning of the second strike dawned squally and overcast. At 0545 the Skate sighted several squadrons of friendly planes searching for Wake. Finally, at 0601, she was circled by four dive bombers who asked the direction and distance to the target. McKinney informed them and they headed in the proper direction. Shortly thereafter antiaircraft fire was heard from the direction of Wake, followed by the thunder of bombs.

This was to be a busy day for the Skate. By 0915, the visibility had cleared, and many planes could be seen depositing their loads of bombs on the unlucky defenders of Wake. Smoke and flames rose all over the island and when a bomb hit a gas tank or an ammunition dump, a mass of flame would shoot five hundred feet into the air. Many buildings remained standing, but most appeared to be gutted by fire.

In spite of this, ack-ack fire still persisted. When the Skate ventured in toward the beach on a rescue mission, she got the surprise of her life. It came in the form of three heavy shells fired from a range of six miles. They whistled over the bridge and slammed into the water uncomfortably close aboard. Needless to say, the submarine made record time in getting down but continued toward her objective.

After forty-five minutes of this, McKinney surfaced and trimmed his ship down until she was awash with practically nothing but the bow and the conning tower out of water. Two aviators could be seen in the sea ahead about two miles off the beach. They were being circled by planes that dropped flares to attract the Skate's attention.

By this time a hail of large- and small-caliber shells was falling around the submarine. Captain McKinney sent everyone on the bridge except himself below, and closed the lower CT (conning tower) hatch. At the same time, he called for a rescue party, and Ensign Francis Kay with two torpedomen, Baugh and Smith, went up the hatch.

"When Baugh and Smith got to the bridge," related Shelton, "the Skipper said he couldn't afford to lose two torpedomen. So, he sent Baugh below and I took his place. I went down on deck with Mr. Kay and torpedoman Arthur G. Smith. We wore life jackets and carried heaving lines and life rings. We waded through almost knee-deep water from the conning tower to the tip of the bow. The latter was just barely out of water.

"Despite the water, the skipper told us to lie flat and we sure did. The Japs were shooting at us with a six-inch gun on a disappearing carriage. And, believe me, when we looked down its muzzle, it looked like a sixteen-inch. As the Skate moved closer, the Japs opened up with everything they had on the beach, shooting at the sub and at the zoomies. We came so close to the shore that we could actually feel the heat from the burning buildings.

"And all this time, the dive bombers were strafing the Jap's six-inch gun. They finally knocked it out while we were picking up our first zoomie."

In discussing this incident later, Captain McKinney recalled that he had no trouble in getting the rescue party to hug the deck even though the seas were breaking over them.

"In fact," said Gene, "I wished I could be down there with them. "On that pass," he continued, "we picked up Lieutenant

Harold Kicker and Ensign Murray H. Tyler, who had been shot down close inshore.

Lieutenant Commander Charles L. Crommelin, a squadron leader from the Lexington, guided us into the spot where the pilots were in the water.

"I had ordered everyone else below and directed Freddy de Arellano, the Executive, to keep me informed of our position by periscope bearings so that I could devote my attention to maneuvering the ship to pick up the pilots. Tyler only had on a Mae West and was so exhausted that he couldn't hold on to the line that we passed him. Torpedoman Smith had to swim out with a couple of heaving lines knotted together and bring him aboard.

"It is of interest that—when Commander Crommelin was so badly wounded and shot up while leading an attack against the Japs sometime later—it was this same 'Tim' Tyler, whom he had helped to save, who flew wing to wing with him and guided him in for a safe carrier landing.

"Altogether, during the course of World War 2, Tyler was picked up three times by submarines, which he said was better than par for the course. After the war I understand he went back to teaching high school in Tyler, Texas."

Kicker and Tyler thus became the first two aviators rescued by the Lifeguard League.

Commander McKinney then went to full speed and headed for an aviator reported down off Peacock Point. A heavy gun straddled the Skate at five miles with three near misses which sent her below in a hurry while three more close ones whanged into the water above. This business of running targets for heavy artillery practice, McKinney felt, could lead to trouble, so he stayed down for forty-five minutes and then surfaced at 1330 to continue his search.

Luck was not with him, however. Twice more, before midnight, the Skate was forced to take cover from enemy planes.

One of these planes dropped two bombs which landed very close to the diving submarine and did considerable minor damage. The DCDI (depth charge direction indicator) was evidently frightened out of its wits and thereafter indicated bombs in all directions whenever the switch was turned on.

In spite of these unwelcome attentions, the Skate continued to search throughout the night, using her Aldis signal lamp to light the seas and hailing regularly into the darkness with her megaphone. Several times, red flares were believed to have been seen. But search in their reported direction was of no avail.

At 0200 of October 8, De Arellano and the Pharmacist's Mate came to the bridge and reported to the Captain that Lieutenant Maxson would die unless he got medical help immediately. Commander McKinney at once headed at full speed for a rendezvous that had been arranged with a doctor proceeding from Midway. Meanwhile, he continued to search the darkness for downed aviators.

The rendezvous was never reached. The dark angel came aboard the Skate shortly before dawn and peace came to Willis Edward Maxson, III.

Lieutenant Maxson was a native of Austin, Texas. He was the only submariner lost in this grim game of saving downed aviators in the entire war. The career thus ended had been brilliant. Young Maxson had been Regimental Commander at the Naval Academy, president of his class (1943), letterman in football and track, and president of the YMCA. He died as he had lived, with courage and with honor. He died trying to save others.

Sadly, the Skate headed back to the vicinity of Wake and with the dawn began searching in expanding rectangles. At noon, a lookout, Seaman Elijah H. Simms, sighted an object in the water about three miles away and the ship changed course toward it. However, as they neared it and definitely identified it as a life raft, a plane was sighted on the port beam coming in fast.

Chief Torpedoman Beck, the Chief of the Boat, and Gunner's Mate Shelton were out on the bow ready to pick up the downed zoomie, so that when Commander McKinney cleared the bridge and shouted to them to lay below, they hesitated. It looked as though they could never make it to the CT hatch in time.

Perhaps it might be better to dive overboard and join the aviator on his raft. But another shout from the skipper to "step on it—we're waiting for you" made up their minds and their speed down the deck as the opening main ballast vents blew spume high into the air about them would have done credit to a Jesse Owens.

"Dive! Dive! Flood negative! Take her down deep," shouted McKinney, as his rescue party reached the bridge and the Skate slid smoothly beneath the waters.

The plane dropped no bombs so, allowing fifteen minutes for it to be on its way, Gene came to periscope depth, sighted the downed pilot, surfaced, and took him aboard.

The rescued aviator, Lieutenant (jg) Richard G. Johnson, was very happy to be aboard; he had been in the water since the previous day. He said he had hidden under his raft flap hoping to avoid strafing and had observed the plane come down to six hundred feet, search carefully about the Skate's position, and then buzz off in the direction of Wake.

Johnson, a former University of California football player, was said to be a "sharp" pilot. While blasting the island of Mili the month before, he had flown so low that he had picked up palm fronds on his wings.

That night, in order not to be interrupted by enemy planes, Commander McKinney, at 2345, stopped all engines and, in the control room, read the simple service for the burial of the dead at sea. Friends and shipmates shuffled quietly into the compartment to pay the last honors to Willis Maxson.

As the service ended, the body, sewn in canvas and draped with the colors, was gently passed up the after-battery room hatch and reverently lowered over the side. Torpedoman Baugh, Seaman Van Horn, Pharmacist's Mate Florshinger, and Gunner's Mate Shelton committed the body of their shipmate to the deep. The white shrouded figure sank silently from sight.

About an hour before dawn, a red flare was sighted. It appeared to be about five miles away. Actually, it proved to be seventeen miles away, but at the end of a two-hour run a raft was brought alongside which contained Lieutenant (jg) Wm. E. McCarthy and Paul T. Bonilla.

No planes interfered with the Skate's search that day and the weather cooperated in keeping the sea fairly smooth so that good coverage was obtained. At 1640 another lookout, Daniel W. Howell, sighted something bobbing in the waves about three miles on the port bow.

As the Skate neared the object, it was seen to be a life raft with its cover flap pulled across it.

"Ahoy, the raft, there!" megaphoned the Officer-of-the-Deck as he brought the Skate's bow close aboard. The cover was flung back violently and a flier, obviously just awakened, stared wild-eyed at the ship. Then with a whoop, overboard he went and fairly flew through the water to the vessel's side and up its steel ladder like a squirrel.

Thus, came aboard Lt. Commander Mark A. Grant, an Air Group Commander from the carrier Cowpens. Sputtering in excitement, he proudly displayed his carefully conserved half-canteen of water and demanded, "How are you fixed for water?"

As McKinney, from the bridge, directed a tommy gunner to sink the raft, Grant yelled, "No, no, Cap'n, it's got my teeth aboard."

Completely forgotten in his haste were Grant's dentures and his "lucky shoes."

Grant had been in the water four days but said he was always confident that he would be picked up. His luck at Wake had been so poisonous that he felt it had to take a turn for the better. As he made a low strafing run on the island, a lone Japanese soldier had fired a rifle at him. The bullet hit the fighter plane's engine and knocked it out.

However, just on the off chance that Lady Luck did not ride with him on that patrol, Grant had taken the precaution to ensure himself against death by thirst and starvation. After unsuccessful shots at seagulls and gooney birds, he had saved one bullet in his pistol.

Some months later, I met Mark Grant's brother, Commodore Grant, Base Commander at Majuro. Our submarines refitting at that base lacked nothing that Commodore Grant could supply.

The carrier Lexington put a splendid seal of approval on the Skate's performance in rescuing some of her fliers, with a dispatch that read: "Anything on the Lexington is yours for the asking. If it's too big to carry away, we will cut it up into small parts."

Months later, I had the pleasure of pinning on some decorations. Among them were a Navy Cross for Commander McKinney and Silver Star Medals for Ensign Kay, Torpedoman Smith, and Gunner's Mate Shelton.

"That Silver Star," Shelton told me later, "sure boosted my standing with my dad, a retired Army major. As a corporal, during the Philippine Insurrection, by saving his sergeant's life under a hail of bullets, he won the Congressional Medal of Honor."

Thus, ended the first chapter of the saga of the Lifeguard League. The Skate had won a star for her Submarine Combat

Pin. The chapter she co-authored was replete with triumph and tragedy, heroism and high endeavor—worthy of the proud services that wrote it.

OCEAN-CAMOUFLAGED F6F-3 HELLCATS IN FLIGHT

4 - Westward Ho with Spruance and Mitscher

OUR NEXT ADVENTURES IN LIFEGUARDING were not so successful as those of the Skate.

The assaults on Tarawa and Makin, by the 2nd Marine Division and the 27th Infantry Division, respectively, began on November 19, 1943. In this connection, the Nautilus, Lt. Commander Wm. D. "Bill" Irvin, was stationed off Tarawa to take pictures and to collect tidal and reef data as well as to perform Lifeguard duty.

The Plunger, Commander R. H. "Benny" Bass, was detailed as Lifeguard off the shores of Mili. The latter, a strong Japanese air base about three hundred miles north of Tarawa, was to be neutralized by a carrier task group.

The Nautilus picked up no downed fliers but was shelled and badly damaged by a "friendly" destroyer—assisted by a cruiser—while proceeding to her next assignment—to land Marines at Apamama.

Everyone had been informed of the sub's movement, but apparently the sight of a target affected Rear Admiral Harry Hills' gunners with something quite the opposite of "buck fever."

The Plunger rescued one zoomie but was strafed by a Japanese Zero which wounded her Executive Officer and five men of the bridge watch.

Taking a lesson from this Nautilus episode, when the Marshalls campaign was launched on January 29, 1944, we stationed no Lifeguard submarines in the vicinity of islands such as Kwajelein, Roi-Namur, and Eniwetok, which were marked for invasion. I felt that the surface forces could handle their own air-sea rescue problems there. In addition, they would be free to attack any submarine encountered with complete assurance that it was Japanese.

However, as soon as Majuro and Kwajelein Atolls had been secured, I flew to the former on February 12, after an overnight stop at Tarawa, for the double mission of selecting a site for a submarine advance base and conferring with Admiral Raymond A. Spruance, Commander Fifth Fleet, and his recently appointed

Commander Task Force 58—the Carrier Force—Rear Admiral Marc A. Mitscher.

The sight from the air of beautiful Majuro Lagoon with its eastern end filled by the tremendous sea power embodied in the Fifth Fleet is one I shall never forget. A long line of new sixteen-inch-gun battleships with a dozen or more CV's or CVL's with seemingly endless rows of jeep carriers, destroyers, destroyer escorts, and fleet auxiliaries jammed the anchorage. Perhaps if Hirohito or Tojo could have seen what I saw then, they would have been ready to toss in the towel.

I arrived on the day of their departure and with me I brought our plans for submarine participation in a carrier raid scheduled for February 17 on Truk, the boasted "Gibraltar of the Pacific."

On the eve of this hazardous and unprecedented operation, in command of such a fleet as no American had ever before beheld, Admiral Spruance was as calm and unperturbed as though he were going on a picnic.

Quiet, soft-spoken, and courteous, but fast as lightning in handling problems, Admiral Spruance was always a most pleasant and inspiring person to work with. The air of capacity which emanated from him and his Chief of Staff, Rear Admiral Charles Moore, was wonderful and gave me full confidence that their bold venture would be a complete success.

Over lunch aboard his flagship, the new and powerful sixteen-inch gunned New Jersey, we discussed my plans. The Admiral approved them, and immediately his communicators spread them throughout the Fleet by blinker light and voice radio, since radio silence would be imposed when the New Jersey weighed anchor at 1600.

In line with my responsibilities for the occasion, nine submarines were stationed in strategic positions near Truk to act as Lifeguards and to sink enemy shipping attempting to escape. Special surface and underwater recognition signals were arranged, and no untoward incidents occurred.

In addition to the excellent services extended by the submarines to surface vessels and aircraft, the Skate sank the cruiser Agano, the Tang downed a fleeing merchantman, and the Searaven rescued a Yorktown torpedo-bomber crew.

In this operation most of the fliers lost were shot down in the Truk lagoon where they were beyond the reach of submarines. However, one flier was lifted out by a cruiser floatplane.

All in all, results that spoke for themselves showed that our coordination with the Fleet was improving.

The big carrier aircraft strike against Palau and the western Carolines was intended by Admiral Nimitz not only to beat down enemy air and naval strength based there but also to remove their potential threat to General MacArthur's advance to Hollandia in northern New Guinea.

For this thrust, our plans for submarine support were even more comprehensive. Confidence in our battleship-carrier task forces had been further increased by their working over of Saipan on February 23.

In addition, the ability of our Lifeguard submarines to save fliers downed at sea had been amply proven at Wake Island and at Truk, while the bag of would-be escapees sunk by other submarines specially stationed to cut off the enemy's retreat at Truk and Saipan included one cruiser, one passenger-cargo ship, and six freighters.

It appeared that this new system was a winner and, after conferences with Admirals Nimitz, Spruance, Mitscher, and their operations officers, Dick Voge and I made and submitted plans of a similar pattern for our submarine participation in the approaching raids.

In the Palau group, the Gar was to Lifeguard off Peleliu, while the Tunny performed a similar service off the main island—Babelthuap. Yap was to be attended by the Pampanito and, finally, the Harder was assigned to Lifeguard duty off Woleai Atoll.

To stop would-be deserters from Kossol Roads in Palau—the only group in which units of the Japanese fleet and merchant marine were expected to be found—we stationed five additional submarines in a line along its northwestern coast.

Most of the submarines selected were already at sea and required only dispatch orders assigning them their designated stations and radio phone code names. By this time our SOP [standard operating procedure], which all submarines carried, contained all the routine Lifeguarding instructions.

With the stage thus set, the Fifth Fleet, on March 22, 1944, stood out from Majuro Lagoon. Its mighty battleships and carriers with a swarm of lighter craft and fleet auxiliaries turned their prows to the westward toward the Rising Sun flag of Japan in whose final setting in the Pacific these very ships had memorable roles to play.

THE SKIPJACK (SS-184) (INBOARD) AND SKATE (SS-305) AT THE PACIFIC RESERVE FLEET MARE ISLAND IN OCTOBER 1947.

5 - HARDER STAGES SURF RESCUE

AS THE SITUATION STOOD ON THIS FIRST of April morning in 1944, Admiral Raymond A. Spruance's powerful Fifth Fleet, with its splendid air arm—the carrier groups of Vice Admiral Marc A. Mitscher's Task Force 58—had just completed strikes at the Palau Islands and Yap, famous as the breeding grounds of typhoons. These attacks began at Palau on March 30 in accordance with the plans we made at Majuro.

While waiting for the Fleet to arrive, the submarine Tunny had sunk a Jap sub, the I-42. When the expected exodus of enemy shipping began on the afternoon before our planes struck, she managed to get in an attack on the giant battleship Musashi, flagship of Admiral Koga. Unfortunately, the big target zigged away.

Only one torpedo hit—and that was too far forward to do vital damage. After this bit of bad luck, the Tunny's horoscope brightened or darkened, depending on how one looks at it.

The next day, while Lifeguarding, she was dive-bombed by a trigger-happy zoomie. His two-thousand-pound bomb, that might have blown her to bits, missed by thirty feet, producing electrical fires and leaks in the hull which forced her return to Pearl.

Meanwhile the Gar, on similar duty, acquired a very creditable bag of eight rescued fliers.

On the homeward trip toward the Majuro base, Yap was hit but no planes found. The entire three carrier groups of TF 58 then converged on luckless Woleai Atoll, which lies about four hundred miles almost due south of Guam and five hundred miles west of Truk.

This armada packed enough explosives to blow the tiny atoll off the map, but the mission was merely to pulverize its planes, runways, and air facilities in preparation for the forthcoming Hollandia campaign. In other words, Woleai was about to receive what was to become famed as a "Mitscher haircut."

Woleai, the main island from which this coral atoll takes its name, lies on the northeastern corner of the group. Its twenty-odd satellites range in size from fairly large palm-covered islets to mere scrub-covered sandspits. Roughly speaking, the atoll has the shape of a reclining figure eight which encloses two lagoons: East and West. These open upon the sea, by means of four fairly wide channels, to all the major points of the compass except the east.

Shaped like a sadiron with a rounded point, the island of Woleai is about a mile long and about three-quarters of a mile broad at its base. Along the shore that skirted the East Lagoon, which furnished excellent anchorage for shipping approaching from the south, ran a narrow road on which fronted the sort of structures rather common to Japanese installations on Pacific islands—warehouses, shops, fuel and oil tanks, a radio tower, and a few dwellings that ranged from ramshackle houses to sun-bleached tents.

Also, present, but rather well hidden by the lush growth of the jungle, was a 3,050-foot concrete runway served by a 1,750-foot taxiway. Along the latter, protected from prying eyes by living screens of vegetation, were the asphalt aprons of medium bombers—the very kind which, with other Japanese air and sea forces based at Palau and other points, constituted a serious threat to General MacArthur's plans in the New Guinea area.

For this strike, the submarine Harder lay awaiting the arrival of the airmen. By now, submarines so stationed were equipped with VHF radio telephone whereby they could communicate with carrier planes.

We had not yet been able to wangle SCAP (Submarine Combat Air Patrols) out of the air commands. But the bombing of the Tunny, by a friendly plane off Palau as related above, was to lead to the achievement of that highly necessary objective at a fairly early date.

The Harder, Commander Samuel David Dealey, of Dallas, Texas, was on its fourth war patrol and was a combat-tested submarine. Under her able skipper, she had won a reputation for skill, daring, and resourcefulness. Even this early in the war, she had established an enviable record that put her in the very forefront in a service where valor was considered SOP.

The Harder arrived in the waters off Woleai during the early morning hours of March 29. This gave her two full days of opportunity to snoop around the edges of the atoll to see what discoveries she could make or targets she could find. She learned through observation that twin-engined enemy bombers operated out of a jungle airstrip that evidently ran into the northeast trade wind on a 200-degree course. She also discovered that there was not a single vessel of any kind in the harbor. Through these two days, during which she made about a dozen contacts with enemy planes, not a single Jap caught sight of the Harder.

However, the submarine slipped boldly out into the open during the wee hours of March 31 when she took station for Lifeguard duty some fifteen miles south of Woleai. The deadly hum of Mitscher's carrier bombers droning through the night skies was heard shortly before 1:00 a.m.

From his surfaced submarine, ready to answer any call for help, Dealey watched four separate bombing runs on the island, all within the space of some two hours. The first of these was so sudden that not a Jap AA [antiaircraft] gun barked in protest. The following runs, however, were met with fairly heavy 20-mm antiaircraft fire.

As dawn came, Sam Dealey wondered how effectively the bombings might have been in wrecking planes and runways. He soon found out. At 0500, he spotted at least four enemy land-based bombers on patrol.

"Some," he said, "came as close as seven thousand yards but without sighting us."

However, later in the morning, the Harder was sighted. At 0959, while he was lowering his periscope after a fifteen-second horizon sweeping observation, an aircraft bomb landed close aboard. The sub was then sixty-two feet below the surface.

"Take her down; one hundred feet; right full rudder," ordered Dealey as his stout little vessel danced a veritable shimmy under the depth bomb's impact. In fact, the ship was so shaken up that several lightbulbs went dark and the bridge talkback was knocked out of order.

Having executed this operation, also known as "let's-get-to-heck-outa-here," Captain Dealey turned, with the wide grin for which he was celebrated, to Lieutenant Frank Lynch, his executive officer, and added: "These boys are on the job, Frank. For the rest of the day we will run at eighty feet, back and forth across the southeast approaches to Woleai—but we'll go up to periscope depth every fifteen minutes just to make sure that nothing slips by."

In the late afternoon, the Harder crept within a half-mile of the Raur Channel entrance to the East Lagoon. Through the sharp lenses of his tallest periscope, Skipper Dealey saw two medium bombers on the runway—now that he knew where to look for planes. A third took off. It was then 1545.

"Looks like last night's harassing raid," he noted, "only served to stir them up."

Little did Sam know—and little did a certain pilot aboard the Aircraft Carrier Bunker Hill know—how prophetically true his conclusion was.

A few minutes later, the Harder returned to periscope depth where she remained until 2012, when she surfaced to recharge her depleted storage batteries. But it was not a placid night. The Japs were restless, uneasy. Time and again, the Harder had to slide beneath the surface when night fliers came uncomfortably close. It seemed as if their scalps itched in anticipation of a "Mitscher haircut."

Meanwhile, throughout the night and hundreds of miles to the west, the huge cavalcade of carriers that bore the brunt of the fighting in Admiral Spruance's Fifth Fleet—surrounded by its formidable escort of battleships, cruisers, destroyers and destroyer escorts—had plowed toward Woleai, the shearing jobs on Palau and Yap having been done to perfection.

As the time for launching the fighters and dive bombers for the Woleai attack arrived, the signal for swinging the carriers into the gently blowing trade wind for takeoff position was given from the "island" aboard the new Lexington, Admiral Mitscher's flagship.

The sea was fairly smooth. The sky was somewhat cloudy. According to the weather Merlins [wizards], the best to hope for—in the line of visibility at Woleai—would be a five-thousand-foot ceiling. It might be much lower than that. Zero even. As some jester—it was April Fool's Day, please remember—in the ready room of Fighter Squadron Eight aboard the Bunker Hill suggested: "The visibility may even be below zero!"

In that pre-dawn morning, the members of Fighter Squadron Eight—like other airmen aboard the Bunker Hill and other Task Force 58 carriers—had gone over the details of the attack mission that awaited them with the coming of daylight.

The task of the Hellcat Fighters, first to move in, was to destroy the enemy's planes in the air or on the ground and to silence his ack-ack fire. The task of the Dauntless Dive Bombers, once the foe's defensive fangs were drawn, was to move in and blow every man-built structure on the island to smithereens. The torpedo bombers were to drop heavy demolition bombs.

Every pilot in Fighter Squadron Eight was a combat-wise veteran. There was not one man among them who had not been through the searing fire of several ack-ack barrages; who had not crossed tracers with some of the best pursuit pilots Japan could produce. In fact, most of the pilots in Squadron Eight had reached a point of easy familiarity with the presence of Sudden Death aloft.

His repeated presence had brought the kind of contempt that familiarity is supposed to bring in the human breast. They listened with perfunctory interest to the usual outline of safety precautions—that seaplanes would be on duty to rescue pilots who either parachuted into or ditched out in the sea.

Also, chances are that most of them gave only superficial thought to the rescue gear they carried along—the Mae West lifesaving jackets tied around their chests, the one-man rafts packed into their parachute equipment. However, most, if not all of them, paid heed to remembering the channels set aside on the VHF voice radio to be used by zoomies in calling for help from the Harder. The latter, in line with instructions, would be near Woleai to serve as Lifeguard for downed aviators.

Still, as an inaudible theme song to all of these preparations for rescue in event of trouble ran the ancient human refrain—as old as mankind itself—"That's the other fellow's worry. It can't happen to me!" And, after all, perhaps that should be so. Fear, in any form, aboard any craft, is a poor shipmate.

Silence had descended upon the ready room of Fighter Squadron Eight. All the talking was over. All the speculations were ended.

"Any last questions?" asked blond and stocky Lieutenant Harlan Gustafson of Norristown, Pennsylvania, as he gave each member of the four-man division of which he was the Leader a quick, searching look. First, Lieutenant John R. Galvin of Burlington, Iowa, (24)—a shake of the head. No more talking. Time for action. Same voiceless sign-off from Lieutenant Christian

Allen (23), and Thomas Brown (25), both of Texas, Freeport and Lubbock, respectively.

Just then came "The Word" from the loudspeaker: "Pilots—man your planes. Pilots—man your planes."

Grabbing their gear, all the fliers in Squadron Eight raced for the exit and headed for the flight deck at full speed. Since Gustafson's Division was assigned to the first-wave fighter sweep, they were among the first to lead the sortie in which, presently, other pilots from other Bunker Hill squadrons would join.

Similar runs from ready rooms to flight decks were taking place aboard some eleven other flattops in Task Force 58. Although it was still dark, daylight was not far off. According to orders, the first wave of attack was to bore in at 0830.

Heading as she did into the trade wind at a speed of better than 25 knots, the Bunker Hill's flight deck was swept by a breeze of almost gale force. But the pilots noted that the sea was fairly smooth. As for the overcast over Woleai? Well, chances were that the clouds would disappear as the sun rose in the sky. Unless it was one of those local clouds that roosts over some Pacific islands, immobile like a hen on a clutch of eggs.

Gustafson, Galvin, Brown, and Allen found their Hellcats, wings uptilted and engines silent, in the very front ranks of the planes stacked well toward the Bunker Hill's wide and open stern. Behind the Hellcats stood the slower Dauntless Dive Bombers. Third and last came the much heavier torpedo bombers.

Even on the equator, dawn winds can have a cutting edge. Therefore, Galvin and his companions scrambled into their sheltering cockpits as rapidly as their cumbersome equipment would let them.

Slim as he was, long-legged, square-chinned Galvin muttered to himself about the lack of room as he sought to adjust the rather tight fit of his anti-blackout suit and pushed his parachute rig with its attached rubber life raft into the metal-framed pilot's seat.

Lastly, he adjusted his Mae West life jacket to minimize the danger of pulling the air cord by accident. Once in his seat with the safety belt secured, Galvin plugged in his connecting lines and began his one-man check-out routine.

This done, he ended up by checking the canopy. It should not be locked, and it was not. This rule, rather new, was to prevent pilots who fell into the sea during takeoff from drowning as captives in their own cockpits.

Suddenly—above the hubbub of mechanics and deck crew members shouting at each other to override the wind and the noises of the carrier's racing turbines—came the metallic voice on the loudspeakers: "Pilots—start your engines. Pilots—start your engines."

Leaning toward his instrument board, Galvin made the electric connection that exploded the starter cartridge. Like a lazy camel, making angry noises because it has to travel with a heavy burden, the engine started off with spitting groans and protesting moans. But the hackings and coughings of the cold motor lasted only a few seconds. It changed into a smooth, musical roar.

Soon the Take-Off Director stepped into place with his green-glowing baton. Next came the "launch planes" signal.

One by one the aircraft were rolled forward, the wings were locked into place, and off they went into the wild blue yonder. As he swung to the starboard to join up with the rest of his four-plane division, Galvin's eyes swept the ocean, near and far.

All around, beyond the far horizons, were the silhouettes of men o' war—the bulky outlines of battleships, the husky forms of cruisers, the slim lines of destroyers. As would the heart of any man who saw this great panorama of might, Galvin's beat with pride.

After an uneventful run over empty seas under clouded skies, the leading division of Squadron Eight reached the target. There Galvin and his companions found that the low cloud cover compelled them to make their strafing runs low. From the very start, they ran into heavy antiaircraft fire.

Explained Lieutenant Galvin, in a later letter to relatives of Captain Dealey of the Harder—whom he was still to meet: "The four of us in our Hellcat division went sporting up the runway with all guns blazing. We were about twenty-five to fifty feet off the concrete. I was firing at a plane on the taxiway when I was peppered with 20-mm cannon shells. I heard the shells hit and immediately kicked the plane over and out to sea."

Smoke filled the cockpit of Galvin's plane. Flames were shooting out around him as he pulled back on the stick and climbed to about a thousand feet. Any hope that he might be able to make it back to the carrier—or even to nose around in search of the Harder—were almost instantaneously blasted. In fact, he did not even have time to reach his Division Leader, Lieutenant Gustafson, on the inter-plane wavelength... But let Galvin continue:

"The engine was running smoothly but smoke and fire filled the cockpit, so I had to bail out. Since both wing tanks were on fire, I was afraid to roll the plane on its back, so out I went, head-first. Correct procedure would have called for slowing the plane down below 100 knots for jumping. However, I was making somewhere near 200 knots. The excessive speed did not give me clearance time and the tail hit me in the back and all along the right side of my body.

"That is all I remember until I suddenly found myself about to hit the water. I grabbed for the ripcord and it came free with no pull. At the same time, I looked up and saw that the chute was already spread above me. Evidently, when I hit the tail it tore the chute pack open. Anyway, Lieutenant Brown, who saw me go down, said my chute opened immediately after I left the plane. While I was going down, Brown told Lieutenant Gustafson that I had been shot down. Gus didn't believe it and kept trying to reach me by radio."

In the meantime, Galvin hit the water. At first, he was dragged a good distance through the water by his chute but, after some effort, he got out of the harness.

Next, he pulled the toggles for his life jacket gas cartridge only to see gas bubble up all around him. This was bad news. But worse was to come. Even as his life jacket was completely useless, so, Galvin discovered, was his rubber raft. It would not hold air. It had been deeply gashed when he was flung against the plane's tail surfaces.

Still somewhat stunned from the shocks of being struck by his plane's tail assembly and his none-too-gentle crash into the ocean, Galvin—when lifted by cresting waves—saw a line of trees quite a distance to the south. He did not know it at the time, but he was some five miles off the northern coastline of Tagaulap, the second island westward from Woleai. Galvin had but one of two choices—sink or swim. So, crippled and numb with pain though he was, he swam. He discarded his pistol, knife, shoes, and cartridge belt.

But try as he would, he could not unzip the cumbersome anti-blackout suit. His back, right arm, and right leg were practically paralyzed. While he was not an expert swimmer, desperation and determination to live kept Galvin paddling slowly toward shore. He found that by staying on his back, wiggling his hands, and kicking with his good leg he could keep moving.

Several times he developed cramps but was able to massage them off. He turned on his stomach only often enough to get his bearings. Even with the help of the prevailing wind and, possibly, some tidal current, it is nothing short of a minor miracle that he ever reached the shore.

Meanwhile, circling overhead—for guidance, protection, encouragement, and assisting possible rescuers—were Galvin's three Division companions. "Gus," his leader, had already contacted the Harder by voice radio, and Skipper Dealey had promised to proceed to the rescue as rapidly as his four engines could take him. It would, he said, be a run of several hours. The Harder, being stationed south of the atoll, had to round Woleai's eastern shore and then proceed westward.

But to continue with Galvin's own story:

"After three hours and fifteen minutes in the water, I finally made the outer reef of Tagaulap Island where I could rest. I removed my life jacket. There are periods of time I do not remember before reaching the reef until I finally realized I was rolling head-over-heels on the bottom. After banging my head on a rock, I kicked free of the bottom to find myself in water only shoulder-high.

"I could not stand up because of my injuries and because I was exhausted from the long swim. However, after a short rest, I managed to cover the hundreds of yards from the reef to the beach by crawling and scooting crablike on my left elbow. I was not able to use my right arm or leg. The water's edge was as far as I could go, and I guess I collapsed. I had been in the water from eight-thirty in the morning until twelve-thirty."

All this time, Lieutenants Gustafson, Brown, and Allen were circling Galvin and communicating with the submarine as well as the Bunker Hill. From the latter, a Kingfisher seaplane was directed to the rescue. By repeated zooming they indicated Galvin's position to the submarine.

For some time, the exhausted flier lay prone upon the sun-baked sands. Thanks to the resiliency of the human mind and body, in time he gathered enough wits to realize that he did not have a raft to aid in his rescue—if he lived that long.

So, laboriously wallowing on his knees, Galvin found a stick and wrote in the sand: "Need raft." One of the Squadron Eight planes dove in acknowledgement of the message.

This done, Galvin, whose face was bleeding heavily from cuts inflicted by sharp-edged coral, pulled himself cautiously higher up on the beach where clusters of rocks gave him shelter from Jap sharpshooters.

As he observed, "I expected to see a bunch of Jap snipers come out of those palms and either shoot or capture me any minute. But there just wasn't anything I could do about it...Gus and the other boys in the division had been covering me all the time, but my eyes were so sore from the saltwater that I didn't even notice them."

Meanwhile the Harder, with Dealey on the bridge and alert for trouble, was making every knot her four Fairbanks-Morse diesels could produce. The news of a downed zoomie came at 0840 and the submarine, on the surface—a big bone in her teeth and a wide wake at her stern—set out to round the southern tip of Raur Island.

By the time she had Woleai itself in plain sight, Dealey, his bridge watch, and lookouts saw a sky full of carrier planes wreak destruction on the main island. As they watched the continuing waves of attack, the installations on Woleai changed from structures to rubble.

So graphic were Commander Dealey's impressions, as recorded in the Harder's log, that they bear repeating here:

"The picture in the skies looked like a gigantic 'Cleveland Air Show.' With dozens of fighters forming a comfortable umbrella above us, we watched a show that made the Hollywood 'Colossals' seem tame. We rounded the coast of Woleai one to two miles off the beach and had perfect ringside seats. The plastering that the airmen gave this Jap base was terrific!

"Bombs of all sizes rained on every structure on the island. Several buildings seemed to be lifted and thrown high in the air.

Causeways between the various islands were bombed. Oil or gasoline storage tanks blew up, covering the islands with heavy clouds of black smoke. The runway on the main island was hit time and again with large and small bombs.

"It was hard to believe that anything could be left on the islands after the first waves of planes had gone over, and yet some bursts of AA fire continued to meet the planes on each attack. The bombers hit Woleai from the south, waited for the smoke to clear, reformed, and then gave it the works from East-West courses! Fighters seemed to hit the place from all directions, peeling off and diving straight into the AA fire that still persisted.

"Many looked as if they would go right on through the blanket of smoke and crash on the islands, but all managed to pull out just above the trees. Fires blazed intermittently on Woleai and most of its adjacent islands and gradually the AA defense was reduced to a few sporadic bursts."

The sun, now in a clear sky, was nearing its zenith when the Harder approached the end of her run toward Tagaulap. With fighters zooming overhead and surface battle stations manned, the vessel turned toward the beach. At 1145, the figure of Galvin, sheltered among the rocks, was sighted. Just about this time, too—awakened perhaps by the inner voice that somehow always seems to be on the alert—Galvin had pulled out of his stupor.

"I did not see the Harder until she was heading my way as I was lying on the beach," he observed. "With the aid of a pole, however, I got to my feet and waved. The sub came up to the reef and then backed off. For a time, my heart stood still. I saw rescue go aglimmering. Soon I realized that it was looking for a better approach. After what seemed to be an eternity—fifteen to thirty minutes at least—the sub reappeared and came right toward the shore.

"Just then a torpedo bomber dropped me a raft in response to the request I had written in the sand. I inflated it and pushed off from shore, paddling in the direction of the sub. It all took time. However, the tide and wind carried me in the opposite direction."

Actually, Galvin was making a surprisingly accurate guess when he concluded that the Harder's skipper was looking for another and safer place to make his approach. With the ship flooded down to aid the execution of the rescue, the vessel had been maneuvered into a spot about 1500 yards off the beach. White water was breaking over the shoals only twenty yards off the bow of the ship and the fathometer had ceased to record.

Planes now advised Captain Dealey that if rescue looked too difficult from where he was—and it certainly did look dangerous—a better approach might be made through what seemed to be a narrow channel between Tagaulap and Mariaon, its eastern neighbor. As the Harder backed off to make an approach from another angle, Dealey saw the aviator—who had been standing on the beach—fall and lie outstretched on the sand.

"His collapse," noted Dealey, "was undoubtedly due not only to physical exhaustion, but also to the disappointment in thinking that he saw his chances of rescue fade away. As this went on, we were advised by a plane that further air reconnaissance showed our first approach to the beach was best after all. We reversed course and headed back at full speed."

At this moment, it was proper for Skipper Dealey to go into executive session with himself. He was sticking not only his own neck away out, but the necks of all aboard, plus, of course, the Harder's. To him she was more than a mere submarine. She was his life and blood. He had taken her off the ways in New London back in 1942 and the sub, through fair weather and foul, had never known another skipper.

In fact, almost all of the officers and men aboard had been on the Harder since she was commissioned. They were tried hands and true friends. As he later informed Lieutenant Galvin:

"How could I be sure, first of all, that you were the lost carrier airman? Our lookout had warned that you might be a decoy put in by the Japs to lure us within easy range. Or the Japs might have left you there just to act as bait for them—a trap to be sprung at the right moment, when the 'take' would be bigger?

"When I got a good look at you through the binoculars, I had to agree with the forward lookout who had you under constant observation—we even watched you through the sights of our forward deck gun. Gun Captain Thomason said he could not make you out. Your face was black from sea and sun and smoke. And last, but not least—throughout the entire operation—a native was calmly sitting among the rocks watching you and the whole show. On top of that, sniper fire began to show up, in steadily increasing volume, as the Harder headed toward shore. By then the air attack had slowed down and the Japs were probably crawling out of their holes."

Suspicion hung heavily over Dealey's head as he selected three volunteers to take a raft ashore in order to bring the flier safely aboard. Since all hands stepped forward as one man, the Skipper selected his Gunnery Officer, Lieutenant Sam Logan of Owensboro, Kentucky (26); John W. Thomason of Fort Worth, Texas (24), Gun Captain; and Frank X. Ryan of Shenandoah, Pennsylvania (20), Motor Machinist's Mate. As the sub moved closer inshore toward a spot where the breakers were spuming high, the three men made ready a raft and a long, long spool of light but strong line with which to maintain contact with the Harder.

By now, sniper bullets were buzzing like bees from the coverts on nearby islands. However, steady ground strafing by fighter planes made it unhealthy for Jap gunners to advance closer. By way of the bridge watch, Captain Dealey was kept advised on depth conditions through constant relays of fathometer readings.

Crewmen, on duty in various parts of the sub, stood frozen-faced as they heard the announcements: "Three fathoms—two fathoms—one fathom—zero fathoms."

And still the Harder moved shoreward—at creeping speed, to be sure, but still forward. Then—from the Torpedo Officer in the forward torpedo room: "Scraping bottom forward, sir!"

White water foamed around the Harder's blunt snout as it rested on a reef. "Keep working both screws," Dealey ordered his Chief Engineer, "just hard enough to keep her bow against the reef." He wanted to be sure that the Harder did not risk destruction by swinging broadside to the seas. There were stern Navy regulations, dating back to the days of sail, regarding risking ships—needlessly...Well, under the circumstances, that was a matter of opinion.

"If I live to be a thousand, I shall never forget that moment," related Gun Captain Thomason about a decade after the event when he, now a successful businessman in Southern California, recalled the rescue. "It was a truly terrifying sight to see the Harder lying there with her bow uptilted on the reef. In a moment like that, any sailor would have a feeling of desperate insecurity.

But not Captain Dealey. He walked up that slanting deck to where we stood near the forward torpedo hatch, as if it were the most commonplace thing in the world—and under sniper fire, too. But the big thing was putting that sub on the reef and keeping it there for more than an hour—that took not only deep-down guts but also real seamanship. Captain Dealey had lots of both and to spare.

"He was cool as a cucumber as he approached. The ever-present pipe was clamped in his teeth, but his usual cheer-inspiring grin was gone. He was more serious than any of us had ever seen him. After looking us and our gear over, he nodded and said: 'Remember, now, none of you have to do this. Anything can happen. The Japs may be up to something—and if they throw a lot of heavy stuff at us—in case of really dangerous fire from the shore—chances are that I may have to back away and leave you to your own resources. Not only that, I may not be able to come back for you. And if I should, it might be too late.'"

Slowly, carefully, he looked at Logan, Thomason, and Ryan. To his unasked question, they answered with grimly set lips and without batting an eye. A fleeting grin swept over Dealey's face as he told them to proceed. Without further ado the three volunteers dove over the side and commenced pushing and towing their rubber boat toward the beach some 1,200 yards away. The line attached to the rubber raft was payed out from the sub so the flier could be pulled back from the beach.

Meanwhile Galvin was feebly paddling his rubber boat against the tide. When Logan, Ryan, and Thomason reached a spot where they could stand up, Thomason held the raft while Logan and Ryan, alternately swimming and wading, caught up with the aviator whose boat had meanwhile drifted farther away.

By this time, he was thoroughly exhausted. Noted Dealey's log: "Logan and Ryan, by alternately pushing and swimming, headed back toward their rubber boat from which a line led to the submarine about five hundred yards away. Just at this critical moment a floatplane, also attempting the rescue, taxied over the line to the raft between Thomason and the sub and the line parted!"

The entire rescue party was now stranded. Thomason was recalled. He managed to swim back to the sub after a hard battle against the tide.

Another volunteer swimmer, Gunner's Mate Freeman Paquet, Jr., Milford, Connecticut (24), then dove over the side with a line and swam to the three men standing just inshore of the heavy breakers. This line was made fast to the wildly bobbing rubber shell and, little by little, the four men were pulled through the breakers and back to the ship.

Throughout the entire rescue, observed Dealey, the co-operation of the aviators was superb. They kept up a continuous pounding of the islands with bombs and flew in low to strafe the Japs and divert their attention from the rescue. In spite of this, Jap snipers concealed in the trees along the beach continued shooting at the ship and rescue party, and their bullets whined over the bridge, uncomfortably close.

"The rescue could never have been attempted without the protection afforded by the planes," wrote the Harder's valiant skipper. "Too much praise cannot be given to the officer and three men who effected this rescue. Its daring execution, under the noses of the Japs and subject to sniper fire from the beach, can be classified as a truly courageous accomplishment, and Lieutenant John R. Galvin, though physically exhausted, showed a character that refused to admit defeat. It is a privilege to serve with men such as these."

With aviator and rescue party recovered, the sub was backed clear of the reef and headed out to sea.

So concludes this incident in the Harder's colorful career. But that is not the end of the Galvin story. Not only did he escape from an extra-narrow squeeze, but—because of his being aboard the Harder during a patrol that inflicted heavy Japanese losses, destroyers as well as cargo vessels—Galvin's war decorations include a Submarine Combat Insignia, the Submarine Silhouette, which all submariners prize and which I and many other swivel-chair strategists would give our eye teeth to possess.

With this trophy added to his "lettuce salad" Galvin returned to the Bunker Hill. Before the war ended, he was credited with seven Jap planes and two probables—as well as a 5,500-ton Jap transport by skipbombing.

In recommending the award of a Presidential Citation for the Harder's performance of duty at Woleai, Fleet Admiral Nimitz gave the final accolade to a day of heroic accomplishment in his endorsement:

"The Commander-in-Chief, Pacific Fleet, considers the performance of the Commanding Officer, the Officers and Crew of the U.S.S. Harder one of the outstanding rescue feats accomplished to date in the Pacific area and in keeping with the high traditions of the entire submarine force.

"The cooperation between the attacking force and the rescue vessel is an example of a courageous fighting spirit and mutual support doctrine which will enable the Naval Service to overcome the greatest odds in Successfully accomplishing its mission."

6 - Tang Gets a Steel Umbrella

ADMIRAL SPRUANCE'S FIFTH FLEET, flushed with the success of its operations against the Western Carolines—Palau, Yap and Woleai—returned to the anchorage in Majuro Lagoon on April 6, 1944. Admiral Nimitz, equally flushed with pride and enthusiasm, was champing at the bit to get down to Majuro and hear at first hand the full story of its adventures.

Also, the matters of General MacArthur's Hollandia campaign in northern New Guinea, scheduled to begin about April 21, and of our naval support for it were items which required immediate attention. Final plans had to be whipped into shape.

With characteristic thoughtfulness the Big Boss invited me to fly down with him, which I was delighted to do. We took off April 7 in his big amphibian, the "Blue Goose." Along with us went Rear Admiral Forrest Sherman, the Cincpac Operations Officer, and other members of the Headquarters operational brain trust.

As soon as the plane was airborne, Forrest Sherman opened up his briefcase of tentative plans and we all turned to on them. Naturally, the Fifth Fleet, and especially TF 58, were involved, although much of the naval cooperation and fire support was to be furnished by Admiral Kinkaid's Seventh Fleet operating from its Australian bases under the Supreme Commander in the Southwest Pacific, General MacArthur. Additionally, Admiral Nimitz had tossed in a plan for a backhanded slap, by Mitscher's carriers, to give the *coup de grâce* to battered Truk on the return trip to Majuro.

This would call for more Lifeguarding, and forthwith I produced the dispositions which Dick Voge and his lads had drafted. They provided for Commander Dick O'Kane of New Hampshire to take station in his sharpshooting Tang off Truk Atoll while Commander Slade Cutter of Illinois located his fighting Seahorse at nearby Satawan Island.

Both of these skippers had piled up impressive scores; it would be hard to say which had the higher record in ships sunk per days at sea. Dick O'Kane had won his spurs as trigger man for another fighter, Commander Mush Morton of the Wahoo.

Since no shipping was expected to be found at either place, it was not necessary to station the usual killer submarines at the channel exits. Already a saying was being coined among us submarine sailors to the effect that when enemy-held islands were being bobbed with the effective, even if unattractive, Spruance and/or Mitscher haircut, "the Fly-Boys zoom from sun to sun, but the Lifeguard's work is never done."

As we have seen at Wake, this was no stretching of the truth, but the rescues Tang performed during the span of a single day from long before sunup to long after sunset was something of a record.

Since the "Blue Goose" had gotten a late start from Pearl, the Admiral elected to spend the night at Johnson Island, about eight hundred miles southwest of Pearl. Arriving there in the late afternoon, we were struck by a heat wave from its treeless, grassless sand and its concrete runways that might well have come from a blast furnace.

Unperturbed by the prospect of a hot, sweaty night, Admiral Nimitz announced, with typical youthful zest, that he was going to take his daily exercise by having a swim from the hangar's seaplane ramp. We had no bathing suits.

"But," announced the Admiral, "I don't need a bathing suit. I have nothing to be ashamed of."

Whereupon, to the wide-eyed surprise of passing officers and enlisted men, we all piled our clothing on the ramp and dived in. It took me back forty years to the happy days of the old swimmin' hole in the creek near my home town of Lamar, Missouri. The only thing lacking was some misbegotten practical jokester to sneak out and tie knots in our underwear.

We arrived at Majuro the next afternoon and again I thrilled to the sight of our splendid Fifth Fleet at anchor. But something new had been added. My own little outfit, two submarine tenders, four or five submarines, and an ARD (2,500-ton floating drydock), lay to the northward of the Fleet in the lee of beautiful Myrna Island.

There, practically overnight, the ever-eager-for-work Seabees had thrown up our newest Recuperation Center, complete with Quonset huts, baseball field, and a pontoon landing pier. The detonation of a couple of tons of dynamite had served to excavate two swimming pools just below the low-tide mark.

The "Blue Goose" sat down near the New Jersey which flew the flag of Admiral Spruance, and the conference began as soon as we were ferried aboard. Present were a dozen or so task group commanders, including the newly promoted Vice Admiral "Pete" Mitscher, Commander TF 58, genial Vice Admiral "Ching" Lee, Commander Battleships and Rear Admirals Ike Giffen, Johnny Hoover, Swede Hanson, Ole Oldendorf, and Ernie Small.

With a string of daring successes behind them, they were all in excellent spirits. The banter of the men about the decks also reflected high morale. The Fifth Fleet was rarin' to go.

Plans for the various Task Groups were presented by their operations officers and approved by Admiral Spruance and the Big Boss. The Fleet filled fuel tanks, magazines, and cold storages and, on April 13, seven days after completion of its last big strike, it sortied for the Hollandia battle.

The war in the Pacific was definitely in full gear, and American troops were no longer hanging on by their teeth and toenails while enemy planes used them for target practice.

Guadalcanal and the Solomons Islands were now secure in Allied hands, and Bloody Tarawa was a bustling American airfield.

The Marshall Islands were now our major operating bases. The forthcoming Hollandia operation held every promise of the complete success which it turned out to be.

Then came the sideswipe at Truk as the Fifth Fleet returned homeward. The Tang and Seahorse were alerted and given the "stand by" signal. The Tang reached her station off Truk without incident, but the Seahorse, proceeding to Satawan at full speed, was bombed, but not hit, by a so-called friendly B-24 from Eniwetok. (Slade Cutter, Commanding Officer of the Seahorse, commented: "That was no friend of mine.")

Recognition between planes and submarines was still not foolproof—especially when the "fool" was also trigger-happy. However, submarines now carried very quick-acting recognition flares and a surface-search ten-centimeter SJ radar which was an aid in spotting low-flying aircraft.

While SCAP had not yet been made official, the air cover given during her Truk rescues left nothing to be desired.

The air strikes began on April 29, and on May 1, the Tang, with Commander Richard H. O'Kane as her skipper, rescued no less than nineteen floaters in six separate rescue operations staged under the threat of Japanese artillery fire from Ollan, which is one of a cluster of small islands in the vicinity of Truk, the center target of heavy carrier strikes.

Strictly speaking, the rescue operation began on the morning of April 30 when the Tang located a raft with three survivors some four miles west of its reported position near Ollan Island. The raftees proved to be Lieutenant (jg) S. Scammell, AMN J. D. Gendron, and ARM H. B. Gemmell, none of whom suffered ill effects because of their rather brief rafting experience after their plane was shot down.

By mid-afternoon the Tang's air-cover headed home and, since another one did not take its place, O'Kane thought that it was up to him to try to offset the rather naked condition of the Tang—so as to avoid prolonged submerged retirement and thus miss out on possible rescue calls—by opening fire on the gun emplacement he knew to lie hidden under a group of phony trees on the southwestern end of Ollan Island.

No sooner decided than done. With skill and enthusiasm, the crew of the four-inch gun on the Tang's after-deck started lobbing shells into the hidden enemy battery. The very first shell burst nicely low among the trees concealing the guns. Now followed a steady stream of shells as the proud Tang pursued its surface course—twenty rounds in all—and not a Jap showed his peaked cap or fired a single shot in an effort to force the Tang to submerge.

After a run of some 8,500 yards, O'Kane ceased fire. The sun was getting low and he figured the Japs would call it quits. But such was not the case. As soon as the Tang stopped firing, the Nips crawled out of their holes and let fly.

"Their first splash," noted O'Kane, "was a little short. The second, we did not spot. We ran submerged for forty minutes, then surfaced and proceeded into the sheltering night at emergency speed."

Long before the dawning of May 1—which was to be the Tang's busiest day—its action-filled program began. A message reported that a raft with two men aboard had been spotted a couple of miles southwest of good old Ollan Island.

During the pre-dawn run, Tang lookouts reported sighting a Jap submarine and clinched their observation by sighting the trail of a torpedo which, luckily, was not well enough aimed to cause any harm to the Tang. The use of the word harm at this point is purely academic. One torpedo hit on a submarine equals: no submarine. This unexpected encounter took place near the island of Kuop, a neighbor of Ollan.

About daybreak the Tang spread her largest flag on the forward deck for purposes of identification; next she reported the enemy sub to the Commander of the Carrier Force for possible airplane hunt and attack.

Meanwhile, O'Kane was heading at emergency speed for the raft reported near Ollan Island. However, before it reached the scene, the pilot of a floatplane from the USS North Carolina had tried to cut himself into the deal, but with disastrous results. The would-be rescuer's plane capsized in the cross chop.

Fortunately, it did not sink. And fortunately, another North Carolina floatplane was flying right along. The pilot of this second ship made a heroic and highly precarious landing close to the raft and the companion plane.

In the interim the latter's pilot had joined the two zoomies on the raft. As the Tang hove into sight, the second North Carolina pilot was engaged in towing both raft and plane clear of the island. To O'Kane this action was highly helpful because he was again under the guns of Ollan. These would surely have been hosing shells at him were it not for the fact that the planes that constituted the Tang's morning umbrella were holding the Japs inactive by strafing the gun emplacements.

It was still in the cool of the morning when O'Kane welcomed Lieutenant J. J. Dowdle, Lieutenant (jg) R. Kanze, and ARM R. E. Hill aboard his ship. While the second North Carolina floatplane with Lieutenant Burns at the controls made a tricky takeoff, the capsized crate was sunk by 20-mm gunfire. Just as the plane was sinking a lookout sang out: "Plane contact—a torpedo bomber—bearing zero nine zero—it's smoking—is hitting the water—range about seven miles."

Alertly ready, the Tang ran down the bearing at emergency speed. The course again took her past the Ollan battery, and again the Tang opened fire as she passed. The camouflaging trees had been removed, which gave O'Kane's gunners an unobstructed point of aim.

The sub's fire, plus the hammering delivered by the air-cover fighter planes and two bombers that had joined the fray, held the Jap guns silent. In due course the vessel sighted and reached a raft from which Commander A. R. Matter, ARM J. J. Menahan, and AOM H. A. Thompson were hauled aboard without ceremony. This because, while en route, O'Kane had word that a cluster of three rafts had been sighted on the eastern reef of Kuop Island. Since this track would take his boat close to the place where the Jap submarine had been sighted earlier that morning, O'Kane asked for and received the fullest possible air coverage.

This time the Tang was called upon to give every ounce of power at her command. Riding high in the seas with all tanks blown dry—and even her engines smoking a bit—the sub rolled through the danger zone at 21 knots with a monstrous bone in her teeth.

"I was fairly confident," reported O'Kane, "that the Japs would get no more than a fleeting glimpse of us—that is, if they were looking."

When the raft-sprouting reef was in sight, O'Kane received a pleasant surprise. Lieutenant Burns, pilot of the North Carolina floatplane, had not only landed near the rafts but actually transferred their seven occupants to the wings and floats of his plane. As the Tang hove into sight, Burns was taxiing toward her.

The two "ships" were almost within shouting distance when an emergency flash came over the air from one of the escorting planes. A fighter pilot had hit the silk and landed in a raft just off Mesegon Island, which lies between Kuop and Truk. The fighting was hot and heavy in that sector—bombs, bullets, and ack-ack flying. Although friendly fighters formed a protective ceiling, the downed airman was in an unpleasant position. Since the seven men were relatively safe on the floatplane, O'Kane told them to hang on. He would come back—he hoped.

"What with friend and foe banging away at each other, it was a nasty spot for a sub to head into," explained O'Kane. "In fact, the least we expected was to be driven down by shellfire. Anticipating that, we rigged a free running line and a life ring to the top of our S-D radar mast. In that way we could still tow the zoomie clear if we had to go in for him submerged. But somehow—I cannot explain why—unless our strafing escorts discouraged the Nips—we met no opposition. It was just one of those things."

Having rescued Lieutenant H. E. Hill, the sub had to head for another pilot who had parachuted from his burning plane into the sea. Before the Tang arrived, one of the pilot's comrades had dropped him a rubber raft. But the youngster was so weak from the landing impact on the water that he could barely crawl onto the raft. He was rapidly drifting toward the razor-sharp outcroppings of a coral reef when the Tang reached him. In a matter of minutes Lieutenant (jg) J. G. Cole might have been in Davy Jones's locker instead of on the spray-swept deck of the Tang.

Many hours had slipped by since the floatplane had been left to its own resources with its seven hangers-on. Finally, in mid-afternoon, the Tang pulled alongside and took aboard Lieutenant R. S. Nelson, Ensign C. L. Farrell, ARM J. Livingston, AMN R. W. Gruebel, ARM J. Haranek, AMN O. F. Tabrum, and ARM R. E. Hill. The floatplane's tail surfaces had been so battered by the waves that she was no longer flyable; so Pilot Burns kissed his sleek little Kingfisher goodbye and went aboard the Tang, where he was a heavy-hearted witness to its destruction by gunfire.

In a separate report, Commander O'Kane expressed high admiration for the brave action taken by Lieutenant Burns in making the rescue possible by deliberately placing himself in as precarious a position as any of the downed airmen.

Up to now, there had been no time aboard the Tang for either food or rest. Just as O'Kane and his men thought that their long day's work was over, in came another SOS.

A raft with two men aboard had been sighted just south of Ollan. It was now 1515 and the sub could not reach its new objective earlier than 1830. This meant close to sunset. On top of that, the protective planes would be recalled at 1630. All O'Kane could hope for was a night fighter escort that would pick him up about sunset near the spot where the raft had been sighted.

Again, the Tang drummed at high speed through the submarine-infested spot in the region of Kuop. His passage through that area was not as comfortable as it had been with a fighter escort. But again, 21 knots took him through in a hurry. One has to feel sorry for any benighted Japanese submarine skipper who tried to get a shot at the Tang that day. Her unrehearsed, unpredictable changes in course and speed could have bowled him off his rocker.

"Two night fighters joined us at sunset," said O'Kane, "just as we were approaching the raft's last reported position, three and a half miles south of Ollan. They began their search at once. Fifteen minutes later, one of them began circling and fired several red Very stars [flares] four miles to the northwest of us. It was quite dark by now but as we headed toward the circling plane, we sighted the raft from the top of the periscope shears."

With Lieutenant D. Kirkpatrick and AOM R. L. Bentley aboard, the Tang dismissed the planes and set its course at slow speed for a clean-up search west of Truk. Tired they were, bone-weary, but I know that Dick O'Kane and his lads looked just as proud and happy as they did when I met them at the dock on their return to Pearl Harbor.

In their tiny galley, the cooks were crowding every facility to prepare food for a sizable batch of very hungry extra hands; while in the already crowded wardroom as well as in the forward and after-torpedo rooms, officers and crewmen tried to figure out how to look after the creature comforts of twenty-two unexpected but very, very welcome guests.

Yes, indeed..."Fly-Boys zoom from sun to sun, but Lifeguard's work is never done."

One of my most treasured souvenirs of the war is a watercolor of the Tang picking up aviators off Truk. The artist, Lieutenant Commander Edward T. Grigware, USNR, was on the staff of Rear Admiral "Black Jack" Reeves, who commanded Carrier Division Four during that strike. The letter which accompanied it from Admiral Reeves made especially pleasant reading:

"The work of your ship was an outstanding example of efficiency, coolness under fire, and resulted in the saving of a number of valuable lives. Equally important was the boost in morale which comes from the knowledge that the plane may be down but the occupants aren't necessarily out."

I sent the original to Commander Dick O'Kane and a color copy to the Big Boss.

The Tang's record bag of rescued zoomies stood for over a year.

7 - Stingray Gives First 'Scope Ride'

"Lookouts below! Clear the bridge! Dive, dive! Take her deep! Flood Negative!" shouted Skipper Sam Loomis. A Jap "Betty" type bomber [Mitsubishi G4M] was screaming in from cloud cover to attack his ship, the Lifeguard submarine Stingray.

"Damn that Betty," he muttered, as the sub slipped below the protecting surface. "I hope our chickens [Submarine Combat Air Patrol fighters] get him."

Machine gun bullets thudded into the sea or ricocheted off the steel hull. The conning tower crew, faces strained, were clutching handy supports and waiting for the crash of the first bomb. It might be their last...None came.

"Bring 'er up to periscope depth," ordered Sam. "Guess he didn't have one left."

"Up to periscope depth," repeated the Diving Officer.

As the 'scope eyepiece rose from the periscope well, Loomis squatted, unfolded the training handles, pressed his eyes to the rubber eye-guard, and followed the upward movement until the object lens broke water.

"Hold 'er there," he called, as he rapidly swept around the horizon.

"Oh, boy! Look at that—our fighters are on him—right on his tail! Have a look, Randy."

The Executive Officer, Lieutenant Commander R. A. Moore, glued his eyes to the eye-guard and continued the running narrative: "He's right down to water level! Three of 'em are making passes. He's smoking! There he goes! He splashes! Look, Captain!"

"Scratch one Betty," said Loomis. "Stand by to surface. Sound three blasts."

It had been a hot morning for the Stingray. Lieutenant Commander Sam C. Loomis, Jr., of Aurora, Illinois, had spotted his ship on her Lifeguard station west of rugged Orote Point at early dawn. While waiting for the carrier planes to come roaring in from the sea, three times had he been forced to dive to avoid strafing or bombs from Japanese planes.

The target for today, June 12, 1944, was Guam, our own Guam. The thought of bombing it was painful to everyone—especially to the two Chamorro mess boys aboard the Stingray. Their chins were really down on their chests.

The Chamorros, as the natives of Guam are called, are a clean, friendly, and warm-hearted people. Their sons, serving usually in the steward's department, have long been favorites in Navy ships. However, Operation Forager (the invasion of the Marianas) was on, and the soldiers and marines were due to storm the beaches at Saipan on the fifteenth. It was imperative therefore that every plane and air facility on Guam be destroyed. We could only hope the Chamorros would keep away from the airfields.

Later, in July, when Rear Admiral Dick Connolly's amphibious forces shelled the beaches of Guam prior to invasion, leaflets were dropped, telling the native population to take to the hills.

The war had taken great strategic strides since the Harder and Tang rescues recorded in the preceding chapters. Top-level decisions had been made to bypass such major roadblocks as Kaviang, Rabaul, and Truk. The cost of taking these strong points, in American and allied lives, would have been terrific. Instead, battered to harmless pulps, they were left to "die on the vine," as Admiral Nimitz expressed it.

Similar top-level decisions had turned the line of our attack northward toward Japan instead of toward the establishment of air bases in China. Saipan, Tinian, and Guam were to be taken for use as major bases for air offensives against the home islands of the Empire.

In the lower echelons, ours was not to reason why, but these changes in plans sure made sense to our "do or die" level.

No sooner had the Stingray popped up to the surface than her business began to pick up.

"As I remember it," said Sam Loomis, telling me of his adventures a decade later, "our first customer was a Lieutenant Searcy. He had burned up his engine trying to catch the Betty which had strafed us. Just too eager a beaver."

The strike against Guam had reached full concert pitch. The flash and flare of exploding bombs, the dull roar of bursting steel casings, the whine of dropping bombs, the chatter of machine guns, and the slam-slam of antiaircraft cannon created a pattern of noise that was united into one solid Niagara of sound by the ever-present—nearby and far off—ear-dinning snarl and whine of powerful aircraft engines and swirling propellers.

Loomis was an old hand at submarine warfare. But this drama of sound and motion was his first sight of a carrier strike. He had heard how such an attack by our mighty Task Force 58 would denude an island of houses and trees in a matter of minutes and reduce the ruins to flame-eaten ashes. The so-called "Mitscher haircut," which many denuded islands wore in those days, was not a subject for light humor. A carrier strike, as seen from the deck of a submarine a few miles offshore, was a dramatic sight. Inspiring. But also frightening.

From his position near the machine gun on the after end of the cigarette deck, the sub's Executive was watching for Jap Bettys and Yank fighters, hoping against hope that—if they came at all—the first would be the last. Then suddenly, on the stroke of nine o'clock, two fighters peeled off from high above the Stingray and plummeted toward the submarine. They zoomed at such speed that, in seconds, they changed from small black dots into easily recognized F6F fighters.

"There's our chickens!" shouted Moore with obvious relief to Loomis on the navigating bridge.

"Chickens" was one of the many colloquial names for covering planes detailed to keep enemy aircraft out of a Lifeguard submarine's hair. All hands on the bridge watch grinned at the sight of the swiftly diving fighters. The thinly veiled tension that had held all the men on the Stingray's deck in its grip vanished in an instant. They had felt pretty naked and defenseless before that fighter cover arrived.

Eight minutes after the Stingray's "chickens" arrived, word came over the VHF (very high frequency) voice radio from the leader of a F6F Squadron that one of his fighter pilots was in trouble.

"He won't attempt to bail out," continued the unidentified voice, "he can see your sub and will make a water landing as near you as he can. If any Bettys are around, we'll protect him on the way down. Over."

The voice had barely stopped when the lookout on the starboard side of the periscope shears sang out: "Fighter plane in sight! F6F is zooming in for a water landing on our starboard quarter. Several friendly planes are circling him. There he is—he is down—about a mile and a half away."

"All ahead, flank. Right full rudder," shouted Loomis from his position on the bridge to the helmsman in the Stingray's conning tower below. In seconds the submarine's four main engines added their roaring song to the overall noise pattern and within five minutes the Stingray reached the spot where the fighter pilot had landed on the sea. The plane, having no buoyancy whatever, sank almost instantly. However, the pilot had enough time to clamber out and pull the air bottle that inflated his Mae West life jacket.

From a spot along the life rail near the forward torpedo hatch, Lieutenant E. G. Weed stood ready to heave a line to the pilot whose head and shoulders bobbed on the gently rolling sea. However, in making its approach, the sub had a little too much way on, although Loomis had killed most of its speed as his human target came within easy range. The line Weed threw to the downed flier fell squarely on the man's shoulder. He grabbed it, but in his weakened condition could not hang onto it against the pull of the sub.

Now that they had a good look at him—eyes closed, arms hanging limp, head lolling on his left shoulder—it was obvious that the airman was completely exhausted and only semi-conscious. Loomis waited until his vessel was clear. Then he backed down toward the pilot, slowly, carefully. When he was some fifty feet off the quarter, Weed, with a line around his waist, jumped into the sea and towed the pilot to the sub's side. From this point, willing hands lifted the now unconscious flier aboard, took him below, and placed him in the competent care of the sub's experienced Pharmacist's Mate.

The latter found the pilot to be suffering from cuts about the head, shock, and too much saltwater. None of these conditions was serious and, before too long, their new shipmate, Lieutenant John Moore Searcy, was able to join the coding and decoding watch—the customary duty assigned to visiting firemen. He seemed glad to be aboard.

Needless to say, the officers and crew of the Stingray were glad to have the flier aboard. Submariners had an intense admiration and respect for their brothers of the flying services, even though they liked to rib them about the kid glove features of piloting—and frequently cursed them for trigger-happy tendencies to shoot up our own submarines.

Nevertheless, the sheer abandon with which these youngsters drove home their attacks and the casual manner in which they faced death in a blazing plane or in the water on limitless stretches of the Pacific won the hearts of our lads in the Lifeguard League. They considered it a high honor to save the life of a comrade in arms even at the grave risk of placing their own lives and their ship in jeopardy.

The alert enthusiasm and skill which submariners had shown in wiping the surface of the sea clean of enemy ships was now given full play in rescuing men who, without the daring, resourcefulness, and skillful seamanship displayed by Lifeguarding submarines, were almost certain to meet tortured deaths.

That afternoon, Skipper Loomis and his sub chalked up another rescue that saved the lives of two men—Lieutenant Richard Edwin James, pilot, and David Hamblin Smith, radioman, of an SB2C that had been shot down and made a forced landing in Apra Harbor about a mile from Orote Point. Their Hellcat fighter-bomber plunged down with a flaring trail of smoke and the blood-chilling swansong of a dying plane screaming around its metal body.

By miraculous luck and good airmanship, Pilot James managed to make a belly landing in Apra Harbor. It saved his life and that of his radioman tailgunner. The resulting geyser of water and smoke was so impressive that the enemy evidently concluded that the crew had been liquidated. At any rate, the Japs were too busy fighting off other American planes to pay attention to two dazed fliers who managed to squirm out of their sinking plane, inflate a rubber life raft, and scramble aboard it.

At first, Lieutenant James and Radioman Smith just lay doggo, getting their breath, thanking God that they were still alive and wondering how they were going to get out of their predicament. It looked hopeless. Jap ships were anchored not five hundred yards away. Orote Point, studded with large- and small-caliber guns, was looking down their throats.

They lay panting, waiting for the inevitable strafing which would spell their doom or for the sound of an approaching motor boat which would mean the same thing but more slowly, more painfully. Nothing happened. The Japs apparently were not wasting ammo on a pair of dead-looking zoomies. Let nature take its course.

They exchanged whispered doubts and fears. James lifted his head for a peek around.

"My God," he whispered, "those ships are getting farther away. We are drifting out of the harbor. The wind is pushing us out to sea!"

"The sea, sir! It's a long way to the Philippines—and we got no chow—no water," protested Smith.

"One gets you five there will be a sub out there to pick us up," replied James.

"Could be a Jap sub, too," gloomed Smith.

"No bloody fear, Smitty, they have a Lifeguard submarine out there whose job is to pick us up—and her station is a few miles off Orote Point. And those boys eat good!"

Presently James thought it would be safe to use the paddles. A few whining rifle bullets greeted this step, but the range was too long for accurate shooting. Eventually they set their tiny sail and, with eyes peering into the sunwash on the brine, into the wild blue yonder they had just left, they flashed their signal mirror at every plane they sighted. None appeared to see them. They had other things to worry about.

At 1351 Pilot James said to Radioman Smith: "Hey, Smitty, there's our submarine. Almost dead ahead. Waggle your mirror, big boy. Waggle it good so they'll catch its flash or we'll be late for lunch."

At 1353, Torpedoman R. E. Waterman, standing starboard lookout on the Stingray, saw something glitter on the water at a distance of two miles. As Loomis headed for the spot full speed, it looked to him, because of the glare on the water, as if he had two Japs on a raft.

As the sub approached, its skipper had two men with tommy guns standing by. The short, ugly snouts of the weapons were trained on the men on the raft. If they were of the Kamikaze breed—one tricky move and they'd get it.

"What's this," muttered Smitty, observing the heavily armed reception committee on the submarine's deck, "beans or bullets?"

As soon as Loomis recognized his would-be guests for what they were, he struck the guns below on the double and gave a rip-roaring "Ha-ha!" to his "chickens" who were now zooming on the sub. This was a big moment. The Stingray had actually seen and practically rescued two surviving fly-fly boys before their protective escorts saw them from aloft.

Just who had found them mattered little to Lieutenant James and Radioman Smith. They were down in the innards of the Stingray stowing away submarine food, than which none is finer.

"See what I told you, Smitty," said James between bites. "Nothing but the best on these packets."

What with three zoomies rescued in one day, one might think that the Stingray would have had more than its share of good fortune on any single patrol. But starting the next morning, it was to participate in a rescue that required men with hair on their chests. Or, as General Holland Smith used to say, a job that would separate the men from the boys.

It was to give the submarine service and the zoomies the first example of our newly devised periscope rescue—a tactic first suggested, as I remember it, by Lieutenant Commander G. W. Lautrup, Skipper of the Gar.

While making some close-in rescues at Peleliu Island in April, Commander Lautrup had planned to use it if the shore batteries opened fire. Rear Admiral John Brown, who trained all our submarines prior to their patrols, immediately seized the idea and incorporated it in his programs. The flying services were also informed of its possibilities. Necessarily, its employment involved a pretty tough toboggan ride for the zoomie, but it might save his life where no other method could.

The incident began during the dawn hours of June 13 while the Stingray was prowling along the west coast of Guam near the southern tip of the island. A message came over the air that a pilot had parachuted from his plane—destroyed in mid-flight at high altitude by enemy AA fire—into the waters of Agana Bay, right under the noses of the shore batteries.

In order to prepare himself, his ship, and his crew for whatever lay ahead, Loomis asked the "chickens" that were circling over the position of the downed pilot what condition the shore batteries were in. He was told that one dual-purpose battery was still in action. All the other guns had been silenced by the previous day's bombing.

According to the first firm word—in which the downed pilot was changed from an indefinite rumor to a definite report by air-cover—the pilot was floating in his Mae West some five hundred yards off Agana airstrip which, at that point, ran close to and parallel with the flat sandy beach.

Sometime later, while the Stingray was rolling up knots to reach the downed man, Loomis asked the air-cover that protected the zoomie from Jap attack if the downed pilot had increased the gap between himself and the shore batteries.

"No, I don't think so," came the hesitant reply. "It is still about five hundred yards and we are undergoing rather heavy ack-ack fire."

"Hey, you dumbo," cut in another voice in a near whisper, "don't tell that pig-boat feller that—or he'll never go in to pick our guy up."

There was a brief pause—after which Loomis' voice-partner came back and added: "Say, that report about being five hundred yards off the beach was haywire. He is now about a mile off the beach—maybe even more than a mile—and he is drifting nicely. Yes, siree, very nicely indeed."

"Oh, yeah," replied the chuckling Loomis. He knew exactly how bad the score was. Anyhow, a matter of a few hundred yards makes little difference to an artillery gunner.

To make his fairly long run to Agana Bay and to reach the dunked pilot, Loomis had to stand well out to sea and give Orote Point a wide berth. It was past noon when he changed course and pointed the submarine's nose southeastward into the shallow indentation known as Agana Bay.

Whatever plans the skipper might have had to take the Stingray in on the surface were changed by the early arrival of Japanese calling cards in the shape of shells that slashed into the sea a bare four hundred yards ahead. At that moment, the Stingray was some two miles from shore in fairly deep water.

"Lookouts below. Clear the bridge!" shouted Loomis. The lookouts shielded their binoculars inside their jackets and scrambled down from their stations and through the conning tower hatch.

The Officer-of-the-Deck and his Quartermaster were right on their heels—in fact, practically rode down on their shoulders. Loomis himself, pausing only to sound two blasts on the diving alarm, beat gravity, as the expression was, down the hatch, shouting to his Diving Officer: "Take her down fast! Flood negative!"

With a nod to the seaman who served as periscope jockey, the skipper went into a deep crouch before the attack periscope which rose to meet him almost instantly. After stealing a swift look at the waters ahead, he rose from his haunches. "Down periscope! Hold her at fifty-two feet. All ahead two-thirds. The bottom shelves fairly fast here. But we are okay for depth at this tide all the way we have to go in...Not bad gunners, those Japs who are still alive," he muttered to all concerned. "They just sent us two more shells as I peeked. The first was only two hundred yards short. The second was even closer. Crawling right toward us, they are. ... Up periscope! But keep it low. Only a few feet. Don't want to stick our necks out too far."

Again, the skipper's narrow hips swung toward the conning tower's deck. A brief look and again: "Down periscope! I can't see our boy as yet. But I know about where he is. I just saw a TBF drop him a rubber boat, the bearing was 150° T."

The minutes ticked by slowly as the Stingray, equally slowly, picked its steady course close to a sea bottom which, with every yard, rose higher and higher under the submarine's rounded hull.

1233—"Up periscope!" ordered Loomis. Then after a careful search ahead and on both bows he exclaimed, "I see our boy—dead ahead—he's on the raft—he looks all right—maybe a little pale around the gills—but no wonder. Who wouldn't? Down 'scope!"

Loomis straightened and grinned at the ship's Talker who, standing in the forward end of the conning tower, relayed the Captain's words to all compartments of the ship. This system, designed to keep everyone informed, is standard procedure on our submarines.

"Up periscope!" A snappy look and: "Our boy sees us. Knows we are looking at him. Gave us a wave and a wide grin. Good lad. Down 'scope!"

A few minutes later. Loomis again: "Up 'scope. We are almost upon him. Have to approach from lee side or crosswind. Wind velocity is from 10 to 12 knots... Pilot is waving. He has seen us again. So have the Nips—two shell splashes in the drink and both quite close. Two more. Much closer. Now they are throwing ack-ack at the pilot. Poor kid—the stuff is close and he tried to duck it. Damn their souls! Down 'scope."

Captain Loomis, mad through and through, turned to his Executive, Lieutenant Commander Moore: "Damn it, Randy, we are going to get that boy, if there's anything left of him, in spite of all the Japs in Asia. But we can't surface here. Not with all those guns going. We might get by with it . . . and we might send the ship and eighty men to Davy Jones. We'll have to use that new PRP—periscope rescue procedure."

"Hope he'll get the idea," replied Moore, "and take a turn with his bow line around our 'scope, so we can tow him out. All pilots must have been briefed on that deal."

"Well, whether he has been briefed or not, we'll simply have to risk it," answered Loomis. "There is no other way. Okay—here we go!"

Turning toward the Talker so that his orders would be repeated for execution in various parts of the ship as required, Loomis continued: "All ahead, creeping speed. I want to keep us barely moving. Hold course steady as you go. Control: Keep her steady at fifty-two feet. That will give me plenty of 'scope exposed. I want him to have the best chance to grab it. Stand by—up 'scope."

Watching through the eyepiece of Number One scope, Loomis continued: "The pilot sees us and is waving. He is holding up his left hand. There is a deep cut across its palm. We are very, very close—but the pilot shows no sign of making his bow line ready to hitch on to the 'scope."

The skipper shifted from Number One to Number Two 'scope, explaining: "I have lost him in the Number One field. Will have to try Number Two; it is lower and wider. Yes, I see him. We are heading directly for him. On the nose... We missed him. Damn!" Turning to Moore, the skipper continued: "Looks like he never heard of PRP."

Loomis was annoyed and with good reason. To take a submarine submerged into the shallow depths five hundred yards offshore—less than half a mile—smack under enemy guns and maybe even subject to enemy air attack, is no picnic.

And now, in these shallow waters, he had to swing the Stingray in a full circle and make another approach. Submarines do not handle well when backing submerged. They usually tend to broach the surface—which might have been fatal in this instance. Valuable time was lost while the ship was maneuvered into a new position. During this ticklish period, about half a dozen shells landed close aboard on the starboard quarter.

The first approach on the rubber boat was made at 1303. The next at 1352. As the sub crept toward its objective, Loomis, at the periscope, reported: "We are almost on top of him. We are right on him. (Pause) Oh, God—dear God—now he is paddling away from the 'scope. Way out of the way. We have missed again. Left full rudder. Down periscopes. Light the smoking lamp!"

The last command referred to the old naval custom of the days before matches were commonplace or permitted aboard ship. In those times, ships carried a lamp at which men could light their pipes. When the word was passed that "the smoking lamp is lighted," the men were permitted to smoke. In submarines on long dives the lamp was usually "out" in order to avoid fouling the air but generally lighted once a watch or once an hour. Loomis lighted it at this time to give his—and others'—nerves a bit of relaxation from the high tension of the operation.

"What do you do with a guy like that?" he asked in deep desperation. For every minute that passed by in this extremely dangerous position, Loomis could feel deadly danger close in upon his vessel, jeopardizing the life of every man aboard it.

"Stand by for another approach," he ordered with a wry grin. It had to be a dismal day indeed when Sam Loomis could not muster a smile. "We'll waltz Matilda around again, as the Aussies say down under."

During the preliminary operations, Moore ran up the periscope and discovered that carrier planes were bombing Agana Airfield and the shore batteries. Unfortunately, this harassment was not enough to stop the Jap gunners from throwing shells in the general direction of the raft and the spot where they believed the rescue submarine would be. Seven projectiles splashed into the sea uncomfortably close to the periscope.

At 1453, Loomis staged his third try. Again, his exposed periscopes stood in open defiance to enemy gunners. Again, the pilot missed the bus. "Well, anyhow," mused Loomis, "he seems to be learning. Our training course in blindman's buff is evidently taking hold. This time he showed the first sign of trying to reach the periscope. Maybe this steady dose of shellfire has made him realize that a periscope ride may be okay after all. But I am getting damned disgusted—plus a stiff neck and a blind eye—peering and peering into that confounded 'scope. Blast him—I'll give him one more chance. If he doesn't take it, he'll spend the rest of this war in a Jap prison camp. And if we get him aboard, I sure am going to make that zoomie Captain of the Head (toilet)."

Wham! Topside splashed another close shell followed by a burst of ack-ack.

At 1516—Fourth rescue try. "Well, what d'ye know," yelled Loomis in rank violation of traditions that call for bland manners on the part of submarine skippers. "He finally got the word! We've got him. We've got him hooked. He's on the Number One periscope and he is hanging on for dear life. Randy, reverse course and head us for deep water. Keep your speed to two knots or slower if you can."

For almost a solid hour, the Stingray towed the rubber raft to seaward at two knots. It must have been extremely painful for the pilot bumping along over the white caps and holding desperately on to the bitter end of the bow line while saltwater deluged the raw cut in his wounded hand.

His face was a veritable mask of pain and he signaled frantically to be taken aboard, but that was not to be thought of. Loomis was adamant. And rightly so, for the Stingray would have been a sitting duck for one of those Jap 5.5-inch guns. She had spent several hours in waters too shallow to get below the lethal range of aircraft bombs.

Now that that stomach-fluttering experience was over, Loomis was not going to take unnecessary chances on the lives of his crew and his ship.

And so it was not until 1611 by the Stingray's conning tower clock that Loomis gave the order to lower Number One periscope—the one which had been towing the raft. The amazed expression of the wounded pilot seen through the other 'scope was certainly one for study. He probably thought, "Well, now they are going to abandon me! Where do I go from here?"

At the Number Two periscope, Loomis watched the pilot's face which presently changed its expression from one of pain, to amazement, to visible delight, as he gradually realized that this twentieth century version of the old-time Nantucket Sleigh Ride—

wherein whalers in dinghies were hauled over the waves at racing speeds by harpooned whales—had come to an end.

"Stand by to surface," ordered Sam. "Control: Take her up gently so we don't hang him up on the periscope shears. Also, leave the deck aft awash so we can get him aboard more easily in case he's passed out. Quartermaster: Sound three blasts."

As the three raucous blasts of the surfacing signal rasped through the ship, ready hands brought her up and a sigh of relief could be heard in her control room—or was it perhaps the air pressure exhausting through the opening conning tower hatch?

It had been a hard day, a grand day, and the first periscope rescue in history had now been successfully completed.

But Ensign Donald Carol Brandt of Cincinnati, Ohio, did not pass out—cold or otherwise. The stamina he had shown throughout the ordeal stood by him to the end. While the Pharmacist's Mate tended his wounded hand, the youngster explained to the Skipper and his Executive that during the first and third approaches, he was afraid the periscope would hit him, perhaps rip his boat and sink it.

"I tried to get out of the way," he added, "and come astern of you. As for being briefed on Periscope Rescue Procedure—sure; but somehow it is not quite the same thing to learn about it in a briefing room and come face to face with it five hundred yards from an enemy shore with shells splashing all around."

In all truth, Ensign Brandt had several points in his favor. The shock of getting belted out of a plane at fourteen thousand feet, followed by an upside-down fall because he had gotten tangled up in his parachute shrouds, had landed him in the water in a dazed condition. Acting as a live target for the nearby Jap battery hadn't helped his state of mind either. These were not conditions one hears about in briefing-bees.

"He has taken quite a beating," wrote Loomis in his log, "and taken it well." Then, as a closing touch in the lighter vein, he added: "We're on speaking terms now, but after our third approach on him, I was about ready to let him stay right where he was."

Our troops stormed ashore over the shell-blasted beaches of Guam a few days later. In the diary of a dead Japanese soldier was found an entry stating that two enemy fliers had been shot down in Apra Harbor and that an American submarine had come into the anchorage and rescued them.

"I believe," said Captain Loomis, "that the Jap soldier had these last two rescues confused and, writing from hearsay, was actually combining them into one yarn. Certainly, the periscope rescue in Agana Bay got much more attention from the enemy."

In any case, the story really gave the Lifeguard League a build-up. It was a grand piece of morale-lifting propaganda for both zoomies and submariners and in the same vein as an article about a rescue off Tokyo Bay written later by the war's most beloved correspondent, [famous roving Pulitzer Prize-winning reporter] Ernie Pyle [killed by enemy fire in the Battle of Okinawa, 1945].

ERNIE PYLE IN 1945

8 - Finback Also 'Scopes Zoomie'

WHILE SOLDIERS AND MARINES UNDER Generals Holland Smith and Roy Geiger were storming the beaches and conquering or liberating Saipan, Tinian, and Guam, Vice Admiral Marc Mitscher's big flat-tops of Task Force 58 were not idle.

Sometimes they were called upon to blast diehard enemy positions ashore, but their main endeavor was to neutralize all Japanese installations—air facilities in particular—which might interfere with the master plan for future operations in the Marianas and Central Pacific.

Since that plan called for use of long-range bombers, based in the Marianas, to strike the Japanese homeland, it was important that all enemy-held islands to northward—Iwo Jima, the Bonins, and Marcus—be rendered impotent. Hence carrier groups were dispatched from time to time to do the job. Even after Saipan, Tinian, and Guam were secured, there remained a vast amount of work to be done. Landing strips, roads, barracks, workshops, and all the air facilities required by the Army Air Force and its B-29 superforts had to be prepared.

The islands literally crawled with bulldozers and heavy equipment. Thousands of Seabees and Army Engineers swarmed ashore from transports and LST's. At Guam, for instance, it was the top Seabee, Commodore Wm. O. Hiltabidle, Civil Engineer Corps, as I recall it, who said his men had moved more dirt there than was moved in digging the Panama Canal.

Implementing the long-range bombing plan had top priority. Nothing was allowed to interfere—not even the Japanese. To ensure such non-interference, the gun-studded Rock of Iwo Jima and the beautiful Bonin Islands—once the home of a colony of Americans and Hawaiians hopeful of growing sugar cane—were blasted almost continually during the late summer and fall of 1944.

Occasionally the enemy retaliated with wave-skimming night bombings of Saipan, but the force employed was small and our losses from such attacks were light.

As our TF 58 carrier strikes became almost routine training exercises for new air groups against live targets, one of them set the stage for a unique and thrilling rescue, somewhat after the Stingray pattern. This was accomplished off Haha Jima in the Bonins about a month after the Gato made a determined but unsuccessful bid to snatch a zoomie right from under the noses of the Nips who guarded Okimura Bay.

This other incident, in which the Finback shared starring honors with Ensign James W. Beckman of the Enterprise, took place in mid-afternoon on September 2, 1944, about one mile west-southwest off Megane Island, which lies a skip and a jump as bombers fly from Haha and Chichi Jima.

The show began fairly early that forenoon, when Lieutenant Commander R. B. Williams, skipper of the Finback, had word from one of the two F6F fighter planes which were flying air cover. The message was that a fighter bomber of the carrier San Jacinto had crashed nine miles east of Minami Jima.

As Captain Williams started for this reported position, he gave the guns along that coast a good wide berth. He was in a hurry and did not want to be forced down as he had been the day before off Iwo Jima by a couple of shells which smacked uncomfortably close into the Finback's wake.

The sub reached her destination after a two-hour run and just as the Navigator was about to report the noon position to his skipper, as per Navy regulations. There, waiting on the pinpoint, so to speak, was Lieutenant (jg) George H. W. Bush, but no sign of his two-man crew. Bush had not seen his crewmen parachute. They could have jumped, he said, when the disintegrating ship was wobbling over Chichi Jima—or they might have gone down with it.

However, before writing the men off as lost, Williams and his lookouts began a surface search on the chance that the fliers might have jumped and had the good luck to land in the sea. The air-cover planes were requested to keep a sharp lookout.

This search had been in progress about half an hour when word came that a plane had sighted a rubber boat. A quick checkup revealed that the position given would place the raft high in the hills of Haha Jima! Nothing daunted, the Finback started south anyway, asking for jigs, repetitions, and confirmations until Williams overheard one plane say that it was actually circling over a raft some nine miles west of Haha.

"We decided to head for that position because it was as good as any dope we had," reported Williams. "At any rate, it made our cover feel better. In fact, they were so full of happy daydreams that they tried to steer us right through the middle of the island—just to save time, I guess! Later we heard from one of the planes that the pilot on the raft was being shelled—about one and a half miles from the beach of Megane Iwa. That was bad news, and the spirits of all hands dove below three hundred feet."

So it was that the Finback approached its objective, hoping that the Good Lord would protect the zoomie against shrapnel, for at that point only the J-factor could save him. The J-factor, it should be mentioned, was a very real thing to our submariners and reverently spoken of. It recognized the fact that some situations can be resolved only by the divine intervention of Jesus.

About three o'clock in the afternoon the sub was close enough to the scene for Williams to take in the overall picture. Some five miles off he saw several planes circle over a spot in the water quite close to the beach. In the air, near that spot, he saw bursts of ack-ack. Through his Talker, Williams sent word throughout the Finback that their zoomie was still afloat and intact. This welcome news lifted the spirit through the ship no end.

Consulting his chart, Williams found that the water was deep enough to allow him to make his approach submerged. To approach any other way would have been suicidal. "Too much shell fire for us to attempt a rescue while surfaced," announced the skipper. "All ahead full!"

A moment later he cleared the bridge and sounded the diving alarm. "Hold her at shallow depth," he instructed the Diving Officer. "I want plenty of periscope up to search with."

At 1530, Williams slowed to one-third speed, so as not to have too much vibration in the periscope, and motioned to the periscope jockey for up-periscope. A quick look all around, a tense search around the bow; then, "Bearing, mark!"

"Zero nine seven, true," noted the Executive.

"Down periscope," ordered the skipper with a grin. "I saw him a little on the starboard bow—quite a ways off—and catching hell, poor devil. That ack-ack up there is really thick. Change course to zero nine seven."

"Zero nine seven, sir," repeated the steerman, easing his wheel to starboard.

Captain Williams misjudged his range to the life raft—not a hard thing to do—and as a result when he took his next periscope peep at 1550 he was right on top of the raft and, in spite of backing full speed, roared by the astonished zoomie at four knots.

"Guess I must have misjudged the masthead height of that pilot," grinned the skipper to his appreciative audience. "We'll swing around and come down to him from upwind."

After a bit of stalking which was definitely not facilitated by the usual trade wind breeze and choppy sea, contact was successfully made. This pilot evidently remembered what he had been told in the briefing room.

"With Number Two scope," reported Williams, "I watched him lean out of his raft and hook an arm around the Number One scope. Then he was all set... Oh, yeah? You should have seen what happened—and it shouldn't have happened to a Jap. With the pilot hanging on, we headed away from the beach. With all that shrapnel in the air, I wanted to get him away, pronto. First, I tried two-thirds speed. But that was much too fast for the zoomie and the raft. What a sight! Like the daring young man on the flying trapeze, the zoomie hung in a horizontal position, barging from wave-top to wave-top. One arm hung on to the scope barrel; the other hung on to the life raft; and the bailing bucket skittered over the sea, bringing up the rear. Meanwhile, overhead the jubilant air-cover was doing some crazy kind of a way-up-yonder-in-the-blue dance.

"Sprays of hot steel were still spilling all around us when I stopped to see if the pilot would want to change the procedure. I was hoping that he would get into the boat and hitch on with the bowline. And, sure enough, he did that very thing. We got underway again. But even at two-thirds speed, waves tumbled into the boat and the pilot was in the water again. Another stop. Finally, to keep him out of the ocean, we came up to thirty-eight feet so that he could ride on top of the periscope shears. And, at long last, when we were out of gun range at five miles, we planed up, opened the hatch, and rolled out the red carpet to welcome Lieutenant James W. Beckman of the carrier Enterprise."

He was water soaked and weary but otherwise okay. "This is not at all like landing on the Enterprise" acknowledged the Finback's newest guest with a grin. Incidentally, he took a load of worry off the Skipper's mind. Beckman had seen Bush's plane shot down and had noted that only one parachute left it before the craft smacked into the ocean.

"This decided us to discontinue any further search near the shore," reported Williams, "particularly as the Japs were still throwing ammunition and our air-cover had gone home."

The Finback's crew, with two weeks' patrol still to do, thought of our well-stocked recuperation center at Guam and envied the aviators. "That's the nice thing about aviation," said Williams, "either you get home every night or you don't get back at all!"

On the morning of September 8, 1944, at 0535—just as it arrived on Lifeguard station in connection with strikes on the Palau Islands—the submarine Grouper, commanded by Lieutenant Commander F. H. Wahlig, lost its voice.

By this time Admiral W. F. Halsey, after a breathing spell in Pearl, had relieved Admiral Spruance in command of the U.S. Pacific Fleet, and its designation had been changed to Third Fleet.

The Fleet was always ready for a fight whatever its designation, and on this occasion, it was definitely on the rampage. The islands of Peleliu and Anguar were to be given the standard working-over preparatory to soldiers and marines hitting their beaches on September 15. Communications were a top requirement for a Lifeguard.

A singer, awaiting the rising curtain of "South Pacific," could not have been more embarrassed than was the sub's radio chief when he discovered that one of his VHF voice frequency tubes had gone bad. Being resourceful souls, the Grouper's radio specialists established communication with escorting planes by hooking in the APR-I receiver—this they used for listening to incoming VHF messages. All outgoing stuff was sent on the primary carrier frequency. In this rather roundabout fashion, the sub maintained connection with its escorting planes. Its first message was frantic: "Get us an 832 tube as fast as you can—hurry—hurry—hurry!"

From the escort plane, back went word to the carrier Lexington. Without delay, a tube was wrapped up in a float-box, put aboard a fighter that awaited takeoff, and, in fairly short order, dropped near the Grouper. Under cover of a couple of night fighters, the sub was keeping station about three and a half miles west of the sunlit shores of Peleliu Island, a veritable Pacific paradise.

But on this morning, what with the thick black plumes of smoke and the white smears of ack-ack that filled the skies over the heavily bombarded islands, Peleliu looked much more like a highly active corner of Hades than an earthly outpost of Heaven.

At 1005, the Grouper began maneuvering to retrieve the tube that had been dropped near her. At 1012, just as the vessel was in position to pick up the tube, came a lookout's warning cry: "Burning airplane approaching, dead ahead!"

Before Skipper Wahlig had time to call his rescue crew to stations, a burning torpedo bomber plunged in a mad fall straight toward the sub's bow. It was a paralyzing moment. For one split second it seemed as if the plane would make a smash-landing right on the submarine's deck. All hands on the deck cringed involuntarily. Here was death on wings; unless the pilot of that plane took quick and drastic action. There was no time to swerve the sub. It had no steerage way and could only sit and take it.

Fortunately, the plane's pilot, Lieutenant William H. Craven, had enough margin of control over his plunging craft to nose it into the water some five hundred yards short of the Grouper's port bow. The plane hit the water with a thunderous crash. Wings crumpled. Tail-surfaces broke off. For thirty breathless seconds the smoking fuselage rested on the top of the gently heaving sea.

Then it went down. So swift were the dramatic events that Lieutenant Craven and Radioman Ira G. Gray were almost dragged down by their crippled ship. But they escaped from the wreckage just as the ocean closed above them. Without delay, they were pulled aboard the Grouper, where it was found that they had suffered no harm beyond near drowning, slight shock, and minor cuts. Both were assisted below into the capable hands of the Grouper's Pharmacist's Mate, and their rescue was reported to the Lexington.

Meanwhile the submarine radiomen were well-nigh frantic for fear their precious tube might be lost. "Let's get that 832," they urged their Communications Officer. "We'll be in a heck of a fix if something really breaks loose."

The Skipper was equally anxious to restore normal communications, and at 1025 the Grouper resumed the recovery of the

VHF tube, and while the jittery radiomen looked on—casting anxious eyes now and then toward the skies lest another zoomie should interrupt the operation—the float-box that contained the priceless tube was pulled out of the drink.

Rushing below into the control room, the radiomen took it out of its box, placed it in their set, and turned on the juice. No dice. The Grouper did not regain its voice. The trouble lay not in that particular tube. Before anything could be done about it, word came that a plane was down six miles east of Anguar Island.

Off went the Grouper in pursuit of more zoomies! By sunset the sub had rescued Charles D. Webb, only surviving member of a torpedo bomber crew from the carrier Essex, and the crew of another Essex bomber: Lieutenant Walter E. Harper, pilot; Radioman John F. Dold, and Gunner George F. Burkett.

This crew earned the following entry in the Grouper's log: "The three men were sitting very comfortably in their raft when we came upon them. They could have looked no more satisfied with life in general if they had been out on a very successful fishing trip."

Speaking of fishing—the Grouper's radiomen, in the course of the day, caught themselves the right kind of a VHF tube, and the submarine regained its voice.

Now and then—in searching through the records of submarine sinkings and rescues—we came upon incidents where submarine commanders declined to roll out the red carpet for the reception of enemy floaters. This required a toughness of mind one meets only in time of war, and it always exists by virtue of good cause.

Chances are that this attitude had its starting point in the night of September 12, 1944, when the Rakuyo Maru, a transport in a northbound Japanese convoy was sunk with five other vessels. The sinkings took place in the so-called Convoy College, a much sought-after and highly productive patrol area which included the waters from the northern tip of Luzon to the southern point of Formosa. Its western boundary was the Asiatic coast. The attack on the convoy was launched by a wolfpack made up of the Sealion, the Growler, and the Pampanito.

Having sunk four ships and two escorts, the subs went in pursuit of the remaining ships, leaving the crews of the torpedoed vessels to their own, usually adequate, devices. It was not until the late afternoon of September 15, three days later, that the Pampanito, in cruising back through the area to finish off any cripples, discovered that it was strewn with scores of makeshift rafts on which several hundred men had sought refuge.

It developed that the Rakuyo Maru had been carrying some 1,300 English and Australian prisoners of war from slave labor camps on the Malayan Peninsula to the home islands, where they were to work in factories and mines. Most of these pitiable prisoners, too weak to save themselves, had drowned. Nearly all of the survivors were suffering from malnutrition, beriberi, pellagra, and malaria—on top of which were piled the sufferings from starvation, thirst, and exposure incurred during three days of ocean drifting.

Immediately Lieutenant Commander P. E. Summers, skipper of the Pampanito, sent out a flash for Lifeguard subs that brought the nearby Sealion, with Commander Eli T. Reich in command, within a few hours. The Barb and Queenfish joined the rescuers later. Within forty-eight hours, it is believed, all survivors were picked up. They were a wretched handful of some 150 souls.

It was learned that on being hit, the Japs left the slowly sinking ship and the prisoners of war to their own pathetic resources. The strongest men among them built rafts of whatever would float. From these, the POW's saw rescue vessels come to the aid of their Jap masters. There was plenty of room aboard them, but not one single prisoner was picked up. This conduct dovetailed perfectly with another gruesome story these POW's had to tell. When their work camps in the Malayan jungles were moved, all the sick, those unable to march, were bayoneted to death. In his log, the skipper of the Sealion wrote:

"We took a total of fifty-four men aboard until space limitations prohibited further rescue. The men were in pitiful shape—starved, ill, thirsty, and utterly without hope. All were coated with thick layers of oil. It was heartbreaking to leave so many dying men behind. But we had no choice. Fifty-four extra hands—hardly anyone able to help himself—is a serious burden aboard a sub. Two died the next day."

The reasoning of Commander Eli T. Reich of New York City whose torpedoes, it develops, sank the Rakuyo Maru in the melee of night battle, is understandable and his decision was correct. His first duty was to his own crew and to his own ship, which was in enemy waters, vulnerable to enemy air, surface, and submarine attack. Her ability to dive and to fight had to be preserved.

A Mitsubishi G4M "Betty" or what the Japanese Navy called a *Hamaki* ('cigar' or 'tube') after its shape

9 - Haddo and Mingo as Angels

Two factors in the performance of Lifeguarding—factors that changed this type of duty in the minds of submariners of all ranks and ratings who performed it, from uneasy, even fearful anticipation, to one packed with thrills, some pleasure, and a lot of pride—were those of air-cover (SCAP) and very high frequency (VHF) telephones.

From long before World War II, submarine doctrine had emphasized the danger, the foolhardiness, of remaining on surface during daylight.

There a submarine, even one zigzagging at speed, was more or less a shooting-gallery target for lurking enemy submarines and a mark for swiftly plummeting enemy planes. And our own aircraft, eager to repeat that well-known super-laconic message: "Sighted sub: sank same," were at times an equally dangerous consideration. I have referred to this hazard in a previous chapter.

When submarines had the highly essential protection of two or three fighters with whom they had instant communication, they could venture blithely in where even the proverbial angels feared to tread. Also, their search area was greatly extended by the keen eyes of the pilots aloft. And incidentally they got to witness air strikes and air battles—the greatest shows on earth.

To put it plainly, among submariners only a first-class, double-dyed fool would remain on the surface with an unidentified aircraft approaching in a menacing manner. Supplying vital information and keeping all planes off the Lifeguard's neck—plus extending the search area—was a job for SCAP, and most of them made a splendid go of it.

In the early morning of September 22, 1944, thoughts of the Commanding Officer of the submarine Haddo, Lieutenant Commander Chester W. Nimitz, Jr., of Wellfleet, Mass., could have been pretty black. The Haddo, on her seventh war patrol, was assigned as Lifeguard off Subic Bay in western Luzon for one of Vice Admiral Marc Mitscher's carrier strikes launched from the powerful Task Force 38 east of the Philippines and aimed at

Japanese strongholds, shipping, and airfields in the vicinity of Manila.

Tojo's defenses were being softened up for the landing at Leyte Gulf, which was to take place in October. MacArthur's promise, "I shall return," was about to be redeemed.

The Haddo boasted no VHF and she had been assigned no air-cover. There she was, unprotected as a London matron without an umbrella! Submarines of the Seventh Fleet, sometimes dubbed "General MacArthur's Navy," were a long way from the west coast supply centers. For that reason, they frequently had to do things the hard way, but they got them done, nonetheless.

As a final fly in its early morning ointment, the Haddo had been assigned the unflattering code name of "Sallow Face" for this strike.

But it was hard to dampen the spirits of young Chester Nimitz—son of the Big Boss and chip off the old block—on this particular morning. He was just about to complete a patrol that had been one of the Haddo's best and would add to the luster of her name. After the war the official record was to show that, by September 21, 1944, he had sunk five ships, including a frigate and a destroyer, for a total of 14,636 tons.

The disappointment resulting from one attack still rankled in his mind. In a submerged "down the throat" attack on a destroyer escorting a tanker, the torpedo, the last but one in the Haddo's racks, knocked the target's bow off up to the bridge. But the last torpedo—aimed as the "kill" shot—was a complete miss.

Through his periscope, Commander Nimitz had the heartbreaking experience of watching the damaged vessel towed into shallow water. However, he had the comforting thought that the badly damaged DD would either sink before reaching home or be an awful headache in some Japanese shipyard.

But to get back to Subic Bay... Perhaps the sweetest music Nimitz and his men ever heard came over the various radio sets in the wardroom and crew's quarters when at 0601 excited Japanese voices were heard to announce the beginning of an American air raid on Manila. Almost without break, Nimitz observed enemy planes flying along the coast in a fairly steady but uneven procession.

However, they were too far off to give him cause for worry. An hour or so later, the Haddo tuned in on airwaves that produced the welcome chatter of victorious American carrier pilots talking to each other over the radio as they returned to their flat-tops.

A few minutes later, Nimitz had cause to wish that some of those chatty carrier fly-boys were circling over the Haddo. At 0715, two enemy Bettys tried to sneak attack on the sub by coming in at it from seaward at an altitude of only fifty feet.

But the sharp lookouts foiled them. It took only the words: "Two Bettys, bearing 270—angle on bow, zero—range four thousand yards," to send the Haddo into a record-breaking dive. The sub had barely surfaced some five minutes later—for Lifeguard subs to stay submerged during a strike meant failure to receive emergency rescue calls—when it heard plane pilots say that they thought they saw a life raft in the water. At that very moment a lookout saw a plane zoom the ocean over a spot some fifteen miles to the north, right off the Capones Islands.

Sweeping northward on all four engines at what would have been called forced draft in the days of steam, the Haddo was on the way when—out of the blue—nine fighters came roaring at her in tight battle formation and evidently ready for trouble.

"I did not want to waste time diving if they were friends," said Commander Nimitz. "So, we stayed up and tried to identify them, but they kept heading right at us—so we never caught their silhouettes."

So as not to delay his dive if it should become necessary, the Skipper sent his lookouts and the bridge watch below. Only Chester remained on deck, and he stood close to the conning tower hatch with one foot on the ladder and one hand on the diving alarm handle.

"When the range fell below a mile and a half," explained Nimitz, "my nerve failed. I pulled the diving alarm, jumped down into the conning tower, and yanked the hatch lanyard. We were almost submerged when our radio antennae, still above water, picked up these words: 'Hello, Sallow Face, down there!' "

That was the "friendly" tip-off—that name "sallow face" was one of the favorite taunts suntanned airmen flung at submariners whose long submergences tended to keep their faces on the pale side.

"That was fighting talk," said Nimitz, "and the Haddo fairly bounced to the surface!"

Continuing its course on the surface toward the Capones Islands, the Haddo soon established contact with two carrier fighters who agreed to serve as air-cover. From that moment, one fighter circled the Haddo continuously. The other flew ahead to point out the location of a raft from which a pilot, Lieutenant H. H. Hills, was eventually rescued.

That run to the raft, from the moment one of the fighters began to circle over the sub, was a very pleasant one for Nimitz and his bridge crew. With that nice F6F flying overhead, the naked and helpless feeling a submariner has without a winged umbrella was wholly absent.

All hands were sublimely happy and secure—until the pilot shouted over the voice radio: "Say, you on the sub down there—please fire a couple of rockets if your lookouts sight any planes. I'd sure hate like hell to be caught up here by myself."

"And we thought he was protecting us!" mused Nimitz. In commenting on this episode a decade later, Commander (now Captain) Nimitz wrote to me:

"The downed aviator's two wingmen escorted us over to Hill's raft, several miles from our station. We swept alongside and Hills climbed aboard as his wingmates zoomed jubilantly back and forth over us. The first thing Hills did was to yell up and ask me where we were headed. Leaning over the bridge, I gestured in the general direction of Australia—thinking to myself that the question wasn't too pertinent since there were no other busses on that route.

"Hills promptly turned and gave an emphatic wave off to his two cohorts who immediately lit out to the eastward to begin their long trek back over the Philippines to their carrier in the Pacific. Then Hills came up to the bridge and said sorrowfully that he wished he'd hit an Aussie-based boat. I told him we were based in Fremantle and that I'd pointed to the south in answer to his question from the deck. It seems he had misinterpreted my gesture.

"He was dreadfully upset because he and his teammates had arranged that if one of the three was shot down and recovered by a Perth boat, the other two would ditch their planes and come along for the ride! I was amazed that they seemed to have so little regard for their aircraft, but Holly pointed out that his wingmen had long overstayed their normal on-station endurance and would be hard pressed for gas to make it back to the carrier as it was."

The doctrine was that where a rescue sub was at hand, a wingman was justified in staying to the last gasp to help a downed friend with the understanding that if in doubt as to his ability to make it home he was to ditch also and join his buddy. In this case the wingmen's judgment was somewhat colored by their mistaken belief that to come aboard was to go back to Midway—might as well try to get back to the carrier. Anyhow, a misunderstood thumb signal saved the US Navy a couple of Hellcats. I hope.

All hands aboard the Mingo were mighty proud of themselves that morning of October 4, 1944, when their sub, at standard speed on all four engines, cruised slowly north along the east coast of Borneo. The day was hot, humid, and still, as the days usually are in Makassar Strait smack on the equator.

The day before—in the region of Paternoster Island—the Mingo, Lieutenant Commander J. R. Madison commanding, had come upon a flotilla of five small life rafts harboring six Army aviators. They were all that remained of a Liberator crew which had been shot down on September 30 by Japanese Zeros. The other four men of the original ten-man team had been butchered in mid-air with machine-gun bursts while they hung defenseless under their slowly descending parachutes.

These six survivors—Captain J. R. Elder, pilot, and Sergeants M. H. Schmidtke, E. H. Comstock, T. L. Farley, T. W. Borur, and J. F. Menzie—were given into the care of George R. Anderson, Chief Pharmacist's Mate.

With this fine batting average as a start in the Lifeguard League, the Mingo went in search of other zoomies. In one small bay near Cape Biroe, Skipper Madison saw signs that could spell human activities. Captain Elder, who had suffered no ill effects as the result of three days of rafting that the Mingo's chow and coffee could not cure, warned the sub commander against having anything to do with the local natives. They were, according to his briefing, unfriendly.

At 0801, the lookout sighted several natives along the shore on the starboard hand. No airmen there. Nothing but natives.

At 0807 a port lookout reported a small fire on the beach at the eastern end of a little bay. Presently the fire sent up an extraordinarily large amount of smoke. A signal fire, and no doubt about it. When Madison and Lieutenant Commander Bill Kitch, his executive officer, saw something wave—tan, like a shirt—they decided to investigate.

Kitch and two crewmen—Harry H. Anderson and Richard H. Ahrens—all armed with tommy guns, broke out the sub's rubber boat and paddled shoreward where they soon shook hands with five jubilant Army airmen, members of a Liberator crew that had had to jump when their crippled plane gave up the ghost. The rest of the bomber's crew had also bailed out and should not be far away.

The airmen brought aboard by the rescue party were: Lieutenant H. L. Drollinger; Sergeant R. G. Avenius; and Corporals R. C. Van Corder, R. M. Blake, and P. I. Wingert.

While this meeting took place ashore, the Mingo stood by just inside the one hundred fathom curve in eighty-three fathoms of water. Even though this was plenty of water for a quick dive, the fact that rugged hills marched right down to the sea rendered the ship's radar useless and laid her wide open to surprise air attack. All Madison could do was to post extra lookouts and hope.

Next came the job of finding the rest of the Liberator crew. Since it was impossible to stage a search along the narrow, twisting beach, Madison hung the Mingo's largest flag on the fully raised Number One periscope. This was to convince any observers ashore that the sub was not a Jap. Less than half an hour later, a lookout detected movement on the beach. A flashing light was sighted. Then a parachute was spread on the beach. Through his strong binoculars the eager lookout sighted three men perched on a rock.

"They're Yanks!" he shouted. A boat was put over the side and manned. It was headed toward the shore when, out from among the offshore rocks, came a yellow rubber boat with five of the missing members of the Liberator crew: Lieutenants C. B. Baldwin and R. E. Connell, and Corporals W. W. Smith, J. S. Morrison, and B. Rodrigues.

The last named had a chunk of shrapnel in his leg. The eleventh member was reported to have gone down into the sea and was presumed drowned.

As the last of the five zoomies vanished into the sub through the forward torpedo hatch, Skipper Madison turned to his executive and said, "Know something? This was a real global rescue!" Greeting Kitch's amazed expression with a chuckle, he continued, "Half these lads were picked up at 00-00.5 North. Half of that bomber crew landed just south of the equator; the other half just north of it. How's that for distribution, Mr. Kitch? No living soul could do that if he tried!"

Madison was ready to have his Talker relay this interesting bit of information to all hands when his attention was called to a high-flying Liberator which was pursuing a parallel but opposite course to that of the submarine on the latter's starboard bow about twelve miles away.

"Keep a sharp eye on that plane," directed Madison. "Something tells me that he looks upon us with grave suspicion."

The skipper's hunch was a good one. Our commanders had learned not to take anything for granted. A sub skipper who lost his sense of suspicion was apt to lose his life, his ship, and the lives of the men with him. Presently it was self-evident that the Liberator did not like the Mingo's looks. This despite the fact that the sub still displayed the large flag it had hoisted on its periscope to identify itself to the zoomies.

By now, the Liberator had changed course. It swooped around the submarine overhead but at a respectful distance. Time and again, from the pilot's window, came light flashes from a signal lamp demanding that the submarine identify itself.

This, according to Madison, the submarine did to the best of its ability. In fact, it used every card in the deck. But, evidently, with unsatisfactory results. After trying its Aldis lamp without getting the desired acknowledgment, the Mingo turned to its twelve-inch searchlight. Clatter-clatter-clatter went the Venetian blinds over the lens. No answer.

Next, the sub tried all five channels from A to D inclusive on the VHF. No answer. Now came semaphore signals. No answer. Last resort was radio, both channels, 4475 KC and 8455 KC. No answer.

Maintaining its threatening, not to say truculent, silence, the bomber, after twenty minutes of circling, headed away. But, instead of continuing to whatever point it was heading, the four-engined battle craft turned around, made a deliberate run on the Mingo, and dropped a hundred-pound bomb that landed a hundred yards from the sub, board on the starboard beam.

"Write that Liberator's number down! 444-877," shouted Madison from the bridge through the conning tower hatch to his Yeoman. "If we get out of this alive—if that oaf doesn't sink us, he'll hear of this. I'll fry his ears!"

At this moment, Captain Elder—commander of one of the downed Liberators—asked permission to use the voice radio. Permission was gladly granted. Over Channel B of the VHF voice frequency, the Army pilot spoke to his comrade overhead. He identified himself as a member of the Thirteenth Air Force. He mentioned names and places that no Jap could possibly know anything about. He spoke a language that was plainly that of an Army flier. He told how he and fifteen other crew members of two shot-down Liberators owed their lives to the very submariners the other plane was trying to sink.

"This is a helluva note!" he concluded. "Here these sub-boys stick their necks' way out to rescue us—and you, you blankety-blank egghead, try to scuttle them. And us too! Lay off!"

"Cut it," snapped a cold voice on the loudspeaker. The man upstairs had finally melted to the point of speaking. "Repeat that helluva word, will you?"

"Sure," answered Elder. "I said it is a helluva note and I'll say it again. It is a helluva note!"

"Good! Your sub is okay in my book."

"But—but—what has helluva note got to do with it?" stuttered Elder with a note of sharp amazement in his voice.

"Because if you were a Jap, you couldn't say it right. You wouldn't be able to handle the 'L's."

The Mingo's last message to the Liberator, after making a formal report covering names and numbers of the sixteen rescued, was: "Please go to 'L' home and take your bombs with you!"

And he did.

10 - SAILFISH LAYS GHOST OF SQUALUS

IN THE BOOKS OF MANY SUBMARINERS of all ranks and rates, the Sailfish was written down as a hard-luck ship. This because in the early part of her career, under her original name of Squalus, while diving off Portsmouth, New Hampshire, her main engine induction valve failed to close, and she went to the bottom with the loss of about half her crew. Her sister ship Sculpin spotted the distress buoy and gave the alarm which resulted in saving thirty-three officers and men of the Squalus crew.

In time, by heroic efforts of Navy divers, the Squalus was salvaged. In time, the twenty-six lads who died in her were committed to Mother Earth and, in time, the Squalus was refitted and recommissioned as the Sailfish. It was hoped that with a new name her disastrous past might be forgotten. Most of us forgot; but there were those who could not.

One who could not forget said to me, "Admiral, I never dive in that ship without the haunting fear that I will hear the crash of water coming in through the main induction."

I recommended a transfer for him.

Others felt that hard luck pursued the Sailfish even when, after a heroic fight against the sea as well as against the enemy, she sank the Japanese escort carrier Chuyo. The Chuyo was carrying twenty-one American submariners as prisoners. These prisoners came from the submarine Sculpin—the same boat which had discovered the Squalus' telephone buoy after she sank off Portsmouth. Thus, works the irony of Fate!

Twenty of those twenty-one P.O.W.'s went down with the Chuyo. Sure, it was a heartbreaking piece of bad luck. But, if it was bad luck for us, an unavoidable misfortune of war, it was certainly a double-barreled dose of hard luck for the Japs.

Those who knew the Sailfish—Dick Voge had been one of her skippers—loved the faithful, rugged little ship. She not only earned her place in submarine annals by sinking seven enemy ships but also emerged from the war with a splendid record as a member of the Lifeguard League.

Certainly, to the twelve aviators who were rescued from almost certain death by drowning or by Jap bullets, she was anything but a hard-luck vessel. And if she were haunted—as some otherwise completely sane submariners insisted—then I know that her ghosts were of the kind that fill the Halls of Valhalla—ghosts that inspired the members of her living crew to reach for new heights of adventure and daring.

To me as Commander Submarines Pacific, the results of the twelfth War Patrol of the Sailfish, skippered by Lieutenant Commander R. E. M. "Bob" Ward, of Antioch, California, made particularly satisfactory and inspiring fare.

The Sailfish—on October 12, 1944—had been assigned the Lifeguard job off Takao, Formosa, during one of the famous Third Fleet strikes conducted by Admiral Bill Halsey and Vice Admiral Marc Mitscher and designed to knock out enemy airfields and fleet bases through which reinforcements might be channeled southward from Japan. Eight days later, General MacArthur was due to make his long-promised return to the Philippines by way of the landing craft at Leyte Gulf.

At this point—during those feverish days when Uncle Bill, always on very short notice to me, was working-over such widely spaced targets as Marcus, Okinawa, Formosa, the Pescadores Islands, and northern Luzon—my submarine Lifeguards were kept hopping like the proverbial flea on a griddle.

Fortunately, by this time we had pretty well worked out a standard procedure for the Lifeguard League. Hence, we at Subpac Headquarters in Pearl Harbor had only to select the nearest submarine, assign a reference point and a VHF voice call name well saturated with 'L's, and give the required time on station. Willing hands and sharp minds in the submarines did the rest.

The Sailfish, when assigned to station on this particular occasion during a regular patrol in Convoy College, not only had willing hands and high hearts but she also had a system.

With vision and thoroughness, Bob Ward had brought expert efficiency methods into the Lifeguard League. On the patrol in question, he had set a record which stood for the remainder of World War Two, when her crew, during the afternoon hours of October 12, yanked aviators out of the drink at the rate of one every eleven minutes.

This speed, which hardly allowed time for a full-blown zoomie to get a thorough soaking, was the result of smart thinking and clever organizing on the part of Ward and his crew. Soon after he left his base, Ward organized a rescue team that consisted of four men, one of whom was a top-notch swimmer. This team was equipped with a life ring, to which a long, strong line had been attached, and with a short but quickly maneuverable Jacob's ladder.

Day after day, on the run to station, the Sailfish's rescue team practiced its technique. Kinks in the plan were ironed out and she arrived on her reference point fully ready and able to perform her duties. The procedure was like this:

On sighting a zoomie, the sub would approach at high speed until close aboard. Then, as she slowed down for a pick-up, the life ring would be thrown to the aviator who hung on while the submariners, by means of the lifeline, pulled him alongside their vessel up to the Jacob's ladder. There the swimmer, already in the water, would start the flier up the ladder while the others reached down to give him a helping hand up on deck.

It frequently happened that downed aviators were suffering from shock or wounds and had to be pulled or lifted gently aboard. With a well-directed slash or two by a sharp knife, the swimmer deflated the raft and started it sinking. Then everyone tumbled down the hatch as, from the bridge, the speed of the Sailfish was built up again.

Ward and his boys were mighty proud of this technique which, if nothing else, reduced those very dangerous moments when their surfaced submarine was more or less immobile in a hostile area.

These pretty theories were put to the test of practice on Columbus Day in 1944. The morning had been dull, what with only one or two erroneous rescue calls. In addition, the dawn and forenoon air-covers never showed up. In fact, the sub's winged umbrella did not appear until just after midday. Since 0925, when more than a hundred planes had passed over the Sailfish, Ward knew the strike was on, but he felt a little naked sitting on the surface so close to a big enemy base.

"We have been running at high speeds on the surface with planes all over the sky," wrote Commander Ward, "and just hoping that the Japs are too busy to sneak in on us. When, at last, it came, the air-cover immediately organized itself into two sections of two planes each—one to search for and help us locate downed aviators, the other to circle over us and keep us happily supplied with local control of the air."

That much-welcomed arrival of air-cover happened at 1215. Five minutes earlier a smoking carrier plane was seen to crash into the sea at quite a distance.

"All ahead—full," ordered Ward.

At 1235 the Sailfish made its well-practiced rescue approach on a raft from which its team, quicker than a duck can shake its tail, rescued Lieutenant S. M. Tharp and Radioman R. H. Hodel.

"Plane about to crash—bearing zero four five," sang out a lookout.

At 1257 Ensign A. R. Arnold was snatched from possible death or, at best, a wet ride in a rubber boat.

At 1314 Ensign H. R. Copeland, Radioman R. J. Bradley, and Gunner W. C. Poppel were hauled aboard the time-making Sailfish. Bradley was quite set up and spent minutes congratulating Pilot Copeland. It appeared that he was the first pilot to come back with Bradley from a crash. "I've outlived seven pilots since Pearl Harbor Day," he boasted.

At 1353 Ensign G. Munich, Jr., and Radioman C. W. Anderson joined the wet parade down to the wardroom and mess room of the Sailfish. All wet. All hungry. All happy. None hurt.

In making its last rescue, the Sailfish had competition. A large Jap patrol boat tried to beat the submarine to the rescue of Munich and Anderson. The sub's gun crew manned the forward four-inch gun, but just then the planes that served as air-cover, plus other planes in the vicinity, deciding that the submarine needed support, began strafing and bombing the Jap.

Ward and his boys would have none of that. Over the voice VHF, he sent out this message: "Leave that Jap alone. We want him."

In his report, Ward wrote: "We fired three rounds of four-inch stuff. The second stopped him dead. We then ceased fire and kept the range free for our own planes who put on a good dive-bombing and strafing show that left the wreck of the Jap aflame and sinking. In the middle of this show, a fighter plane came barging down, its pilot shouting over VHF that he was out of gas. He made a spectacular landing smack across our bow. It was close. We had to back emergency to avoid ramming him."

At 1430 the rescue team pulled Ensign D. W. Fisher aboard over the sub's starboard bow.

At 1435 the team swung into action again and pulled Lieutenant (jg) D. N. Scatuorchio and Radioman J. C. Seeley over their vessel's port bow. Just one zoomie after another. And every one of them came aboard by speedy special delivery.

The Sailfish now had six officers, five radiomen, and a gunner aboard. Meanwhile the Jap patrol boat had sunk. "Air-coverage," concluded Ward's report, "is essential and, when well-organized like it was today, it certainly aids the submarine in her work. Except for the possibility of Jap submarines, we felt that our submarine-plane combination had everything well in hand."

Thus, did the Sailfish demonstrate with the hearty cooperation of her SCAP just how simple Lifeguarding can be. Thus, did she lay in their graves any remaining hexes which were reportedly bequeathed to her by that fatal sinking off Portsmouth under her ill-fated original name.

It should be mentioned here that all of these rescues were made in waters which, because of probable mining, the Sailfish had been forbidden, by her Lifeguard orders, to enter. But none of the zoomies had been briefed about avoiding mined areas. Said Bob Ward: "After all, what else could I do?"

My answer is: "You did all right, sailor."

On the subject of minefields and as proof of the truth of the old saying that "familiarity breeds contempt," I submit the log of the Bream's Sixth War Patrol. Commanded by Commander James L. P. McCallum, a lad appointed to the Naval Academy from the state of Missouri, the Bream staged this patrol in the Java Sea and the Gulf of Siam in the spring of 1945.

It could be that the spirit of spring gave the Bream a feeling of confidence and exuberance. Or possibly her soaring spirits were born of what Commander McCallum believed to be a major victory.

On April 29, from 0747 to 1957, the Skipper and his tracking team conducted a well-planned and cleverly executed daylight end-around and moonlight submerged attack against what they believed to be a German blockade-running tanker. The end of the chase came when two torpedo hits transformed the target into a flaming pyre which sank in ninety-eight seconds.

Post-war reports identify the Bream's tanker-target as an ex-submarine tender—a nice bag for any submarine at that stage of the war.

On May 19 the sub was told a pilot was down at 22-02N and 120-15E. On checking his chart, McCallum learned that the spot designated was in the heart of a minefield. But he was too elated over his victory to let that deter him.

Reads the log: "Headed for reported position on four main engines. This position is in a minefield but believe that we can safely go between the lines of the mines." Later: "Picked up pilot in minefield three miles southeast of Shoryuky Island."

A few days later: "Received word of a B-25 crew down in minefield southwest of Takao Harbor. Believe we can get in fairly safely."

Three hours later: "Picked up four survivors of B-25 crew, all badly dazed and bruised. We are mighty glad to get these boys, but wish they wouldn't pick minefields to ditch in."

To me, the intriguing part of that report is the line: "Believe we can get in fairly safely." When one is dealing with a minefield, how does he traverse it fairly safely? The confidence of youth is a marvelous thing. We old folks need more of it.

11 - Archerfish in Big League

THE GODS EVIDENTLY SMILED UPON THE just cause of American fighting men in the Pacific during the fall of 1944 and blessed their arms with victories. On October 20, General MacArthur's divisions swept ashore at Leyte Gulf to wrest Leyte and the island of Samar from the grasp of the Nipponese.

Then followed disastrous defeats of the enemy fleets at Surigao Strait, in the Sibuyan Sea, and at Cape Engano—defeats inflicted by the forces of Admirals Oldendorf, Mitscher, and Halsey, respectively. These almost wholly destroyed the once-vaunted power of the Imperial Japanese Navy.

My own submarine force and that of Rear Admiral Ralph Christie in the Seventh Fleet had made important contributions to these victories by timely reports of enemy fleet movements, by sinking the heavy cruisers Maya and Atago, and half a dozen light craft, including a submarine, frigates, and destroyers.

Last, but not least, our boats had contributed by filling the Straits of Luzon, the South China Sea, and the East China Sea with the sunken wrecks of southbound transports and cargo ships which were desperately needed in the Philippines to bolster the crumbling defenses of the Empire.

The maimed survivors of these battles with our Third and Seventh Fleets, fleeing northward, met further disaster when the Jallao sank the new cruiser Tama on October 25 and the Sealion II sank the battleship Kongo on November 21.

At the time of which I write—November 1944, when the Archerfish began her historic tour of duty in the approaches to Tokyo Bay—Lifeguarding for the B-29 bombers, during their strikes against the parts and munition centers of Japan, was in its infancy.

Lifeguarding for carrier task force strikes, at this stage, was a well-developed activity. As a result of numerous unfortunate bombing incidents—such as those of the Tunny, the Seahorse, and the Mingo—Standard Operating Procedure—Number Two (SOP-Two) had been issued under date of October 28, 1944.

This order established simple procedures for identification, communication, and all necessary operations of Lifeguard submarines and those whom they served. Copies were furnished to all submarines and to all surface and air commands.

With this doctrine in the hands of all interested units, arrangements for Lifeguard at any point at any time required only one or two dispatches whereby the submarine nearest the projected strike would be alerted and placed on station.

From that point onward, her operations and those of the planes for whom she was Lifeguarding would be conducted as per the provisions of SOP-Two. This policy continued in effect, with slight alterations, until the end of the war.

Immediately after Saipan and Tinian had been secured, Isley and Kobler Fields were built; the USAF moved in bombers and girded itself for bomb warfare against Iwo Jima, the Bonin Islands, and the Japanese home islands.

Soon afterward the Twenty-first Bomber Command, headed by Brigadier General Haywood S. Hansell, moved in with the new superforts, the B-29's, and plans were laid for training runs against selected targets.

Representatives of the USAF called on me in Pearl Harbor, requesting Lifeguard cooperation, and in a few minutes time we had expanded our business into what was to be, eventually, its most active department.

Because of the time element and the distances involved, we delegated handling of Lifeguard operations in Saipan, Tinian, and Guam to the senior submarine squadron commander in Tanapeg Harbor, Saipan. This job was handled by Captain George E. "Pete" Peterson until I moved Subpac H.Q. to Guam in January 1945.

During a hasty visit to Saipan in these earlier days, General Hansell very courteously met my plane at Isley Field and, with great pride, showed me through a brand-new B-29. It impressed me as being a very great weapon, but I still preferred my submarines.

The General promised me an enemy raid from Iwo Jima that night, as the moon was just right. I assured him that I had seen all the air raids I required in London in '41—and I was not disappointed when the promised strike failed to materialize.

High adventure, almost unbelievable attainment, and flat failure were among the seasonings that Fate dished out for Commander Joseph F. Enright of North Dakota and his men aboard the Archerfish on the Fifth War Patrol of that submarine. Her Lifeguard and attack missions took the ship into the home waters of Japan south of Honshu, the heart and nerve center of the Japanese Empire.

The tall adventure, accompanied by high attainment, came to the Archerfish during the middle part of its patrol. On the night of November 28, some twelve miles west of Inamba Shima—an island speck about 120 miles south of Tokyo—the sub picked up an extra-large pip on its radar scope. The Archerfish was running on the surface at the time, charging its depleted batteries. The sky was overcast with a dark horizon to the north.

After more than an hour of tracking, it was decided that the pip on the screen was that of a Japanese aircraft carrier which was stealing out from its base under cover of night, accompanied by four fast destroyer escorts. The carrier, steaming at 20 knots, was trailed by the sub for almost seven hours.

At times, Enright's chances of making an attack appeared hopeless and he sent out frantic contact reports, hoping to draw in nearby teammates.

In answer to one of these, our Subpac Operations Officer, Captain Dick Voge wrote, with my enthusiastic concurrence, a message typical of his humor and unfailing cheer and one which will live in the memory of submariners: "Hang onto him, Joe. Your picture is on the piano."

Toward the end of this chase, there was a favorable change of enemy base course. At the time, Enright concluded that his target was a carrier of the 28,000-ton Hayataka class. He was to learn months later that his quarry was the huge 59,000-ton Shinano—a ship about the size of our recently commissioned James V. Forrestal.

As a result of the carrier's change of course, the Archerfish found itself actually ahead of the target group. Fearful lest one of the escorts should pick him up, Joe Enright dove and made ready for a periscope attack. By now the cloud cover was thinning and the moon was coming out.

At long last, after a thrilling chase, Joe let all six forward torpedoes go. He saw and heard the first two hit while he was still at periscope depth. The remaining four slammed into their target as the Archerfish, anticipating swift reprisal in the form of depth-charge attacks by the destroyers, went deep in search of some measure of security.

To be sure, the avenging escorts arrived within five minutes. But they came too late and with too little. After dropping a mere fourteen depth charges (the nearest at three hundred yards), they rushed back to the wrecked carrier presumably to pick up survivors.

With the coming of daylight at 0610, Joe made his first periscope observation. The sea was empty. Nothing in sight. For all the surface of the sea revealed, there might never have been a carrier and a sinking. Enright's elated message to me ended with, "I think that baby sank." How right he was—but we did not know the full importance of his triumph for several months.

Naturally, the spirit of officers and crew soared sky-high. A carrier is a target in a thousand. And to sink it—nothing short of a grand slam! With this auspicious start, the Archerfish re-dedicated herself to the primary objective: namely, to watch for and to pick up zoomies knocked down in B-29 bomber strikes against Japan.

Several days went by. Bad weather and no strikes. Finally, on December 3, the submarine's radio picked up a lot of high-pitched yapping from Radio Tokyo. In the background of the hysteria, he could hear sirens and bells. No one needed to tell the Archerfish gang what was going on. Our bombers were over Japan's most important target—Tokyo.

As the afternoon dragged on, the weather worsened. Finally, at 1630, Enright got word that a B 29 was in trouble some 120 miles southeast at Hachijo Shima. Joe's heart fell. There was not much chance for those unhappy fliers. Full speed on all engines—bucking the sea that was running that day—gave him, at best, only 10 knots—barely half of what the Archerfish could do under better conditions.

"We clenched our teeth, secured all loose gear, and put double lashings where required, for we knew it was going to be a rough and punishing ride," Joe Enright told me a few weeks later when we met just before Christmas at Camp Dealey on Guam. "I knew—all hands knew—that those poor devils didn't have a chance. In that sea no plane could have landed without smashing into a thousand pieces. Even if they had hit the silk, there wasn't much chance of a life raft living among those towering seas."

At 1656 another message came from the plane, asking for assistance but giving a new position. The submarine replied that she was on the way and got the plane's "Roger." Then, just to ensure no mistake had been made, the Archerfish conducted a sweep of the first reported position and continued on toward the second. During the night the Scabbardfish arrived and took up the search at the first location.

After a terrific night, in which the Archerfish took tons of water down the main induction and drowned out one auxiliary generator, the submarine reached the second reported position to discover only mountainous seas. Unless a life raft had been spotted right on the crest of a wave, it would have been impossible to sight it at more than a few hundred yards.

"It looked like a hopeless chance," said Enright, "but we went into an expanding square search, praying that we might lick this apparently futile setup, as we had been lucky enough to do in the chase of that carrier."

But the J-Factor was not right this time. After two more days of combing the area and following the drift line, the search was abandoned. It was a bitter blow to the Archerfish.

Failure—defeat—is hard to take in any game, but in this game where defeat meant failure to save men who were at the mercy of the cruel sea, it was especially sobering and heartbreaking. Even the thought of their wonderful achievement in the sinking of a carrier brought little consolation.

But God knows they had done their best. No man—no angels—could do more.

12 - Pomfret Braves Tokyo's Defenses

EARLY IN JANUARY 1945, we dispatched my Headquarters ship, the veteran submarine tender Holland, to Apra Harbor, Guam, preparatory to moving down myself with the operational members of my staff.

Two tenders were already on the job there, and our recuperation center on the windward side of Guam was operating full blast. It had been named Camp Dealey in honor of the heroic and beloved Commander Samuel David Dealey, lost with all hands in the Harder.

On arrival in Guam and while getting established aboard the Holland in the last days of January, I made contact with Major General Curtis LeMay of the Twenty-First Bomber Command, who was at the time the senior USAF officer on that station.

Command relationships in the AAF Pacific Ocean Areas seemed somewhat involved to us sailormen—and later became more so with the arrival of topflight talent from the European Theatre, such as Generals Spaatz, Harmon, Giles, and Twining. However, all of my own conferences were held with General LeMay and later with General Barney Giles, so that no duplication of effort or conflicting directives resulted.

Admiral Nimitz believed in maintaining the shortest and most direct lines of communication among operating forces in the field; hence my orders were to arrange services direct with Admiral Halsey, Admiral Spruance, the Army Air Force, and others. His review of our plans seldom directed changes. As a "Big Boss" to work for, Admiral Nimitz, in my opinion, left nothing to be desired.

General LeMay had recently moved his headquarters to Guam and knew the elementary facts of Lifeguarding, since some of our submarines had stood by in the Yellow and East China Seas during his June 1944, bombing raids on Kyushu from Chungking.

As related in a previous chapter, plans for Lifeguarding had been made with Brigadier General Hansell on Saipan in November 1944. The Commander Forward Area, Vice Admiral G. H. Hoover, contributed surface ships (known as "Birddogs") and amphibians—PBM's or PBY's (known as "Dumbos") to supplement the submarine effort. At that time Japanese-held Iwo Jima was the division point between Subpac and other rescue units.

The submarines were responsible for the areas north of Iwo Jima all the way to Japan; the "Birddogs" were stationed south of that dividing point; while the "Dumbos" either stood by on Saipan for calls or roamed the skies over "Birddog" areas.

Nearly all large air-cover planes carried droppable equipment for the use of men afloat on life belts. There were rafts that would hold from one to seven men as well as motor-propelled boats. These latter, fully equipped, were dropped from B-17's toward the end of the war.

The results of these early arrangements were not highly successful, chiefly because of the aviators' desire to bring their ships home. They always seemed to believe that they could pull through on a wing and a prayer unless, of course, the aircraft was shot all to pieces.

As a result, a damaged plane might pass up a chance to ditch near an available Lifeguard and then be forced to bail out or crash land before the next one could be reached. Faulty navigation, with consequent erroneous ditching position reports, and lack of VHF telephones at the outset cost many lives, but gradually these handicaps were lessened or eliminated altogether.

As we have seen in previous chapters, communication procedures were simplified and standardized. Foolproof and enemy-baffling code calls were set up, and pilots made a practice of pasting Lifeguard positions and calls on their instrument panels. Likewise, SCAP (Submarine Combat Air Patrols) now came under the head of standard equipment for close-in work.

At our first conference, General LeMay, with his ever-present, Churchill-type cigar, was not in a happy frame of mind nor an expansive mood. Ditchings of superforts in strikes against the Empire had, for November, December, and January, averaged fifteen planes per month.

"Admiral," said General LeMay, "we are losing a lot of bombers on these Empire strikes. Sometimes ditchings are due to mechanical failures—sometimes to enemy action. These losses can and will be reduced. But the thing which concerns me most is the small percentage rescued from those who go down at sea."

"General," I assured him, "I am just as concerned about these losses at sea as you are. My staff and I have done a lot of thinking about the problems involved and have come up with some of the answers.

"To pick an aviator up before he drowns or dies of exposure, we have to know approximately where he is. That means a ditching plane must give us a fairly accurate position report or we must have air-cover aloft to extend the scope of our search quickly. To accomplish any of this, we must have thoroughly workable VHF communications.

"Above all," I continued, "we have to gain the confidence of your pilots by education and performance so they will realize the wisdom of ditching when in bad trouble near a Lifeguard rather than take a chance on getting home and wind up in a spot where no one can locate them.

"Bombers can be built in a matter of months, but it takes a lot of years to build an airman!"

With our basic positions established, our staffs went to work on "Gibson Girls" (hand-powered transmitters for life rafts), homing beams from "Dumbos" and "Super Dumbos" to submarines, "corners" (aluminum targets for rafts that could be picked up by submarine radars), indoctrination, briefing, and many other angles.

The liaison officer attached to the Twenty-First Bomber Command, Lieutenant Wm. H. McGhee, USNR, worked tirelessly with my staff on these projects. Lifeguard business began to boom. The rescues for February were almost 50 percent.

In January 1945, time was on the march—and so were American forces in the Pacific. After the Marianas were in the bag, General MacArthur's troops landed at Leyte Gulf on October 20 and finally hit the beaches of Luzon in three or four places simultaneously. The major one of these assaults was at Lingayen Gulf on January 9, 1945.

I followed that part of the campaign with keen interest because Lingayen was the same gulf through which the Japanese had invaded in December 1941—the same gulf whose defense against that very same type of invasion we youngsters of the Navy and shavetail lieutenants of the Army had studied and argued about in Manila in 1914. I was then the proud skipper of my first submarine, and plowed Philippine waters in a diminutive A-boat armed with one torpedo tube! Times, ships, and weapons had changed since those distant days, but Lingayen Gulf was still 42nd Street and Broadway so far as invasions of Luzon were concerned.

The desperate Japanese Imperial army was squeezed into the north end of Luzon's wild mountain provinces. The time was ripe for American arms to move nearer their ultimate goal—Tokyo. Two new objectives already had been designated and, for months, plans for their assault had been built in Fleet Admiral Nimitz's H.Q. and in General MacArthur's G-4 (Plans). Our Submarines Pacific had spent many tedious and dangerous hours in making periscopic photographic reconnaissance of the target islands and in searching their waters with our new mine-detection gear.

I recall one motion picture strip taken through a submarine periscope which showed a machine-gun emplacement being constructed on the beach at Iwo Jima, the first objective marked for attack, taken at such close range that the busy enemy personnel photographed should have been recognizable to their friends.

The submarine Swordfish was lost with all hands in the early part of January off Okinawa, the second objective for the scheduled invasions, while on a photographic reconnaissance mission. Her loss was due most probably to depth charges, but it is possible she was mined.

These two objectives, Iwo and Okinawa, were musts in our Pacific Army and Navy calendars because the former was required as a fighter base and the latter as a fighter and bomber base—also as a harbor and jumping-off place for the invasion of the Japanese home islands.

The Army Air Force bombers, which were striking strategic points in Japan from bases in the Marianas, urgently required fighter cover in order to reduce the serious losses they were incurring at the hands of Japanese Zero fighters. Iwo Jima—some six hundred miles from Tokyo—was well located to provide this protective service and had airstrips which could be utilized.

After Iwo was secured—D-day was set for February 19, 1945—Okinawa would be assaulted beginning April 1. Its capture would provide harbors for the Fleet and a bomber base only four hundred miles from Japan—a murderously close, point-blank range for softening up the defenses of the enemy homeland.

At the time of which I am writing, the submarine Pomfret, skippered by Lieutenant Commander John Borden Hess, of Portland, Oregon, was a part of the overall submarine disposition for the support of the Iwo campaign. Sailing on her Fourth War Patrol, she had been one of eight submarines which conducted an anti-picket boat sweep—for the purpose of eliminating those troublesome tattle-tales—ahead of the Fifth Fleet before its fast carriers struck at the Tokyo area on February 16 and 17.

When the anti-picket boat sweep was completed, the submarines had dispersed to Lifeguard stations while the carrier planes worked-over Tokyo. On this patrol, Lieutenant (now commander) W. C. Dozier was Executive; while medical matters were supervised by Chief Pharmacist's Mate (now Hospitalman Chief) P. W. Wood.

It is there aboard the Pomfret, twenty miles south of Tokyo Bay entrance, that our story opens. War can reach a pitch so intense that human perspectives change to a point where death and man's defiance of death become routine. That cold contempt of consequences which we call courage was the trademark of submariners of the Lifeguard League. It is not cowardice for humans to have a hankering to live—to want to emerge from war's grim adventure with sound limbs and a whole skin. And yet I dare say that the Lifeguarders who entered so wholeheartedly into the fray of the moment give little thought to the comforts and security of a tomorrow that might never come.

On the whole they were men of exceptional spiritual strength and iron morale. If they had not possessed those characteristics, the man-killing hours and days of inactive waiting that were mixed in with the rather brief but spectacularly hectic moments of rescue operations might easily have adversely affected their performance of duty'.

What gave them that strength and iron morale—that J-Factor of daring, self-sacrifice, and fortitude? I have often sought for the answer. I still do. And the only conclusion I have been able to reach, which seems tenable, is that Lifeguards were convinced that, on those missions, they were in the service of humanity and thereby panoplied with a special spiritual armor.

To be sure, numerous rescues were of a routine nature; others were accomplished in the face of overwhelming dangers against heavy odds; some required the use of just average good seamanship; others called for superb ingenuity developed on the spur of the moment—occasions where there was no time to think; only opportunity to do—and in doing, to be right on the beam the first and only time. Violent death seldom takes time out for a trial run.

Such an adventure briefly held the lives of all hands aboard the Pomfret in the balance on the afternoon of February 17, 1945, when death and the enemy were defied in order that the life of Ensign R. L. Buchanan, a fighter pilot of the carrier Cabot, might be saved. The flier, because of a disabled plane, had been compelled to seek refuge in the frigid waters of Sagami Nada, a wide, windswept stretch of water that lies just around Joga Shim, a tiny island to the south westward of the entrance to Tokyo Bay.

Before the war against Japan came to an atom-punctuated end in August 1945, our Lifeguard League submariners were to become well acquainted with the dangerous areas that lie as close as the Ten Fathom Line to the Japs' home islands. But on the day when Ensign Buchanan was rescued—right under the nose of the Mikado, so to speak—the inshore home waters of Japan had seldom been violated by enemy keels.

The honor of making the first invasion of Sagami Wan belongs to the Pomfret, which staged a brilliant penetration during its Fourth War Patrol. Conceivably, Daibutsu—the Great Buddha of the nearby shrine at Kamakura—could have watched this startling event with inscrutable, unblinking eyes.

However, before we get underway with the Pomfret's adventure, let me attempt to draw a picture of the stage upon which our maritime drama was enacted.

To begin with, let us try to visualize the water approaches to Tokyo, the gem of the Japanese nation, the shrine of their emperor-god. Opening wide upon the ocean is a broad body of water known as Sagami Nada (meaning 'sea'). In the very center of its outer edge lies O Shima, a small island that serves mainly to support the tall tower of Kazehaya Saki lighthouse. Where Sagami Nada passes to northward of the entrance to Tokyo Bay, it changes its name to Sagami Wan (wan – 'bay') and goes on to lave the beautiful bathing beaches of Kamakura and Atami, the picture isle of Ino Shima, and beautiful Hayama, the site of one of the Emperor's summer palaces.

Across the hilly Yokosuka peninsula, along the Tokyo Bay side, just a good cannon shot away, lie Yokohama, Yokosuka Naval Base, and Uraga Bay—the last better known to Americans as Mississippi Bay. There, in 1853, Commodore Matthew Perry and the ruling Shogun signed the first treaty that "opened up" Japan and guaranteed that no more of our shipwrecked sailors would be murdered for the mere crime of swimming ashore to Japan.

Tokyo, with its defending fighter and bomber fields, lies not more than fifty miles north of the center of Sagami Nada. Joga Shima Island, mentioned above, lies just off the end of Yokosuka Peninsula guarding the entrance to Tokyo Bay. Suno Saki is on the opposite side of the channel.

This mid-February day was bleak and ugly in all respects. The wind coming out of the north had been honed keen as the edge of the High Executioner's sword on the icy peaks of the so-called Japanese Alps, the Hida range, where many allied POW's were even then working in enemy copper mines. On its cold current rode clouds that delivered alternating downpours of rain, snow, and sleet. And from the clouds hung unbroken curtains of fog-like mist that left a ceiling of less than five hundred feet over the wild, spume-crested waves.

At sea, beyond Sagami Wan, it was the kind of day when submariners sigh for the comfortable solitude of three hundred feet down. In the air, it was the kind of day when pilots long for the sight of a carrier's deck.

To be on the surface of the ocean on a day like that—on the insecure footing of the bridge of a rolling, heaving, pitching, yawing submarine—was no privilege.

On the insecure air-blown fabric of a raft no larger than a bridge table—a raft that conforms to every slant of the foam-capped wave it rides, soaring high on every cresting, sliding deep with every dip—life was even less enjoyable. And yet some four-score men in a submarine sailed such a sea in closely guarded enemy waters that February afternoon to save the life of a single soul—a flier who had lost his power of flight.

That afternoon Commander Hess and his gallant crew gave proof that the Lifeguard League meant every word of their reassuring boast: "Go ahead, pilots. Do your stuff. And if they clip you—we'll pick you up. Even if we have to go into Tokyo Bay to get you!"

For all practical purposes, our show begins on the morning of February 16. At 0756 on that day, while preparing to surface to Lifeguard a carrier strike, the Pomfret sighted the first waves of fighters coming in toward Sagami Wan.

The visibility on her station—a few miles east of O Shima—was so poor and the ceiling so low that the planes seemed to fly on the tops of the waves. Just as the Pomfret surfaced, the Junior Officer of the Deck shouted: "There is a Jap Betty at eight thousand yards. He's turning toward us. He's firing at us. I see his gun-flashes!"

Before anyone could touch the diving alarm for a swift ducking, a group of friendly fighters swung out of the nearest wave and jumped the Jap. Then all were lost in the haze. Said the Pomfret's log: "Saw no more of Betty. Weather is miserable. Ceiling about six hundred feet, solid overcast. Alternate rain, snow, and hail. Force Three sea and twenty-knot wind from the northeast. No sign of fighter cover. Sighted wave after wave of fighters coming in from the southeast—a truly impressive picture."

At 0940, a little later in the day, the sub's fighter cover appeared. But no one aboard the vessel showed boredom waiting for it. Too much was going on aloft and at sea; all hands aboard the Pomfret had grandstand seats for one of the largest and noisiest shows on earth. In anticipation of its staging, Commander Hess had the ship's public address system tapped in for the benefit of all hands.

"We could hear," said Hess, "hysterical Japs jabbering over 4475 KHz. They would start saying something and their voices would get higher and higher as they grew more and more excited.

"Finally, we began hearing American voices over the same frequency. We picked up fragments, such as: 'There is nothing here but flame and wreckage,' or 'I am strafing sixty parked planes. They're all on fire. No opposition.'

"All over the screen we had radar contacts on planes that we could not see. Most of the time our fighter escorts were off looking for targets; so we just had to hope that all the planes that zoomed around us were friendly and keep plugging along.

"We patrolled back and forth halfway between our station and the beach with Honshu about twelve miles away. We felt pretty cocky, I reckon, just like we were blockading the place with about thirty first-line battleships."

In the midst of this hubbub came a flash that transformed the Pomfret and its men from spectators to participants in the great drama that was being staged all around them. At 1030 the Skipper received a report of a fighter down on a shoreward bearing.

The contents of this message were in keeping with the pell-mell activity of that morning—flocks of fighter planes shooting all over the place like streams of angry bees erupting from their hives. The reporting pilot continued: "No life raft, no dye marker, no lifebelt." ... Fine mess! ... "Quote—he ain't got nothing! Unquote."

Neither the Pomfret's air escorts nor its vigilant lookouts could find trace of this flier whose luck had run out. It was a bitter pill to swallow.

Two hours later—when the lusty mills of the gods of war had almost ceased their noisy grinding—came another message: "Fighter down in the northern tip of Sagami Nada!"

This position was deep in the heart of the enemy's home waters—a forty-nine-mile run and very close to Yokosuka Peninsula. Hess was told that he would not have fighter cover after 1500. That cinched it. It would be impossible for the sub to get in and out of Sagami Wan before the fighter cover departed, leaving her naked as a newborn babe within twenty miles of enemy airfields.

Also, try as hard as the Pomfret might, that luckless zoomie could never be found under existing sea conditions without the aid of an air spotter. Over the voice radio, Commander Hess suggested that an amphibian might be able to pick up the survivor. It was and, reportedly, it did.

At 1515, much to the surprise of all hands, a relief fighter cover showed up. Hess concluded that the show was going so well that the Carrier Command had decided to stage an evening performance. That was okay by him. Eight minutes later the ship's lookouts sighted a rubber raft. Said Hess: "One survivor on the raft. Maneuvered to pick up, believe it or not, a Jap. We have to pick somebody up—don't we?"

For the next half-hour or so, the Jap on the raft put on a show that drew the interest, but almost cracked the patience, of all hands on the sub.

"This Jap," explained the skipper, "apparently remembered all he had been taught about not allowing himself to be taken prisoner. Die first; that was the idea. First, he pulled off his life jacket and made a determined effort to drown himself. But he seemed to find this a very painful process and was unable to hold his head underwater long enough to do the trick.

"Finally, after a thirty-seven-minute fight, he came aboard. I never before realized how hard it is to put a submarine alongside a man who insists on swimming away. After stripping him, we turned him over to Pharmacist's Mate 'Doc' Wood. We found a small memo book about two-thirds full of Japanese writing. He was apparently Navy. He was blue with cold and Doc poured some brandy between his chattering teeth. As warmth once more began to course through his veins, he almost smiled and uttered his first word aboard the Pomfret: 'More!' "

A better rescue was made by the Pomfret a few hours later, after a short but hectic search for a downed carrier pilot. It was dark by then but, aided by the downed pilot's Flight Leader, the lookouts spotted him and got him aboard. Now the Pomfret had a real honest-to-heaven zoomie in the person of Lieutenant (jg) Joe P. Farrell of the Hornet. They found him just in time. He had only a life jacket to sustain him and, in the words of Doc Wood's scientific diagnosis, "the lad was colder than a frozen haddock—and almost as stiff."

Glad to have Farrell aboard and glad that he responded quickly to highly skilled treatment, the Pomfret settled down to the routine of the night and prepared for whatever activity the next day's strikes might bring. As things turned out, they were to be of the stuff from which the pages of inspiring history are made.

"After a very quiet morning," noted the Pomfret's log of February 17, "we finally got some business. At 1207 we received a report of a fighter down in Sagami Wan. We headed for the entrance at flank speed. We are all alone, having seen no trace of our supposed fighter cover since 1100. So, as a last resort, we requested the friendly planes that circled over the downed fighter to give us cover on the way in. They did that and willingly. The zoomie's reported position was five miles up the bay on a 350-degree bearing from O Shima. But after we reached that point, we kept working farther and farther in, being led on by the planes.

"I was beginning to feel plenty uneasy because I was taking the Pomfret into a very dangerous position, when our guide plane directed us to come right another 10 degrees. No raft. Next, we were told to come right another 20 degrees, and so on. A regular blindman's buff in a howling storm and under the nose of Japanese guns."

In the direction of the Yokosuka defenses the constant slamming of AA fire could be heard above the screaming of the wind. And, every moment, the sub came closer and closer to the shallow section in the middle of Sagami Nada. The blinding surface mist was terrific. The bridge watch could see nothing to take cuts on. Hess had to rely entirely on radar for navigation, depending primarily on ranges and bearings on what he believed to be Suno Saki Lighthouse. Throughout this trying period, the lookouts saw three or four enemy barges and sampans to the northwest.

However, the radar screen was full of plane contacts and above the overcast could be heard the angry snarl of dogfights and the heavy pumping of 50-caliber guns. At any moment an enemy might break through and rain bombs and lead on the Pomfret.

Continued Hess: "On the way in, the planes told us that their low fuel supply would force them to leave us shortly. So, we asked them to request special air-cover to get us back out. The pilot came back with a 'Wilco.' Meanwhile, we were coached closer and closer to the shallow section of the bay until at long last we saw a raft and picked up Ensign R. L. Buchanan."

Just as simple as that, but all the while the Pomfret and the aviator knew they were both living on borrowed time. The quiet words of Commander Hess, "We picked up Ensign Buchanan," tell enough for official purposes but do not tell of the expert seamanship that must have been required in a rough sea to get the raft alongside and its occupant aboard the pitching submarine without injury. Nor do they tell of the prayer of thankfulness that went up from all hands that they had rescued their zoomie and the sotto voce plea of the lookout: "Now leave us get the Hell out of here!"

"At that time, we were only 17,500 yards southwest of Yokosuka Peninsula," Hess continues, "and our escort had been reduced to one plane. The moment Buchanan was aboard, the lone pilot overhead dipped his wings, said "Congratulations on a wonderful job well done," and left in haste, since he was not sure he had enough gas left to get back himself. I hope he had not miscalculated.

"It was a lonesome moment as the pip of that friendly pilot's plane faded off the radar screen. We realized we were in the heart of enemy waters and that there was not a friend anywhere. And Tokyo Bay and the Tokyo Plain with all their airfields were right over the hills. Maybe they had problems of their own after our carrier planes had worked them over that day. We now had a total of five or six small vessels in sight to the northwest. Could not definitely identify any of them, except for one at seven thousand yards. It looked like a canal barge. Probably none were armed with more than machine guns and we could have destroyed several, but, candidly, my feet were getting a little cold in more ways than one (the air temperature was 42 degrees, Fahrenheit); so, we headed seaward at flank speed and did not spare our diesel horses.

"The Japs must have listened to our VHF conversations and known that we had no air-cover left to protect us. Still, they never bothered us. Three hours after we started in—and making knots on the way out—we hit the line between the center of O Shima and Nojima Saki Light and felt much better. Slowed to 270 r.p.m. and commenced zig-zagging."

Some two hours later the Pomfret's lookouts sighted one frantically waving Jap in a small swamped rowboat. As the sub pulled close aboard, the rafter realized the character of the rescue vessel. "The sudden look of astonishment and horror on his face was truly pathetic," commented Commander Hess. "Whoever speaks of the inscrutable Oriental never saw this fellow. He stopped waving and held his hands up. When he realized we were going to pick him up instead of shooting him, he jumped out of the boat and swam toward us.

"We took him aboard and he behaved like a friendly and fawning puppy. He was very busy saying, 'Thank you—thank you—me a little Jap newspaper boy.'

"This one is so effervescent that it is going to be very difficult to make the crew treat him purely as a POW for the next five or six weeks."

And thus, within the space of a few hours, on February 17, 1945, the Pomfret performed rescue missions that ran the whole range from the sublime to the ridiculous.

With a mixed bag of passengers and prisoners such as the Pomfret had acquired and with her patrol practically just begun, life might have become a bit complicated.

"However," writes the Executive Officer, Commander W. C. "Bill" Dozier, Jr., looking back across the years, "such was not the case." The two aviators, so Dozier told me, worked like beavers on the coding board, and Ensign Buchanan, the refugee from Sagami Wan, was so interested in this new type of ship that he stuck close alongside Lieutenant (jg) Langam, a brand-new officer aboard, who was working hard to get his notebook ready for his qualification examination.

One day they fell into an argument concerning the operation of the flood and vent manifold. Langam insisted that, as a submarine officer, his interpretation of how the system worked must be the correct one. The situation became tense. These two "old submarine hands"—neither with more than twenty-five summers to his credit, and neither having been aboard more than three or four weeks—glared at each other.

Finally, the rescued aviator, Ensign Buchanan, said, "Look, Langam, be your age. I know as much about this bloody boat as you do—I've been aboard her just as long as you have."

As we have always said, these fly-fly boys are sharp on the ball—they have to be.

As for the prisoners, the Jap airman had to be guarded. Those career lads just never gave up. But the "little Jap newspaper boy" became the pet of the ship and, out of consideration for his topography, was christened "Butterball." He was a survivor of a Japanese picket boat which carried depth charges and hunted American submarines.

Some unfeeling dive bomber had sunk his ship, and he never tired of gleefully dropping empty tin cans on the galley deck—he worked as the cook's assistant—to illustrate the technique of liquidating ships such as the Pomfret.

And before Commander Hess's proud ship arrived at Pearl Harbor, the ship's cook, Cahill, had a convert—Butterball could sing "God Bless America" better than most Americans.

13 - Chub Defies Attacking Zeros

Lifeguard duty was, as I have previously indicated, the most dangerous among submarine assignments. This because their skippers, while performing such duties, were called upon to disregard, when occasion demanded, well-established rules with respect to safety and survival of submarines in enemy waters.

Foremost among these was the rule that called upon submariners to dive—and dive fast and deep—when exposed to bombs or to gunfire from hostile planes. It is true that many German submarines in the Battle of the Atlantic carried impressive batteries of anti-aircraft cannon. Their instructions were to fight aircraft, not dive—but the German losses in submarines were terrific and I wanted no part of such tactics.

Bear in mind that the Lifeguard League invariably operated not only in seas controlled by the Japs but also well within artillery range of coasts studded with Japanese antiaircraft batteries and coast defense guns. Also, remember that the very nature of Lifeguard duty required the submarines to function on the surface.

And yet—thanks to the highly skilled teamwork of all hands—the casualties were remarkably low. Not a single submarine was lost while carrying out missions of the Lifeguard League. And among men on topside duty—such as gun crews, the bridge watch, and lookouts—less than a score were killed or wounded by enemy pilots or gunners.

This achievement by Lifeguarders becomes doubly remarkable when one considers that in other submarine operations, according to enemy post-war reports, possibly eleven of our lost submarines were destroyed by Japanese bombs while on the surface. Survivors were recovered from only one of these eleven unfortunate ships.

Hence the short command "Take her down!" became the title of the theme song of Lifeguard submarine commanders. Honoring the rule, they sang that song early, late, and often to the accompaniment of the raucous two-blast summons of the klaxon which echoed the command.

But, as with all rules, there were exciting exceptions to this one and some of the incidents that rose in their wake were so crowded with hair-raising action that they are almost unbelievable.

An incident that underscores the exception to that well-established policy with respect to submarine commanders diving to avoid machine-gun fire took place aboard the good ship Chub, a belated entrant into the war but determined to win a place for herself on her very first war patrol.

Her commanding officer, Commander Cassius D. "Doug" Rhymes, born and raised in the deep South of Monticello, Mississippi, had cut his eye teeth and won his spurs during five war patrols. As torpedo officer of the Sargo at the beginning of the war in Philippine waters, he went through a hell of frustration with defective torpedo performances. For that frustration and the resultant punishment by depth-charging, Doug Rhymes was determined to make the enemy pay. Rhymes was what I consider an ideal submariner—slow to anger, quick to act, and impossible to stampede.

He was to prove himself a veritable fire-eater on the morning of March 31, 1945, when hot steel flew above the pea-green waters of the South China Sea off Hainan Island, a well-fortified Japanese base. Within the brief span of two hours the men of the Chub crowded enough blood-chilling combat thrills into their lives to last a healthy Tommy half a year, as Kipling says.

On this particular morning, which had begun with Rhymes on the bridge from midnight on, the Skipper was feeling a bit resentful and scornful toward our public enemy number one, the Imperial Japanese Navy. The midnight to 0600 hours of the previous day had been spent as part of a coordinated attack group with the Flounder and the Sea Robin chasing a group of two destroyers and four DE's along the south coast of Hainan Island into Tonkin Gulf.

The enemy vessels had kept the submarines at bay with well-directed, radar-controlled gunfire and unpredictable zigzags, but they had had no heart to carry the fight to the Americans.

As Rhymes recorded in his log: "It appears that pickings are really getting lean when three submarines have to chase a group of six DD's and DE's all over Tonkin Gulf in an effort to get a shot."

The official patrol report is thrilling enough when you interpolate between the lines of laconic entries. But let us see the action through the eyes of Captain Doug Rhymes as he wrote me from London a decade later.

"From reading the factual details of our basic war patrol report you can readily discern that the eventual tenseness of this particular incident actually developed in a drop-by-drop or straw-by-straw manner. For my part, I make no bones about the fact that I was most apprehensive throughout the course of events.

"However, my officers, men, and I as a team accepted bit-by-bit an incremental cumulation of circumstances, rather than face a complex problem presented as a package. From my own emotional point of view the events that made and kept me apprehensive pyramided as follows:

"First, a number of us had stayed up all night, expanding our retiring search curve in quest of three downed Army fliers, peering into the dark and sounding our whistle. (Incidentally, one of the zoomies, Lieutenant Walker, later told me that they heard our whistle—but they were miles away and had expended all their flares.) Dawn found us tired and in uncomfortably shallow water about two miles off the southeast coast of Hainan."

As Comsubpac, I had to re-read from time to time a paragraph in the now outmoded Articles for the Government of the Navy, which prescribed pains and penalties for commanding officers who "improperly hazard their vessels."

I cannot imagine any better way to invite a torpedo or bomb than to race around the approaches to an enemy base blowing one's whistle. They probably also used their Aldis signal lamp to search the waves. Did such conduct demand disciplinary action under the paragraph mentioned?

The borderline between a medal and a court martial is not well delineated. Incidentally, it is amusing to note that the British speak of their next to the highest combat award, the D.S.O., as a "Damned Silly Officer" decoration.

Rhymes came out of the war with one Silver Star and two Bronze Star medals. No court martials.

But this story is only begun: "Shortly after dawn on March 31, 1945," continued Rhymes, "a Navy Patrol plane (Liberator) appeared on the scene—heading straight in. We flashed the proper recognition signals several times, paralleled them by voice radio and fired flares—he kept heading straight in. We had identified him and hoped sincerely that he would correctly identify us. Finally, when he was too close for us to dive, he answered our oft-repeated challenge with a bright Aldis lamp. After coming up on voice radio, the Liberator stated that he hadn't replied to our challenge earlier because he didn't think we would have seen his lamp from far out.

"With our uneasy introduction behind us, the Liberator joined our search, became our pal for life, and proceeded to perform in a manner that exemplified the ideal in air-sea coordinated rescue. He expanded our search tremendously, covering in a matter of minutes miles of area that would have taken us hours. In a seemingly short time, he sighted the two rubber life rafts and started homing us in.

"We headed west at 20 knots, full power on four engines. The sea was like a mill pond with a slight haze. A myriad of flying fish paced our bow wave, and the shoreline appeared much closer than it actually was. What a beautiful morning—but I sure had a naked feeling. I had hoped to sight the life rafts soon, but mile after mile of white wake trailed behind us, and we found ourselves drawing closer and closer to Yulinkan—the Jap base.

"Meanwhile our Liberator pal, in addition to homing us in, was rounding up reinforcements. We soon spotted a second Liberator orbiting over the location of the life rafts—north of the track we were headed on. Shortly thereafter four Army Air Corps medium bombers (Mitchells) materialized out of thin air and commenced circling over us at about two thousand feet as we headed in toward the orbiting Liberator. Our well-organized air cover gave us a most comforting feeling; we would not have been able to accomplish the subsequent rescue without it.

"As we headed in toward the life rafts, which we could see for a long way in the calm and mirage effect, and toward Yulinkan Harbor, the cheese became more binding. We found that we were rapidly approaching the southern boundary of a Jap minefield and could not determine initially, because of our inability to take radar ranges on rubber life rafts, whether our zoomies were inside or outside the minefield.

"Also, the footnotes to our intelligence data sheet stated that our Army Air Corps had dropped mines in these same approaches to Yulinkan, but gave no indication as to just where the mines had been laid. At this stage I slowed to two engines and really began to worry and fret; but LCDR Ralph DeLoach, my topnotch Executive, quickly eased my mounting tension. Ralph, in his own quiet way, made it clear that he considered worrying about navigation more properly his problem. I gratefully dumped this portion of my worries on Ralph's broad shoulders and proceeded with the business in hand—a normal sharing of the load between the Skipper and Executive of a submarine."

The naked feeling, on the skipper's part, changed from speculation to dead certainty when, standing in about 1000, the Chub was tracked by Jap shore-based radar which stuck to it like a postage stamp to an envelope. A few minutes later the Chub lookouts sighted mirror-flashes from life rafts beneath the orbiting planes.

This had to be a surface rescue. The chart showed some thirty fathoms, but Chinese coastal waters are notoriously badly charted. On request of the Chub, one of the cover planes dropped notes to the three zoomies on the rafts urging them to paddle southward and away from shore as rapidly as they could in order that the rescue might be staged out of the range of coast defense guns. The situation, to Rhymes, smelled very, very bad and he wanted to be out of it as soon as possible.

"In the meanwhile," wrote Rhymes, "we had observed a pair of Jap Zeros making feints and attacks from different angles in an attempt to break through our air-cover—the four Mitchells at approximately two thousand feet and the two Liberators at about five hundred feet, circling us tightly. Our air-cover was doing a stellar job of driving the Zeros off. (Later I learned that there were actually six Zeros in pairs involved in this skirmish, rather than an apparently extremely versatile single pair—just as well I didn't know it at the time!)

"We slowed as we approached the three persons in two yellow rubber rafts and exchanged waves with them. About this time two Zeros broke through our air-cover from the west and made a strafing run, splashing bullets all around our downed zoomies, but fortunately injuring no one. In watching the Zeros come in, I could think of no earthly reason why they headed for the life rafts instead of our submarine—I could tell from far out that the Chub, though only slightly off in deflection from their heading, was not their target. From experience in watching bombing raids in Soerabaja, Java—from the receiving end—I knew that the Japs, after choosing their target, normally did not deviate from the beeline approach.

"Soon a lookout called my attention again to the west where, coming in under our air-cover, I saw two Zeros—the angle on the bow was also zero, making the beeline point of aim unmistakable. I cleared the bridge of all personnel except myself. My remaining topside was no ostentatious display of bravado. It was a case of necessity. We were close aboard the rafts and I did not want to run them down. During the few seconds that the bullets peppered away against our plating, I crouched behind the bridge spray shield, wondered how strong the plating was and remembered where I had misplaced my Australian penknife.

"As the two Zeros roared overhead, Ralph stuck his head up the hatch to ask if I was all right, which I was. We immediately set a skeleton watch topside and let Lieutenant Bob Carroll take his rescue team down on the main deck—Bob had been champing at the bit for some time. Lieutenant (jg) Austin Cordray in the conning tower was maintaining excellent voice communications with our Liberator, who lowered and tightened our protective umbrella, as the Zeros circled outside looking for an opening. Bob had reported his gang all set and Ralph was helping me maneuver to bring the rafts alongside.

"Along about this stage of the proceedings our Liberator reported that a DD and DE (or maybe it was two DD—I forget which) were standing out of the harbor. I glanced toward the harbor and saw nothing with my naked eye. I couldn't spare the time or interest to use binoculars. I did not discount the ships as a threat, but I felt that worrying about them could wait its turn. At the moment I was more concerned about Bob and his gang on the exposed main deck, and I hadn't been able to completely dismiss the mines from my thoughts, in spite of Ralph's assurances. The main impact of the DD/DE warning was to accelerate our plans for completing the rescue and returning to deeper water.

"Bob and his gang did a perfect job of fishing the zoomies out of the drink. They were Lieutenant Murphy, Lieutenant Walker, and Warrant Officer Perkins of the Army Air Force. Almost the first thing they asked was where we were based. When we told them, we were headed back to Perth, they ducked below with faces all smiles. Bob called up to ask if we also wanted to recover the rubber boats—my reply was brief and unprintable."

Nobody can successfully contend that the spirit of adventure and travel in foreign lands is dead in American youth. Every man in the Armed Forces—certainly in my outfit—wanted duty in Australia. I learned to expect one of two requests from a submarine skipper after a successful performance: a refit at Brisbane or Perth or a new submarine building at Manitowoc, Wisconsin. At the latter place, the West family built beautiful submarines; in the first named places the Australians built beautiful beer and the good Lord built beautiful girls.

"With the zoomies aboard and stowed below," said Captain Rhymes "we swung left and started opening out to the south at flank speed. Now that we were underway, the Zeros again tackled the bombers, trying to break their tight formation. Good gunnery sent one of the Zeros limping home, but it was replaced by another. As the Chub headed for water deep enough to dive in, the Zeros continued to harass the Liberators and Mitchells but without getting too close to their barking guns. Lord, what a wonderful racket the deeper-toned chatter of American 50-caliber machine guns made—just about the sweetest music I ever heard.

"We stationed lookouts and restored the bridge watch. To be sure, we were still wide open and liable to strafing—but too much was going on aloft for one man to keep track of, and there was nothing to stop the Japs from sending a fighter bomber to the scene in an effort to sink us. Gosh, how we prayed for deep water.

"The reality of our danger from shore batteries came to the fore a moment later when the Quartermaster reported one of our bombers had been hit. But a second observation showed that it was an optical illusion caused by a burst of flack between us and the plane.

"What became of the enemy DD's or DE's, I really don't know. I thought about them as we were pouring on the coal to get out of there, but more pressing business crowded out that worry. I suspect that they would have welcomed catching an unprotected submarine on the surface or in shallow water, but that a sheltered submarine on the surface or an independent one in deep water were horses of a different color."

This was a stage of the war when our submariners had a hard time finding torpedo targets. Likewise, Sam Dealey and others had proved that DD's and DE's can be killed just like other ships. Perhaps these particular Jap antisubmarine vessels had gotten the word. In any case, they bothered Rhymes no further.

"Presently," continued Rhymes, "as we passed into deeper water, the bombers asked us if we needed coverage any longer. I answered in the negative, thanked them for a nice job and gave them the names of our zoomies. The bombers had barely left when we saw Zeros starting in on a second run on us. Lookouts and bridge watch beat gravity getting below; I gave the diving alarm two quick jabs and fairly flew down through the hatch. Those Zeros were swooping down at terrifying speed.

"That dive was the quickest one I ever made. We passed one hundred feet in less time than it takes to tell it, still logging 14 knots, which is going some when your boat is submerged and plenty startling when you aren't too sure of how much water is under you. Even so, we heard machine-gun fire drum a fast tattoo on our periscope shears. On the way down, we told the planes that Zeros were in the offing. They replied, 'Oh, tell 'em to drop dead; we're heading for home sweet home.' As we set our own course southeast for our next assignment, running deep at two-thirds speed, DeLoach and I agreed that we did not blame them. We would like some of that medicine, too."

Ten years after the events chronicled above, Commander DeLoach, back in submarines again, wrote me:

"A few days after picking up the aviators, I was sitting alone with Warrant Officer Perkins in the wardroom when the Chub made a quick dive to avoid enemy A/C and received a bomb close aboard. The ship shook violently with the explosion and a heavy E. B. (Electric Boat Company) ashtray catapulted to the overhead and crashed down in front of Perkins. He asked, wide-eyed and breathlessly, 'What was that?' I replied, 'You just received that which you usually dish out.'

"That morning," continued DeLoach, "was the morning in which we—all of us in the Chub—found ourselves. Our organization was put under fire for the first time. I considered that we had an exceptionally fine group of officers and a good, well-trained crew, but the proof came when the chips were down. I was delighted to find that our reactions were cool, strong, and decisive.

When we finally cleared the scene of the pick-up, I was emotionally exhausted, intensely proud of the Chub, and had absolute faith in our Skipper, Commander Doug Rhymes."

Commander Bob Carroll—then a lieutenant, who was out on the bow with two enlisted men, "Gunner" Specht and "O-Boats" Holmes, picking up the downed zoomies—remembers the entire incident as one might remember a closely fought Army-Navy football game. In this watery, Franklin Field setting, the drumming of machine guns, the whistle of bullets, and the darting of enemy Zeros attempting to break through the Chub's air-cover furnished so many chills and thrills that the thought of being in a minefield had little chance to register.

"The war patrol," wrote Carroll, "up until the rescue of the three aviators, had been quite dull, and this event proved a great stimulant in welding together a fine team. There were very few in the organization that actually knew until later on that we had penetrated a minefield to make the recovery. My confidence in the Skipper and the Executive was complete enough to entirely dispel that particular concern from mind in the excitement of finding and taking the aviators aboard. My only reaction to the event after its completion was a realization that I was serving in a top-notch ship.

"The wardroom and crew all got a kick out of "Navigator" Perkins. He was a fresh-caught, enthusiastic, and very articulate youngster of about twenty years. His total experience in the war zone consisted of that one flight over Yulinkan Bay. He had been assigned his first mission on the day he reported in. Yet to hear "Old Perk" talk you'd have thought he had started out with General Doolittle's boys."

Small wonder my lads liked taking airmen aboard. They surely livened things up.

14 - THE BULLHEAD FINDS A WAY

IT WAS JUST ONE OF THE REGULAR MILK-RUNS—the kind that formed part of the day-to-day routine of the B-25 boys in the Fifth Air Force which, in the spring of 1945, was based at San Marcellino on the island of Luzon in the Philippines. With the first pink rays of the rising sun, wind up the old Mitchells, head for the mainland of Mother China, and whang the daylight out of Japanese installations afloat or ashore.

By and large, it was an easy mission. Japanese sea power had dwindled to a point where few destroyers were left to patrol the long reaches of the Asiatic coast. Similarly, Jap airpower had shrunk to a point where fighters that displayed Hirohito's "meatball" [the big red dot of Japan's flag] were as few as the proverbial hen's teeth. As for ack-ack, it was to be expected only at larger installations, such as Hong Kong and other big maritime targets.

At the briefing session before take-off on the morning of August 16, a formation of five Mitchells had been assigned to attack and destroy a fleet of some thirty junks that had been sighted north of Hong Kong. According to intelligence reports, these innocent-looking vessels were loaded to the gunnels with food, munitions, and other war essentials.

"It is not expected," said the Briefing Officer to the pilots, "that you will run into any aerial opposition. But, just in case, a formation of two P-38 Squadrons will meet up with you over Pratas Reef. On reaching the target, you'll go in abreast for low-level bombing and strafing...

The pilots listened with dutiful patience. It was such an old and oft-repeated performance. Load the planes. Fly to the target. Bomb. Shoot. Return to the airdrome. And then what? Another milk-run, another day.

One of the five Mitchells that stood on the line of San Marcellino airfield that morning was "The Klunk," which, despite its drab-sounding name, was slick as a greased kitty's ear and polished to a T.

There was music in the idling of its engines as its aircrew climbed aboard. Sergeant John J. White of Philadelphia was already strapped into his seat in the tailgunner's cubicle; Sergeant

James Pasledni of Bellaire, Ohio, the engineer, fingered dials on his panels as, with critical ears, he listened to the hum of his motors and the song of his props.

Up in the nose, Lieutenant Harry Cohen of Norfolk, Virginia, the navigator, was putting his instruments in place. There were no navigation problems today, thought Cohen. The sky was clear, and the air was smooth all the way up and back, to and from the target. In a way, he was sorry. A little instrument weather would have been a welcome diversion.

Now Lieutenant Irving Charno and Lieutenant Harold V. Sturm, respectively pilot and co-pilot, put in their appearances. With them was Sergeant Robert Tukel, radio operator and waist-gunner. Three genial youngsters, all in their early twenties, they got on well together and perhaps because they shared one uncommon and most peculiar trait: they were all from Brooklyn but made nothing whatever of it.

Up they went into their proper places, made a brisk run through the takeoff procedure, and—when word was flashed from the tower—goosed the engines up to concert pitch and hit the invisible battle lanes of the blue. Shortly after they were on their course, following their meeting up with their fighter cover, Lieutenant Charno waved Sergeant Tukel up to his seat, lifting his voice above the drone of engines and props he shouted: "What's the watchword for the submarines today?"

"Lovely lady," grinned Tukel. And, after a brief pause: "Why?"

"Dunno!" grinned Charno. "Just wanted to catch you off guard if I could."

"Well," cut in Sturm from the co-pilot's place in the cockpit's right-hand bucket, "it's nice to know there's a sub handy in our own area. But don't forget there's a blind bombing zone all around our target. We can bomb anything we see in it and ask no questions. So, you'd better pray we don't have to use that lovely lady call close to the target. No pig-boat skipper in his right mind would ever stick his neck out and make a pass to pick up any fly-boy in a blind bombing zone."

"Maybe you got something there, Hal—but let's hope not," replied the young, tall, and curly-headed plane commander. He added: "Take the crate while I make a check trip through the ship. I'll be right back."

Time ticked off as "The Klunk" and her brood droned toward their targets. Presently they saw them—a batch of sorry-looking junks. Even at a distance they looked as if a mild breeze would blow them apart—a snare and a delusion, for the ancient junks of China are very sea-worthy ships.

As the P-38's swirled overhead, the five bombers lined up noses in a row and, with bombardiers and gunners at their triggers, went in to blast their targets some forty feet above the slanting mastheads. The run made, the bombers moved off to give the fighters a chance to use their machine guns.

Just as "The Klunk" was about to nose back into its five-plane formation—smoke came up through the flooring—smoke that was quickly followed by flame. In seconds it spread from the fuselage to the port engine. Before a full minute had run its course, the flaming engine, its propeller dead as a doornail, was a dead but burning weight on the left wing.

In swinging off from the target, Charno had gone into a climbing turn. This had taken him to a height of about one thousand feet above the sea. When he discovered that the plane's built-in fire extinguisher did not function, he thought for a moment that he might blow the fire out in a steep dive. But a quick glance downstairs revealed that he did not have enough altitude for that particular trick.

"Get ready to ditch," he yelled on an intercom system that did not work. For seconds that seemed ages, the two pilots fought Old Man Gravity for control of "The Klunk."

Gravity won. Despite full flaps and heavy pulls on the control column, the bomber hit the ocean—nose first. It paused briefly on the surface and then, as if by means of some unholy magic, it vanished without trace from the surface of the sea. There was barely time for the two pilots to leave the wreck by way of a forward emergency window.

Tukel got out through a midships' emergency hatch. Pasledni, White, and Cohen were never seen. There had been no time to release rafts in this high-pressure ditching—no time for anything except for Tukel to send a few fast flashes on the lovely lady signal.

Fortunately, all three had their Mae West life jackets on, but the brutal pounding they had received when the plane hit the ocean—from black eyes to long gashes; from scalp lacerations to bruised legs and feet—made it difficult for them to muster even the strength it required to turn the tight little valve that let CO2 gas into the rubber life jackets.

At long last they succeeded. Now they faced a new danger; oil and fuel flung forth upon the sea by the disintegrating bomber had caught fire. It was hard and exhausting work for the three men to paddle away from the slowly spreading island of flames that sent a black shaft of smoke into the sky. But, to a man, they were all too weak to swim even the few hundred feet that separated them from a life raft dropped for them by Lieutenant Frederick Kluth, their Flight Leader.

Taking stock, the trio consulted on their chance of survival. They agreed that it was none too great. They figured that they were at least twenty-five miles away from the targets. So, there was not much possibility of their being taken prisoners by enraged survivors of their air attack.

Next, how long could they remain afloat considering the elements of thirst, starvation, exposure, and sharks. The coast was fairly near, but China was in Japanese hands.

"Just a milk-run, eh," remarked Tukel with a wry smile, "but look where it took us. Here, lovely lady, pretty lovely lady, come get us," he laughed, but there was an edge of hopelessness in his laughter.

Meanwhile, a new source of danger arose in the form of Japanese search planes. They were evidently looking for lost American airmen. As luck would have it, no Jap eyes looked in their direction. About an hour later, two Chinese junks hove into sight. Much to their happy surprise, the trio, after some anxious moments, discovered that they were manned by friendly native fishermen.

There was not a Japanese aboard either one of the shabby and ill-smelling fishing vessels. But Sturm, Charno, and Tukel were too exhausted, too shaken up by the violence of their crash-landing, to have any clear picture of what was going on as the pair of junks sailed closer—as ragged sails slid down the sturdy masts and long, oar-like poles propelled the junks toward them.

Charno, who had drifted off by himself during the excitement, was picked up by one vessel; Sturm and Tukel were hauled aboard the other.

Don't forget that the crews of these junks—from seven to nine men in each—took their lives in their hands by helping Americans. They saved them out of pure humanitarian instinct.

Now that they had them aboard—what to do with them?

Charno recovered enough consciousness to give some thought to that matter—especially because, whenever a plane soared overhead, their rescuers would hide them under piles of fish nets and grass mats. Once, when the sky was clear, the fishermen shared their skimpy portions of rice and dried fish with their unexpected problem guests. However, if they were worried about the eventual outcome, they showed no sign of it.

Meanwhile, quite a distance out at sea, the submarine Bullhead was cruising through its patrol area under command of Commander Walter T. Griffith of Mansfield, Louisiana. The Bullhead enjoyed the distinction of carrying on this, her first war patrol, a passenger sent down to me from Admiral Nimitz' Headquarters, war correspondent Martin Sheridan—the first reporter allowed to make a trip into the war zones in a submarine.

Just as the Skipper was leaning on the bridge cowling speculating on what might be up for dinner that noon hour—the time was 1120—Lieutenant Donald Hendricksen, his Communications Officer, handed Griffith a radio flash announcing that a Mitchell Bomber of the 71st Tactical Reconnaissance Group of the Fifth Air Force had crash-landed in Bias Bay less than twenty miles from shore and that at least three survivors had been sighted in the water.

A quick consultation with Keith Phillips, his Navigating Officer, showed Commander Griffith that the bomber was out of bounds so far as submarine rescue was concerned.

"Look, sir," said Phillips as he pointed at the chart, "they are down not only in a blind bombing zone, but at a point well inside the one hundred-fathom curve—hardly enough water to dive in."

"Too true," admitted Griffith, as he weighed the factors involved. The crash happened right on the approaches to Hong Kong and the spot could therefore be subject to frequent Japanese air patrols. There might be enough water to hide the submarine, but certainly there was not enough depth for her to evade bombs. In a blind bombing zone, the sub was live bait for any aircraft, friend or foe. Just as these thoughts ran through the

Skipper's mind, another message came: cover would be provided overhead by a PV Ventura.

"We will go in," announced Griffith. "It's a run of about thirty-five miles. We should be there about 1300. Speed up the galley so that all hands will have had chow before we get there. Spread our largest flag on the foredeck—so that American pilots who look before they shoot may know who we are. Also, Hendricksen, if we should be knocked out in very shallow water, I want you to be ready to destroy all secret material and decoding equipment."

Hendricksen's face fell. He loved his expensive and complicated decoding gear. To lessen the anguish of his junior officer, Griffith explained:

"This, Don, is what submariners could well call the Davy Jones Run. For a sub to head into the kind of position where we are going—where it has not a friend in the world—is a new kind of work for subs to undertake. But the reward, in saving lives if we succeed, is so great that we have no choice—so here we go."

With all four engines at flank speed, and selected lookouts high on the periscope shears, the Bullhead plowed her way across the glassy waters of the South China Sea under a sky that was speckless blue. Griffith would have welcomed the protective cover of low clouds and dancing whitecaps.

The Bullhead was quiet, if not actually glum. Every soul aboard knew the ticklish mission that lay ahead—knew how vulnerable his vessel was. There was no joking. No wisecracking. After about an hour's run, the China coast lifted above the horizon. Soon the lookout reported sighting a column of smoke from the oil or fuel burning on the surface of the sea where the bomber had crashed.

Just then a lookout sang out: "Aircraft dead ahead." After a moment of tension, it was identified as a friend—the expected PV Ventura. The mere presence of that plane visibly reduced the emotional pressure on deck and below. Coming still closer, the sub sighted the outlines of two Chinese junks which, with sails lowered, were riding the slow swells of the unruffled sea.

"We've got to move in fast and get out fast," the Skipper told the Ventura's pilot by voice radio.

"You can't be too fast for me, bo," answered the airman, "I am almost out of gas. Twenty minutes more and I won't get home."

Oh Lord, thought Griffith. Will the day ever come when a sub skipper, in a tight squeeze, will meet a zoomie who isn't almost out of gas?"

"The way I dope it out after a couple of swoops on the junks," continued the Ventura pilot, "is that there are two airmen on one of them and one on the other."

"Good," replied the submarine commander. "We'll not bother with rafts. It is too dangerous, and we have no time. We'll simply swing alongside the junks, take the boys aboard, and be off."

It was 1315 before the Bullhead was close aboard the junks. More precious moments were expended before the Chinese fishermen were made to understand that they were to come alongside. With all engines stopped, the Bullhead floated silently, a junk on each side of the bow.

But it was obvious that the three airmen were too done in to climb up the side of the sub that towered above the low-lying junks. Charno was the only survivor who could move under his own power. The other two, Sturm and Tukel, were stretcher cases. So, time was consumed in flooding the forward tanks to lower the nose of the ship to junk level.

Just as the bomber pilot came aboard the sub, the airman overhead thundered in over the Bullhead in a steep dive that was followed by a cheery: "Well, so long boys, I hope we all make it. If I am one pint short of my estimate, I won't—so cross your fingers—Cheerio."

"You know," observed Charno, as he leaned limply on the arms of two sturdy men who guided him toward the forward torpedo hatch, "I wish we could do something for those fishermen who took care of us. They sure have a lot of heart—and a lot of guts."

As Charno spoke, Griffith's head was crowded with thoughts. He was trying to think of some way to express gratitude to the rescuers. Not a soul aboard the Bullhead knew a word of Chinese and the fishermen did not seem to know even pidgin English. There was pity blended with admiration in his eyes as he took in the ancient junks aboard which the fishermen and their families courted the dangers of the sea to make a hard-won and meager living.

Scrawny, almost like scarecrows in their tattered garments, were the men on deck—and the women, some with babies riding astride their hips or slung in shawls upon their backs, looked worn and old before their time in their drab black robes.

Then Griffith's racing thoughts fell into a pattern that produced immediate action. He leaned quickly over the bridge rail and called to the grizzled Chief of the Boat standing by the lines on deck.

"Chief," he said, "I want you and the Commissary Steward to take a quick look through our food supplies—preserved meats and fruit, rice, and canned goods. Have some of the men form a human bucket line and pass everything up on deck that we can possibly spare. These poor devils are starving. We can skimp if we have to. Keep just enough aboard to get us back to port."

"Aye, aye, sir," came the enthusiastic response.

These men were seeing, probably for the first time, the abject squalor and poverty which are the common lot of the Chinese masses and it touched their hearts.

All hands worked quickly and with a will. Food supplies poured up through the hatch and into the hands of the astonished fisherfolk. To the foodstuffs were added those treasured extra packets of cigarettes from the men's lockers and from the wardroom mess. Truly, giving is a blessed thing, a wonderful emotional outlet!

That April 16 was just an ordinary day to many of the billions of people who live upon the earth. But to the Chinese who were on those rescue fishing junks that day, it was a day of days. A day of plenty. A day when unbelievable bounty was showered upon them.

Having paid his tribute of goodwill and friendship to men who had saved American lives at the risk of torture and death, Walt Griffith waved a final salute to the now smiling, bright-eyed Chinese faces and backed away to continue his patrol.

Five months later, under command of Lieutenant Commander Edward R. Holt, Jr., the Bullhead, according to postwar reports, was hit and sunk by two enemy aircraft bombs near the storied Isle of Bali. There were no survivors. Among those lost was Lt. Keith Phillips whose life was spared when he, in the fall of

1944, was transferred from the Harder just before it set out on its sixth patrol, never to return.

I shall always feel that, on the Day of Judgment, when the rolls are called, the warmhearted gifts of the Skipper and the men of the Bullhead will weigh heavily in favor of those who now sleep their last long slumber in the peaceful depths of the Java Sea.

As for Charno, Sturm, and Tukel—they returned to their base on Luzon to learn that "The Klunk" had been hit by a 40-mm shell. Presently they joined the crew of another bomber that flew out of San Marcellino on the day-to-day routine missions of bombing strikes by B-25 boys in the Fifth Air Force—you know, the milk-runs.

15 - Gato's Zoomie Was Weighed and ...

If Jack Cannon, tailgunner aboard a B-29 bomber, had tipped the scales some thirty more pounds than he did on that April day in 1945, he would not have lived to parachute into the life-sustaining comforts of the Gato. The latter, under command of Lieutenant Commander Richard Holden from the old Green Mountain State of Vermont, was the submarine assigned to Lifeguard duty adjacent to the eastern entrance of Van Diemen Strait which, at the southeastern edge of Japan, separates the Nansei Shoto island chain from Kyushu, southernmost of the home islands.

Instead, the chances are that Jack Cannon would have followed his fellow crewmen into the Great Beyond as they bailed out from their B-29, crippled at fifteen thousand feet by ack-ack fire from the belching guns that guarded only too well the munitions plants of Miyazaki on the island of Kyushu.

This story about the tailgunner whose weight saved his life and about Captain Holden, whose submarine made it possible for Cannon to execute his new lease on life, is not the start—nor, for that matter, the end—of the saga of the Gato's Twelfth War Patrol.

Ships, like men, have definite personalities, and the lusty old Gato was of the kind that never did things by halves. When it was smooth, it was smoother than moonlight on a periscope window. When she was on a rampage, she somehow always stuck her blunt old nose into the very spot where the shooting was at its hottest... The Gato! Bless her lucky, cantankerous old soul! Something always happened to her. Something to test the mettle of the men who operated her.

Like the time in December 1943, when she surfaced after serving as an unwilling target for Japanese depth charges. On her deck, big as Tojo and twice as ugly, stood an unexploded ashcan. A one-package deal for swift extinction neatly tied up, triggered up, and ready to explode. Quick thinking and cool action saved the day, the Gato, and her crew... But that is another story for another day. It just goes to show that the Gato can be expected to horn in on the unexpected.

Like the sinister, deadly flashes that began coming in on the Gato's torpedo detector at 2150 on the night of April 22, 1945, when the vessel was on station on the east coast of Kyushu up toward the Bungo Suido entrance to the Inland Sea. And kept on coming in at much too frequent intervals... Torpedoes, and no mistake about it. But where did they come from?

That was the poser. Trust the old girl to spring a mystery in the middle of the night after a day of long, tiring, and unproductive patrols. Nothing in sight on the surface for human eyes. No sound of a prowling submarine below the surface to alert electronic ears.

And still—even now and then came the TDM contacts that spelled enemy torpedoes of which the Gato could afford to take not even one.

At that stage of the war the Gato was on a busy street. The desperate struggle for Okinawa was in progress and hundreds of kamikaze planes were flinging themselves at the ships of Admiral Spruance's Fifth Fleet.

On the night of April 6, in a final banzai charge which never reached its goal, the mighty Japanese battleship Yamato with a cruiser and eight destroyers sortied through Bungo Suido only to be reduced next day by dive bombers and torpedo planes of Admiral Mitscher's carriers to four crippled DD's limping into Sasebo.

Yes, Bungo Suido was a busy ditch, as they say of the Panama Canal, not only for surface ships and aircraft but for enemy submarines. This, Dick Holden well knew when he surfaced at 2101 the night of April 22 to charge batteries. Therefore, he cautioned his sonar man at the Torpedo Detector (TDM) to keep his ears well pricked-up if he wanted to see home and mother again.

Holden knew both his own and the enemy's torpedoes. I first knew him as a torpedo officer down in West Australia in those heartbreaking days of torpedo troubles and marked him down as a lad with guts, determination, and ability. Now, in his first command, he was determined not to lose his ship to any bloody Japanese submarine.

To that same alert sonar man, the Gato and the men aboard her undoubtedly owed their lives. The battery charge had hardly gotten started when the TDM operator sang out: "Contact—torpedo—bearing two eight zero!"

Holden had that situation all figured out in advance, too, and his shout of "Take her down. Right full rudder!" came almost before the startled sound man had finished his report.

The bridge watch and lookouts tumbled down that conning tower hatch as though the Devil himself were right behind them—as indeed he was in the guise of sudden, violent death—and the Gato reached for depth.

From the sonar operator, eyes wide with terror but not too paralyzed to keep his dial centered on the approaching messenger of death, came the hoarse whisper: "Bearing steady on the port beam! Bearing steady! Bearing steady!" until finally the effect of the hard-over rudder began to be felt. The terrifying snarl of the torpedo's propellers began to draw forward and, as all hands held their breath, it raced harmlessly across the Gato's bow. ... A fervent "Thank God" echoed throughout the ship.

"Pretty close," said Dick Holden, cool as the granite of his native Vermont. "Catch her at one hundred feet. Make your course zero nine zero. Let's get away from this damned coast."

An hour later, Holden surfaced to complete the battery charge, but again his pursuer was hot upon his trail, and at 0105 the cry "Torpedo contact" sent the Gato plunging for the depths.

This time the Jap torpedo snarled its angry way down the Gato's port side while hearts thumped in throats and all hands unconsciously leaned toward the starboard side.

"Dammit," exploded Holden, "where do these blankety fish come from?"

Later he wrote in his patrol report: "This is getting exasperating. We cannot get any radar contacts on our 'friends.' They are probably midget subs along whose scouting line we laid the Gato's base course. The ARMA Course Clock (for zigzagging) and the TDM have saved our necks tonight."

That was how the Gato's Twelfth War Patrol began—and that was, more or less, how it ran. Of the thirty days the vessel spent on duty in a Lifeguard area, twenty-three were spent submerged. A fine way to join the Navy and see the world.

This grim and high-stakes game of hide and seek was broken off when the Gato was informed that a plane was down fifty-six miles northwest of the Gato's current position.

"Put all four main engines on the line," called Holden to the steersman as he headed for the bridge from the conning tower. "Blow everything high and dry. Man all the bridge guns—all of 'em. This time I'm not going to be forced down."

Was it the Gato laughing? Or just water gurgling through her upper deck gratings?

The day was cold but sunny. A brisk wind swept the skies clear. State of sea—Two. Force of wind—Two. And overhead, winging in a huge circle, flew the three B-29's that served as the Gato's air-cover as well as her long-range rescue eyes. Once a Zero entered the picture briefly—long enough to be sighted by a Gato lookout, too briefly to be sighted by the air-cover.

The usual suspense, as to whether or not the downed zoomie would be found, ended at 1300 when Corporal Gene Tarn was picked off a one-man raft. At 1310 Sergeant David L. Hirsch came aboard, and at 1332 Lieutenant Frank L. Johnson joined the party. All were from the same plane.

Nosing upwind, Holden held the Gato on the drift-path of the rafts. Scene zero was reached at 1430 when the submarine arrived on the edge of a gasoline slick on which floated the badly wrecked tanks of a once proud airplane. Evidently its bombs, which had failed to drop over the target, had exploded on ocean impact. Four men had jumped before she crashed. One chute did not open.

Three men were rescued. The rest of the crew did not bail out and undoubtedly died in the explosion... Only three men present but, sadly, all accounted for. The plane cover left shortly before 1530 and the Gato submerged. When the submarine surfaced at 1951, there was a bright moon and a flat calm—also a Zero. Now began a nightly procedure that had become almost routine since the first few nights of the Gato's patrol. Whenever it surfaced, bang—up would pop a Jap plane.

At 2115, just after a Jap Betty had passed down the Gato's port side practically within spittin' distance, Holden called it quits. "I decided to stay down all night at fifty-five feet and get some rest. For seven out of the past nine nights we have been chased down by night planes."

That was the way it was, life on the Gato. Seldom a chance for a welcome dull moment.

"0753, April 29—surfaced on new Lifeguard station after a good night's rest."

As though promising a fine day, the weather was beautiful, the air calm, and the sea flat. But, somehow, peaceful promises never worked out for the Gato and before the day ended, she engaged in a most dangerous sport—one that savored strongly of the reckless—a deliberate gun duel with a Jap Zeke.

Now if there is any one thing that a well-behaved submarine is not supposed to do, it is to engage in an open brawl with an airplane on the surface of the sea, thereby exposing herself to falling bombs and flying bullets. It just is not done even in the most intrepid circles—except when the Devil drives. But, as I have hinted with respect to the Gato—well, one could never predict the unpredictable.

The show began at 0947, when Plane Mascot Five reported a disabled B-29 had crashed into the sea at a given position in the area of Van Diemen Strait. "Keep your big blue eyes wide open, baby," came a voice from the Gato's air-cover. "These woods are lousy with bandits ('enemy aircraft')."

Acting on this advice, Holden ordered the 20- and 40-mm guns manned. If any air raiders or Kamikazes showed up, the Gato would be ready. Holden was determined that he would not be forced down until he had collected his zoomies. If it were action he wanted, Holden got it at 1057 when a float-type Zeke was seen on the port beam at a distance of three miles. The sub and the air-cover saw the Zeke and opened fire at the same time.

"Our 20- and 40-mm tracers were meeting him very nicely," noted Skipper Holden, "but he kept on coming. At a 60-degree position angle, he nosed over and headed down at us. We were doing all right until we saw two bombs fall from his belly and with a zero angle on the bow. Giving orders to the bridge watch to put the rudder hard left, I yelled 'Take cover' to the bridge watch and proceeded to carry out my own orders. With taut nerves we watched the falling bombs.

"The first exploded to starboard and the second about ten feet astern. At the time, we were making 19 knots and I had no need at all to issue orders to the gun crews to resume revenge fire. Meanwhile, the Zeke pulled out of his dive, climbed up to a thousand feet, and did a nice wing-over for a strafing run. This time I cleared the bridge. A quick survey revealed that our air-cover 'Dumbo' had only got in an initial burst and was trying to maneuver. Things did not look too well, so I put the rudder amidships, dived, and let 'Dumbo' shoot to his heart's content. This is interesting work, but I felt that the old girl needed a little more firepower to exploit it successfully."

At 1100 the sub arrived at 150 feet to take stock of the situation.

"We discovered," said Holden, "that our camera fan, Ensign Lloyd Greene, had been taking movies of the proceedings up until the time of 'Bombs away.' Our mess-boy, Hold, and also one of the 20-mm loaders beat gravity in clearing the bridge and left the metal part of his helmet up there. We ran through the main power circuits, found everything all right, and at 1125 surfaced to find that we now had two 'Dumbos' and no Zekes. I went to four main engines to reach the survivors. Our new 'Dumbo' told us there were bandits in the area. ... As if we did not know!"

At 1400 the air-cover "Dumbos" bid the Gato goodnight and good luck. Almost an hour later a seven-man raft hove into view. The huge spread of orange-yellow rubber looked empty and deserted. It was not until Holden, for the third time, had shouted: "Hello! Anyone aboard?" that he got results.

A light-haired young man stuck his head out from under a mountain of blankets and whispered with pleased but obvious surprise: "You guys Yanks?"

On being told that such was the case—Skipper Holden hails from Vermont—the zoomie emerged from the blankets and was helped aboard the Gato. His name: Jack B. Cannon. His job: tail-gunner aboard a B-29 that had to be abandoned after it was hit by ack-ack fire just after bombing industrial Miyazaki.

After being checked by the Pharmacist's Mate and found okay, Sergeant Cannon—a small, almost boyish-looking young man—told his story. According to his best knowledge, he was the last of the six men to jump. His chute opened just before he hit the water. Apparently, he had bailed out from five hundred feet at an airspeed of about 240 miles per hour. That would put the other five parachuting zoomies within five miles to the north of the Gato.

Holden sank the rubber raft and continued his search along the best-estimated line of parachute drop. The sea was flat, and visibility was excellent. The Gato searched west three miles and north four miles to within eight miles of land. Next, it headed east and then north, zigzagging across plane track and current set. No zoomies to be seen. Twenty Bettys sighted. Wondering if they were looking for the Gato or for Okinawa, Holden pulled the plug and took stock.

He had found only one of six zoomies. What had happened to the other five? Gone. Lost to the Gato. He had searched an area eighteen by twelve miles.

"By now," said Holden, "it was too dark to see, so I headed away from the beach."

True, the 'Dumbo' had reported only one survivor in the water, but what about the others? The rescued aviator tried to reconstruct the picture and concluded that the following happened:

"Cannon's plane was badly hit over Miyazaki while its formation was bombing from fifteen thousand feet. The plane's right-hand engines were out. As the pilot headed out over water, he lost altitude fast and, at two thousand feet—when he realized that he could not ditch—the alarm bell was sounded. Five men jumped ahead of Cannon, who pulled his ripcord as he jumped. He is small and the high speed of the plane did not cause his shrouds to break when the chute opened. In fact, his chute opened just before he hit the water.

"The other members of the plane crew who jumped were heavier than tailgunner Cannon by thirty pounds. If they delayed pulling their cords too long, they'd be too late. If they pulled their ripcords before their bodies lost their high lateral speeds, the shock of the chute opening would either snap their necks or break their shrouds.

"These luckless fliers had two thousand or less feet in which to balance these two factors at a speed of 240 or more miles per hour. That kind of balancing just could not be done. Cannon, because he was thirty pounds to the good, did not face this problem. Considering this situation, plus the report of the 'Dumbo,' who was at one thousand feet when he located Cannon and dropped him a raft, I do not believe there were any other survivors.

"I write this dissertation," concluded Holden, "for the benefit of others who may have to make the hard decision of breaking off the search."

Before the Gato's Twelfth War Patrol came to a close, the gallant men who manned her snatched six more airmen from the cold-hearted sea, making the score for the run a total of ten. One of these latter rescues had the typical Gato touch. One morning, acting on a hunch and while looking for two downed fliers whose reported position was very vague, Holden decided to hold a course quite different from the one given him.

He told his OOD: "We'll run up the Hundred Fathom Curve and we'll see them at 0815."

What happened? Well, let us quote the Gato's log: "0812—sighted life raft, distant two miles. Fate had the conn [at the helm] and I feel pretty humble about the whole thing."

At 0818, Lieutenant E. B. Fish and Sergeant N. H. Woodville were aboard, and before one bell of the forenoon watch, Sergeants N. Lewis, T. J. Doherty and R. R. Ferry and Lieutenant F. H. Proctor also were aboard the sub... On the Gato, hunches had a way of panning out.

A Boeing SB-17G variant of the B-17 'Dumbo'

16 - Scabbardfish Converts B-29ers

Liaison between the Army Air Forces based at Guam and Submarines Pacific Fleet increased and improved as the spring of 1945 lengthened into summer. Regular bi-monthly round table staff conferences were held. Lieutenant General Barney Giles—who had succeeded to top command of the local AAF in early May—and I were nearly always present to keep in touch with the latest thinking and practice of our representatives and our Lifeguard captains.

Many advancements were made in the methods of locating downed planes and in the technique of supplying flotation and survival gear to aviators in the water—also in getting them aboard the rescue submarines. Twenty-one big Navy seaplanes—PBY's mainly—called "Dumbos," were eventually employed by the air-sea rescue service. In addition, there were nine B-29's, called "Super-Dumbos."

These aircraft were invaluable in searching for downed zoomies and in guiding Lifeguard submarines to the spot. When the state of the sea permitted, the seaplanes themselves landed and rescued personnel. Several planes and their crews were lost in such gallant attempts. All of these types were equipped to drop rafts, survival kits, provisions, and radios to airmen in the water. The AAF also equipped a few B-17's to carry droppable motor lifeboats.

The "Super-Dumbos," because of their long range and endurance, were especially valuable as submarine combat air patrols (SCAP) over Lifeguards along the home coasts of the Empire. Because of their short fuel range, fighter aircraft could remain on such locations for only short periods.

Educational work had to be done by the AAF among the various aircrews themselves to improve ditching and bailing-out techniques and thus increase their chances of survival. When a sixty-five-ton aircraft hits a rough sea at a speed of more than 100 miles per hour, the occupants are often killed or seriously injured—as Colonel Hans Adamson, co-author of these pages, can bear witness.

Had their B-17 been equipped for the parachuting of themselves and their crew members, chances are that Captain Eddie Rickenbacker, Hans Adamson, and their bomber crew of six would have emerged from their twenty-four days of rafting on the South Pacific without loss of life or serious personal injury.

As it was, Sergeant Alex Kaczmarcayk died of starvation, thirst, and exposure; while Colonel Adamson and Sergeants John F. Bartek and James W. Reynolds suffered injuries on crash-landing on the water that kept them hospitalized for weeks and months after they were rescued by a Navy Kingfisher plane on Friday, November 13, 1942, after rafting without food and water since October 21.

In those early days of the war, submarines had not been assigned to Lifeguard duty and parachutes had not been developed for ditching procedure. In fact, the experiences accumulated by the Rickenbacker-Adamson "expedition" were to lead the way in the adoption of air-sea rescue equipment.

In this connection, the widespread aversion of aviators to "hitting the silk" in preference to sticking with the plane had to be overcome.

In order to further promote acquaintance with each other's problems, bomber crews were invited to our Submarine Recuperation Center at Camp Dealey and pilots were taken out for training runs and dives in submarines. The AAF reciprocated with invitations for submariners to fly on training missions.

Later, I found some of this "training" extended to bombing runs over Japan. Boys will be boys!

An interesting comment on the early attitude of B-29 crews toward submarines as rescue factors and how misconceptions based upon lack of familiarity were broken down by friendly intermingling, was a first-hand story given to me by Commander F. A. "Pop" Gunn, skipper of the Scabbardfish:

"An incident occurs to me that gives an amusing sidelight on the workings of our fraternization with the B-29 fliers and on Frank Leahy, famous former Notre Dame coach. The Scabbardfish was on Lifeguard duty off Japan for the very first B-29 raid from Guam. The fliers just would not ditch near us. They tried to get back to Guam and quite a few were lost in the big stretch of water in between.

"On our return to our submarine base of Guam, the General in Command—who took over the Fifth AF in China when General LeMay came to Guam—invited all the submariners to have chow with the USAF at their headquarters. They were practically living in tents at that time and the big macadam highway to Camp Dealey was undreamed of in those early days. The General told us that losses were extremely high, and morale was extremely low as concerned the long trek to Japan and back. He asked us if we would mind inviting his lads out to Camp Dealey for a party and a get-together to see if we working members could convince his boys that their best bet, when hit bad, was to ditch near us and be picked up rather than risk the long run back.

"Well," continued Captain Gunn, "we invited them out and I really think the idea panned out, because we learned what type radio gear they had and also discovered that we had the means to contact them. Meeting each other on that intimate basis also gave them a little more confidence in us, I think."

"Anyway, from that time on, the number of pickups in that area began to increase and the morale of B-29ers began to increase also. Captain Rob Roy McGregor was the only one at the party who didn't make out—he lost his shirt betting against the General while he was rolling the dice that night. After the party, the B-29ers invited the submariners to take a ride up to Saipan in a B-29. The Scabbardfish group, plus Frank Leahy—who was the Recreation Director for Subs at Guam—arrived for the ride and were immediately loaded down with aviation gear (coveralls, Mae Wests, parachutes, helmets, goggles, etc., etc.). It was about 100° in the shade and the submariners nearly melted trying to crawl into the plane with all this stuff on.

"We were stationed in various spots in the plane and were supposed to rotate stations during flight," added "Pop" Gunn. "I was stationed mid-ships with an enlisted gunner who finally took pity on the 'poor submariner' and told me it was okay to take off the hot gear now that we were airborne. Some joke!

"After learning about the remote-controlled 50-caliber guns, I started to crawl through the tunnel toward the cockpit. Just as I got almost there, the plane took a sudden 'up angle' and I slid all the way back down to the mid-ship station. After the plane finally leveled off, I tried again. About halfway through the tunnel the plane took a 'down angle' and I slid right out into the cockpit. As

I looked up from the deck, there was Frank Leahy on the controls. He shouted: 'Hey, Pop—this is easy—to make her go up, you pull back. And to make her go down, you push forward.'

"Holy smoke! If I'd known Frank was on the controls, I would never have taken off the parachute. As it was, we almost scraped the top of Rota Island before I convinced him that the pilot was the right man for the controls." But to return to the sterner side of the picture, further instruction was given by submarine staff rescue members who spoke at bomber fields in all parts of the Pacific.

General Giles himself gave me the grand tour of the AAF facilities on Guam, including inspection of a B-29 about to take off, a B-17 carrying a motor lifeboat, and several satisfied customers—airmen who had been rescued by submarines. They all agreed that submarine chow was tops!

To further improve our communications and liaison—as soon as Iwo Jima was secured—we sent Commander James A. "Caddy" Adkins, a submarine skipper of long experience, to report to the Air-Sea Rescue unit there. This branch of the Lifeguard League we designated as the "National League."

Later, when Okinawa had been secured, we sent Commander Charlie M. Henderson—with 22,000 tons of enemy shipping to his credit—to report to Rear Admiral John Dale Price, the Island Commander, and set up the "Texas League."

Similar arrangements had already been made in March with the Far Eastern Air Force at Clark Field, Luzon, when that island was liberated. Commander Royal L. "Fu" Rutter—ex-submarine Kete—was the liaison officer in that command.

These efforts to increase the understanding by airmen of submarines as rescue mediums bore excellent fruit. And the top percentage of rescues for the war was reached in May 1945, with a figure—for all types of rescue craft—of about 80 percent. The average for the last nine or ten months of the war was about 50 percent.

In Lifeguard operations, the rescue of the aviator—sometimes simple and sometimes under hair-raising circumstances—did not end the submarine's problem. The rescued zoomie then became a passenger, an honored guest for whom the red carpet was rolled out.

Now a submarine represents the ultimate in economy of space. Into it, clever naval constructors and engineers have crammed so much costly and complicated operating gear that a submarine is, ton for ton, the most expensive type of naval craft.

The number of the ship's complement and the number of bunks matched each other. If extra officers or men were carried for training or other purposes, cots or hammocks had to be rigged, or "hot bunking" was resorted to. This last meant that the extra hands, when they came off watch, turned into the bunk of some shipmate who had just gone on watch. It was a simple and workable system when necessity demanded. The Germans, for instance, had bunks for only two-thirds of the crew, but we Americans like more individuality, less regimentation.

And so, rolling out the red carpet and throwing open the VIP suite for zoomies was not always easy aboard submarines, but mutual goodwill and mutual admiration made the system work—these, plus the factor of youth, youth which had grown up in Boy Scout camps and college dormitories.

Illustrating this extremely important point is the following excerpt from comments on that specific subject. Speaking of the day-to-day existence of zoomies on the Sterlet, its skipper, Lieutenant Commander W. V. "Micky" O'Regan wrote:

"The Lifeguard duties performed by this vessel off Okinawa on October 10 were interesting and our association with the four Navy pilots and two crew members was a source of real satisfaction.

"At first, communications with the planes were hampered by a lack of knowledge of air 'slang' or code words. The first pilot rescue, however, soon corrected this. As soon as Lieutenant (jg) R. L. Dana, from the Biloxi, had put on dry clothes and had some coffee, he volunteered to man the VHF on the bridge. He translated the circuit language and, in addition, knew practically all of the air group calls, so that we were able to utilize returning groups to search for reported rafts along their return route. Incidental cruiser scouts also cooperated with great willingness.

"The four pilots stood watch as JOOD and the two gunners stood regular section watches for the remainder of the patrol, as well as filling in on wardroom bridge games when needed. Their desire to inflict damage on the enemy led them to suggest many novel ideas for fighting the Nips, and their unfailing good humor and high spirits were a source of continual pleasure.

"The ship was fortunate enough to make three night attacks after their arrival in which it was possible for them to see the Japs sink. One remark after an attack: 'Gee, you fellows really know when you sink them!'

"All the aviators approved of the submarine food and the two gunners were considering a transfer to submarine duty for this reason alone.

"The crowding in the wardroom was no hardship because of the thoughtfulness and good humor of all hands. Their performance of duty was of the highest order and learning about air operations was extremely interesting."

The report concluded with these words:

"It is hoped and recommended that these men will be awarded a Submarine Combat Pin. They worked for it and, while not regularly attached in the strict meaning of the word, they nevertheless contributed no small amount to the success of this patrol."

When a submariner uses words like that in speaking of the lads from the Wild Blue Yonder, his praise is warm indeed. Incidentally, they did receive the highly desired Combat Pins.

Our English cousins, when they changed from downed British carrier planes to Uncle Sam's submarines, were equally acceptable as round pegs for round holes. Lieutenant Commander T. E. Harper, captain of the Kingfish on its Eleventh War Patrol, rescued four carrier airmen from H.M.S. Illustrious.

Said Skipper Harper's log:

"It was a distinct pleasure to have had them aboard. They were all excellent shipmates and their ability to adapt themselves to a submarine and a different Navy is most commendable. Within a few days after coming aboard, each was standing watches as JOOD. While on Lifeguard station, each was invaluable for communications with British planes.

"While on submerged patrol, each soon qualified as helmsman, planesman, periscope watch officers, and eventually as cruising diving officers. The British Chief Petty Officer we had aboard, having a radioman's rating, sat right in with our radioman on all the circuits, besides standing a lookout watch. We of the Kingfish consider it an honor that we were fortunate enough to bring these British Naval officers back and were most disappointed to see them leave us on our arrival in Saipan."

In many cases, downed fliers were rescued in the early part of submarine patrols. Thus, they were necessarily retained aboard for some weeks, since the normal war patrol was for sixty days. It was most interesting to note the reactions of airmen toward undersea warfare.

When it came to Lifeguard duty, submariners learned to take whistling bullets and exploding shells in their stride. As submariners, they had already learned to accept snarling torpedoes and thunderous depth charges as unavoidable troublemakers.

True, it would be going too far to say that they ever learned to like these terrifying messengers of destruction. But one might say that the men of the subs developed normal attitudes of respectful acceptance and fatalism. Otherwise they might have ended up with the screaming-meemies—[shellshock, PTS] some did. If a submariner or his vessel is hit—if a bullet, shell, torpedo, or depth charge that bears a fatal number comes along—well, that is that. "My ship is my coffin; my grave is the sea" is an old salt's expression which applies particularly to submariners and likewise bears within itself a strong potion of fatalistic comfort.

But let us bear in mind that this attitude of acceptance is strictly professional—and let no one suppose that our submariners planned to accept such a fate without taking plenty of the enemy with them. It is seeded in the individual submariner with his subconscious indoctrination and it grows through the gradual awakening of an attitude of acceptance that is fostered by environment and experience. In a way, this fortitude is a product of native courage, although that is not entirely the case.

Proof of this was found in the fact that many of the airmen who became involuntary passengers on Lifeguard subs—and who as such had to share the dangers that confronted their hosts during surfaced and submerged combats—died a thousand tormenting deaths during moments of submarine action when the margin between death and survival was hairline thin.

However, no one should (and no one did) think that this reaction of airmen to submarine dangers was strange. Men can be conditioned to danger, to terror, to death in any form. But that kind of conditioning requires time and contact with those dangers. To expect men of the air—daring, courageous fighters and cool-headed confronters of death in their own element—to accept terror, danger, and death beneath the sea merely because fate thrust them into a submarine, would be not only unrealistic but lacking in understanding. If these men feared death within the narrow confines of a submarine, it was not death itself they feared but rather the guise in which it came.

Some zoomies, on being picked up by Lifeguarders, took the prospect of spending several days or several weeks on a submarine that looked for combat, as well as for raftees, as a lark. To others, it was disappointing when they learned that, for several days or weeks, they would be incarcerated in a "sea-going sewer pipe."

Of course, in cases where downed aviators had been wounded in air action or disabled in ditching, their rescuers usually sought to place them aboard homebound submarines or the nearest "bird dog" surface ship. However, these were not always available and, unless specifically ordered to the contrary, subs remained on patrol stations as originally directed. This because each sub was part of a well-planned system of coverage. For a sub to leave its station was tantamount to a soldier deserting his place in the firing line.

During these enforced stays in a totally strange environment and under an equally strange element, it was quite obvious that in spite of the famed submarine chow and well-meant hospitality, a rescued zoomie was far from physically safe or mentally at ease.

Again, in all fairness, let me hasten to add that, in all instances, rescued airmen—who had escaped injury in air combat or in ditching—invariably did their level best to fall into the daily pattern of work, rest, and recreation aboard their host submarines. Officers, as a rule, requested assignments to such duties as coding and decoding and junior OOD, while crewmen sought to have their services employed in their specialties—generally radio—or as lookouts, at which they were exceptionally good.

As for the injured, I am truly proud to say that I do not know of a single case where the pharmacist's mate—the "Doc," "Quack," or "Pill-Roller" of the submersibles—failed to provide adequate and proper care for his patients. There is no better proof of the truth of this statement than the universally high rate of recovery and cure among zoomie casualties.

A record of three successful appendectomies performed on their shipmates by pharmacist's mates while in enemy waters also testifies to their competence. The youth of their patients, of course, was on the side of our Docs; it is amazing how much punishment a youthful body can take and still pull through.

While the medical and surgical departments of subs were well prepared for the type of patients they were likely to handle under normal patrol conditions, they were not fully equipped to deal with all kinds of cases.

One of the unusual cases is cited by Commander R. B. Lynch, skipper of the Seawolf, who learned on sick-call one day that one of his men, a red-headed youngster from the forward torpedo room, was in misery with an abscessed tooth.

"There's only one way out of it, sir," reported the Pharmacist's Mate. "Red's tooth is poisoning his system and it's got to come out."

"But, but, but," stuttered Red—he spoke with great difficulty because his features were pulled drum-tight by the abnormal swelling—"look what he wants to use on me!"

"And what are you going to use on him, Doc?" inquired Lynch of his medical expert.

"Well, you see, sir, I have no proper gear for tooth carpentry. So, I looked high and low and came up with these—ain't they just jim-dandies?"

With a smile that was completely saturated by pride, the Doc produced, in a hand he had held behind his back, a very capable, albeit slightly grim-looking, pair of long-nosed plumber's pliers.

"Yes, sir," Doc continued, "if anything will fetch that tooth, these will."

A woebegone expression spread over the Torpedoman's full-blown mug—a face that would have been worth real money in a Keystone comedy [a silent movie with slapstick humor]. Lynch had all he could do to keep from laughing.

"He'll pull my head off, that's what he'll do," moaned the patient. "I've seen smaller tongs used to handle blocks of ice back on the Great Lakes. No sirree—sir—I'll keep my tooth and take a chance on it curing itself."

Unfortunately, or fortunately, perhaps, the patient did not escape the Doc and his pliers. As the day grew older, the pain increased and long before sunset the tooth was extracted with the aid of the king-sized extractors, plus a nip of the stuff that made Kentucky famous, to serve as a painkiller.

"Gimme that tooth," said Red at the end of the operation.

"For what?" asked Doc, who was about to throw it into the garbage.

"For one last bite," was the reply. "I'm gonna tape it onto the warhead of the next torpedo we load into the forward nest with this message to Tojo: 'I hope this bites you right in the seat of the pants.'"

As regards the reaction of zoomies to life aboard submarines in combat, the experiences of Lieutenant (jg) Jack Heath, a carrier pilot based aboard the Wasp, are worthy of mention. His plane had been damaged during a strike on shipping in Manila Bay in September 1944.

When Heath attempted to reach a Lifeguard submarine stationed near Subic Bay, he could not make it. His engine dead, Heath had to ditch his plane a short distance from the Cavite shore.

With the aid of a Filipino fisherman and, later, of Filipino guerrillas, the pilot made his way southward across Luzon. Eventually he reached the island of Mindoro, from which he was evacuated by the Ray, skippered by Commander W. T. Kinsella. But let Heath tell his story:

"We rendezvoused with the Ray just after dark on that evening. We were in a launch, the Ray surfaced, we spotted her, started up our outboard motor, went on over to her, got aboard, and I thought that I had been rescued... Oh, yeah!"

Evidently the airman dreamt of a yachting cruise in the South Seas, now that the danger of capture on land or death in the sky no longer existed.

"I say I thought I had been rescued, that I, at long last, was safe," Heath continued, "but there were occasions when I had my doubts. Once I was aboard his sub, Captain Kinsella took me out and got me bombed and depth-charged. In the course of thirty-four days, he practically made a submariner out of me. To top it all, I was aboard the Ray while it stood Lifeguard duty off Lingayen.

"One day we picked up another zoomie, so I had a little company aboard. He was Lieutenant James Brice, a fighter pilot from the Cowpens. Brice had been shot down and we picked him up after he had been in the water about two days. Oh sure, we both got back okay, and we are really a hundred percent for these submarine men. But they are hogs for danger.

"Honestly, there was one time during my trip on the Ray when I thought the jig was up. Captain Kinsella barged into shallow water and made an attack on a cruiser.

Then we went deep and got in between the cruiser and the beach, the cruiser being only about two thousand yards off the beach. And what do we do but run aground, wipe out one of the sound heads, and spring a leak in the forward torpedo room. As holes go, it was not very big—about an inch in diameter or a little less. But, unfortunately, I happened to be in the forward torpedo room where and when the action took place. It was just like in the movies—the water was pouring in at a pretty good clip and I thought: 'Well, I'll never get back.' But we came up to periscope depth, got the leak stopped, and finally got out of it with whole, though somewhat wet, skins.

"On another occasion, we took an aerial bomb when we were at periscope depth. To submariners, a bomb is nothing much to worry about unless it is very close. This one did not do much damage, but still, I can tell you that I would rather be dropping those cans than catching them. Now don't get me wrong and don't take my joshing too seriously. What I really want to say is that we zoomies certainly appreciate the work that the submarines did in helping rescue our boys."

It so happened that Lieutenant Heath was exposed to submarine travel for the duration of an entire patrol.

As for endurance by survivors on rafts before rescue, I believe that the honors go to Sergeant B. R. Grier of the U.S. Army Air Force. At the time he was picked up, he had been afloat on his one-man raft for twenty-three days. The rescue was performed by the Sealion, commanded by Lieutenant Commander Charles F. Putman, on that sub's Fifth War Patrol. It took place in the South China Sea off the coast of Malaya. The patrol had just about run its course. In fact, the Sealion was en route to base when, on the afternoon of April 2, 1945, a lifeboat was sighted through the high periscope at a distance of five miles—an amazing bit of luck. Closing to investigate, the submariners came upon Sergeant Grier. Despite his long period of rafting, the flier's only loss was forty pounds of weight.

With respect to distances covered by ditched airmen, chances are that Lieutenant W. N. Low, of the U.S. Air Force, holds the long-distance record. In five days, starting July 23, 1945, he drifted and sailed some three hundred miles. Happily, his journey ended when the Hammerhead, skippered by Commander Frank M. Smith, found him and took him aboard on July 28.

Records for zoomie transportation of short duration were established by the crew members of a B-24 that was limping home to Saipan two days after Christmas in 1944. Just as the Blueback and the Sea Fox were standing into the harbor of that island, their lookouts saw the bomber make a sudden ditching.

The craft broke up as it struck the water. The disaster happened so rapidly that there was no time to make rescue calls. But being on the spot and alert, the Sea Fox picked up three survivors while the Blueback gathered four. The rescues were completed at 1715; the men were ashore at 1846. The proximity of land and medical aid saved Corporal J. L. Buatt's life.

Because of a violent sea—no less than Force Five—and because of Buatt's injuries, it was necessary for Commander Merrill K. Clementson of Pennsylvania, skipper of the Blueback, to trim down aft and slide Buatt up on his deck in the rubber raft.

Immediate treatment was administered on the cigarette deck. No attempt was made to take the wounded man below. Had it been necessary to move him, he would probably have died. The work of E. P. Resner, Chief Pharmacist's Mate, in treating these zoomies was worthy of special notice.

In his log, Commander Roy C. Klinker of Sebastopol, California, captain of the Sea Fox, noted that during this rescue, the sea and wind conditions were such that it was impossible to affect the rescue without putting a man over with a line.

Quartermaster, First Class, Clyde L. Reese volunteered to swim out for the man. After an extremely difficult time, the airman was brought aboard. Reese had to be treated for exhaustion himself. He was highly commended for risking his own life to save that of Flight Officer G. I. Sacks, the injured aviator.

All of which goes to prove that neither time nor distance from home base is a factor in determining degrees of danger or the proximity of death.

17 - POW's—Unwanted Guests

In sharp contrast to the latch-string-is-out attitude of our Lifeguards—and other submarines, as well—toward our brethren of the air was their antipathy to transporting prisoners of war.

Occasionally there was light comedy relief, but, in general, POW's were surly, sullen, verminous, ungrateful, often suicidal, and frequently bestial passengers who required constant watching.

Only the dictates of humanity and the urgent requirements of our intelligence officers induced our undersea fighters to bring downed Japs back to base. Our Standard Operating Procedure called for bringing home two POW's, if obtainable.

I recognized the difficulty this imposed, but, especially toward the end of the war, information regarding minefields, shipping routes, fuel reserves, and so on was vitally needed. Our unwilling guests seemed to have little compunction about spilling anything they knew. The search of sinking vessels also contributed valuable documentary information—plus some narrow escapes on the part of the searchers from going down with the enemy ship.

Almost invariably, survivors of our attacks refused invitations to come aboard our submarines. They preferred to remain with the wreckage of their ships or drown. If swimming teams attempted to bring them aboard forcibly, the Japs often deliberately drowned themselves.

An empty five-inch ammunition magazine made a handy prison "cell." Leg irons or handcuffs around a stanchion could provide the necessary security.

The feeding of prisoners had to be supervised because it was found, at times, that officers or petty officers asserted their rank and prerogatives by consuming most of the chow issued to their subordinates.

The career soldiers and sailors were usually surly prisoners, but occasionally a merchant sailor would be picked up who made himself so generally useful and agreeable as to become practically the ship's mascot before the end of the patrol.

One such ideal cruise ended in a narrowly averted clash between the ship's company and the naval base Marines to whom the "mascot" was being delivered, because of alleged rough treatment by his new guards.

All of which goes to prove that the American fighting man is an amazing and wonderful mixture of toughness and chivalry, severity and sentimentality—God bless him!

While, as I have said, our POW's were sometimes good, usually bad, and frequently so poisonous as to arouse retaliatory instincts among the submariners who had to guard them, it remained for the Spearfish to scrape the bottom of the POW barrel.

The Spearfish, skippered by Commander Cyrus C. Cole, was on her Twelfth War Patrol in the Nanpo Shoto area. At the end of the patrol she returned with seven downed B-29 aviators and two Japanese prisoners.

There had been three, but one of the Japs eliminated himself, and that's the story of this particularly unpleasant incident which dates back to December 1944.

Rescued on the nineteenth, just in time to ensure invitations to attend the Spearfish's simple but heartwarming Christmas party, complete with a tiny tree, decorations, and turkey, were the following B-29 survivors of an 881st Bomber Group: Captain Linden O. Brocker; Lieutenants Kenneth R. Chichester, Clifford B. Smith, and Jay L. Meikle; Sergeants Edmond G. Smith, Richard J. Grinstead, and Stephen J. Darienzo.

The new year had reached its second week when the sub overhauled a Jap lugger [small boat; fishing boat] crowded to the gunnels with contraband of war. After sinking the enemy vessel, Captain Cole was checking the wreckage when the sound operator reported that he heard fast screws—destroyer type—dead astern. The sub went ahead at flank speed on the surface, with left full rudder, and the Skipper was debating the wisdom of slipping down under cover when the Quartermaster sang out: "Boarders [those attempting to board the ship], sir, boarders on the starboard bow!"

That was a new one in a new kind of war. Boarders attacking a sub in the open sea?

Looking forward, his eyes following the OOD's pointing finger, Cole saw first one, then another, then a third Jap climbing up onto the forward deck. Three of the lugger's survivors had evidently gained handholds along the submarine's freeing ports and had been able to reach the ladder.

The first head appeared over the deck when the Spearfish was about one thousand yards from the wreckage.

Commander Cole had no particular yen for prisoners. With seven extra men aboard, the ship was pretty well filled up, and his five-inch magazine still contained a lot of ammo. Besides, prisoners from a lugger probably did not [typically] possess any important information.

Still, there they were, and, being the humane and kindhearted soul that Cy Cole is, he had no thought of throwing them back into the sea or even of diving with them still on deck. (Both of those despicable tricks had been played by our enemy earlier in the war.) He therefore had his unwelcome guests stripped (to minimize the intake of lice), shackled, and taken below to be washed, fed, inspected, and stowed away—one in each torpedo room and one in the engine room.

"Our aviation passengers," noted Cole, "jumped into the breach and took over the job of guarding them, which otherwise would have meant extra watches for all hands. Inspection of our prisoners showed them to be a sorry lot. One had a large tropical ulcer on one leg and a diseased-looking tongue; another, a possible oral chancre [ulcer] and a bad cough; and the third, a five-inch bullet gash in his back. One speaks English somewhat and writes in English with a very nice hand—all appear intelligent. Our Pharmacist's Mate again proved his worth by quiet, efficient, and exact treatment and diagnosis and isolation of the prisoners.

"Two prisoners are apparently none the worse for their ordeal and glad to be alive. But the third has tried to commit suicide by self-strangulation and by bashing his head against the torpedo tubes. Gave him sleeping pills to quiet him. That was in the morning, but by midnight our fractious passenger had recovered and again insisted on self-destruction. We administered some morphine tartarate which quieted him."

But the next morning the prisoner was again fractious. He tried to tear up the torpedo room, break his head against the tubes, and strangle himself with his bonds.

"He has bitten his tongue nearly off," continued Cole, "and has transformed his vicinity into a pigsty—a beast could not tolerate the filth he has tried to maintain. Decided to put him out of his misery before he has a chance to do any more damage. Administered a lethal dose of morphine and then jettisoned him over the side, having made sure that he would not suffer."

It was a hard thing to do, but the conduct of the prisoner was a threat to the safety of the ship and, as the official endorsement to the Spearfish's Patrol Report reads, "...the action taken in his case is considered proper."

Speaking of bestial prisoners, Commander Slade Cutter told me a story of a POW he brought home in the Seahorse. He was making the rounds of the ship one night when he found the prisoner guard in the after-torpedo room livid with rage. The POW, a particularly surly, low-browed type, had used his corner of the torpedo room as a latrine, evidently to show his contempt for his captors.

The guard, who was the compartment cleaner of the after room and very proud of his job, had just finished policing the place. He was so mad he could hardly talk.

"Captain," he sputtered, "I should have shot that S.O.B. How 'bout it, Captain, may I?"

As a test, Slade said, "It's okay by me, Smith. Blow his head off."

The Torpedoman's face fell. All the anger drained out of it.

"Aw, now, Cap'n," he pleaded, "you don't want me to mess up this nice compartment."

Commander Paul C. Stimson, a California and Washington lad who wears most of World War 2's naval decorations, skipper of the Sea Robin on its second War Patrol in the Java Sea and South China Sea, had heard about Kamikaze fliers and Kamikaze pilots of explosive boats and Kaitans (human torpedoes), but he hardly expected to find their brand of stoicism among the crew of a lowly trawler.

The Kamikazes were a "corps de elite" in Dai Nippon—glorified, feted, provided with the best geishas and cheered off on their suicide missions by families, friends, and fellow Kamikazes.

Our view of these heroic, but none-the-less misguided, enemies was quite different. We regarded them as a damning admission of failure by the Japanese High Command. Their rulers could not provide them with weapons with which they could fight, destroy their opponents, and live to fight again. They were a disgraceful waste of heroic manpower. American public opinion will never permit such a program in our fighting forces.

Commander Stimson's enlightenment on this subject began on the morning of April 8, 1945, after his sub had destroyed a Jap sea-truck and a trawler by gunfire.

Previously, the Sea Robin had sunk one large transport and three freighters. She had also rescued Lieutenant Wilfred N. Joyal, an Army fighter pilot who, when he tried to bail out from his P-51, had to climb back into his plunging plane to recapture control because his parachute was fouled in the cockpit. As the horrified men aboard the Sea Robin watched, the flier jettisoned his plane canopy, which from the submarine looked like a falling body.

"It certainly was a sickening feeling," wrote Stimson in his log, "to see what we took to be the body of a man plunge toward the sea with no parachute."

After witnessing this show from his bridge, Stimson decided he had experienced the ultimate in emotional suspense.

While examining the sea-truck's wreckage, the submariners took aboard three prisoners who came along without the slightest trouble. They told Commander Stimson that his two most recent gunfire victims had carried 195 Jap soldiers headed for Saigon.

"Well," said the OOD, "there's 195 that won't bother anybody anymore."

That done, the Sea Robin headed for the trawler which had been sunk by gunfire half an hour before the sea-truck. On arriving at the wreckage, Stimson found fires smoldering at the base of the mast. Since there was no sign of life on the wreck, he decided to expedite its burning by adding fuel oil to the flames.

Much to Stimson's surprise, when the fire got going well, two Japs crawled out from under a pile of palm branches. One was badly wounded in the arm. Stimson tried to get them to come aboard the sub, but they refused. One of them—a vinegar-faced chap with deeply hostile eyes—indicated contemptuously that all he wanted was a knife with which to commit hari-kari.

Stimson was in a cooperative mood and the situation intrigued him. Maybe his Nibs was bluffing. Turning to his Executive, the Skipper said, "Shall we call his bluff?"

"I think we should even encourage him, Cap'n."

Stimson called down the hatch: "Send the messenger of the watch to the galley and tell the cook to give us a good sharp butcher-knife."

During the ensuing period of waiting, the suicidal Jap stood with arms folded and regarded Stimson with glowering eyes.

When the lookout returned with a long-bladed butcher-knife—plus an angry-looking cook on his heels—Stimson took the gleaming sliver of steel and tossed it to the hari-kari boy. It hit the deck and slowly slid into the water. But the Jap showed no inclination whatever to catch or recover it.

"Helluva way to waste my best stainless-steel knife," muttered the cook as his head vanished below the bridge hatch.

Simultaneously both Japs sneered contemptuously and disappeared into the wreckage of the forecastle.

"Backed off and put twenty-five rounds of 40-mm into the hull," recorded Stimson in the log.

Maybe his Nibs got his wish.

The Tirante, Commander George L. Street's daredevil submarine, never won any stars in the Lifeguard League. However, she might have been given a half-credit for rescuing, by force, two Japanese aviators. The Tirante won the Presidential Citation and a Medal of Honor for her skipper on her First Patrol in March-April 1945.

During her scourging of the waters of the shallow Yellow Sea, she came upon a downed Japanese floatplane with a crew of three. The zoomies were invited aboard but gave back only sullen, defiant looks.

When the Tirante nosed into their craft, they jumped overboard and swam away. Thereupon Commander Street turned his Executive, Lieutenant Commander Ned Beach, loose with a tommy gun and their transportation vanished beneath the sea. Perhaps now the Japs would be more cooperative. Not so, however. They remained aloof.

These were desirable prisoners—they might have useful information. Besides, Gunner's Mate Howard Spence did not like their attitude.

"Captain," he said, "may I go out and bring in one of those sons [of Heaven; as the Japanese considered themselves]?"

"You may try, Spence," replied Street, "but take a knife or a piece of pipe. They may be armed."

"I'll just use these, Cap'n," said Spence, holding up a very capable looking pair of fists.

And so, he did. He brought in one and then another. The fist-battles were short and to the point—point of the chin.

When the Tirante pursued the third flier and capture was imminent, the Jap took off his Mae West and began doing slow somersaults, going deeper and deeper each time until his body disappeared.

"I watched the whole thing from the tip of the bow," Bob J. Wright—ex-Torpedoman now in business in Syracuse—told me. "It was a sickening thing to watch. Those Japs sure have guts."

That you can say twice, Bob. And so, had the men who beat them.

Worth recounting is one more prisoner incident among Lifeguard submarines, but in a lighter vein. The Pomfret, skippered by Commander John B. Hess, on its Sixth War Patrol, was patrolling for zoomies in the Nanpo Shoto Islands in the East China and Yellow Seas.

In a previous chapter we have already told of Pomfret's heroic dash into Sagami Wan to rescue a flier. Aside from rescuing five members of a bomber crew that had to ditch, the submarine paid close attention to the junks that operated in those waters in fairly large numbers. Those that were obviously Japanese, she sank; those that were not, she gave free passage.

Near sunset on August 8, 1945, the Pomfret sighted and overhauled a small two-masted junk. The sub's deck guns were manned and ready for action. These vessels had been known to carry radio sets and machine guns. As the Pomfret approached, crewmen on the junk raised a huge white flag on a stick. Aboard were what appeared to be about fourteen or fifteen male Japanese civilians.

"All were very anxious to surrender," noted Hess, "and when they thought we were going to go off and leave them, they gestured frantically for food and water. The thought of cold-bloodedly shooting down this crummy collection of non-resisting humanity was very repugnant to me, but I did not feel justified in letting the junk go since it was suitable as an enemy cargo carrier."

Finally, Hess decided to go alongside and take them all prisoners. But, alas, when this horde finally poured up on deck, extra ones crawled out from under the floorboards. The sub ended up with twenty-three of the sorriest-looking prisoners imaginable. Three of the lot were Koreans. An inspection of the junk showed that they had no food or water on board. Hess destroyed the junk, which he estimated at eighty tons. The prisoners were placed in the engine rooms after they had been disinfected and cleaned. A couple of them had bullet holes from some previous plane strafing.

"Due to minor injuries and ailments of various members of our crew," continued Hess, "we found it expedient to put the three Koreans to work as guards, and they have proved very helpful. Their fear and hatred of the Japs was quickly manifest. Our senior Korean kept his charges in check by making repeated and ferocious throat-cutting gestures with his forefinger.

"Once we had the Japs pretty well cleaned up and squared away, we put them to work, using the Koreans—who had been catching on fast—as straw bosses and go-betweens. The previously ever-so-meek Koreans stood for no nonsense, either. We did not treat the Koreans as regular prisoners of war since they are already bitterly anti-Japanese and will gladly give out any information they have. Their presence has had a definite morale value for the crew, and they have been a big help in easing the load on our watch list.

"The only difficulty is that the head man, a character called "Pop," persistently cheats at Casino. He dealt a further blow to morale by offering his nineteen-year-old daughter to us in exchange for his liberty."

The crew was in favor of giving him "the deep six," which is a sailor's expression for throwing some useless article overboard.

No, by and large, prisoners of war won no popularity contests aboard the ships of the Lifeguard League.

18 - Tigrone, Trutta Beat 'Ole Debbil Sea'

"Man proposes, God disposes." The ancient saying holds equally true of the sea and of the storms which scourge its tormented surface. The absolute mastery with which those tremendous, awe-inspiring demonstrations of Nature's power rule the great waters can balk the best-laid plans of mortals, even though these be buttressed by the armored might of battle fleets.

By what miracle, then, may helpless, terrified men, seemingly forsaken by God and man, hope to survive their fury?

Such miracles, two of our Lifeguard submarines were destined to witness.

In May 1945, the submarine Tigrone, under command of the redoubtable Commander Hiram Cassedy of Brookhaven, Mississippi, was assigned to Lifeguard duty off the home islands of Japan. Cassedy, in April 1942, had cut his eye teeth in the rescue business when the Searaven, under his command, picked up thirty-three Royal Australian Air Force personnel from under the very noses of the Japs on the Malay Barrier island of Timor.

The Tigrone had hardly arrived on station when a tough problem in guiding a lost and disabled bomber—which, so to speak, had flown off the map—to a submarine afloat in an area off the east coast of Honshu was dropped in Hiram's lap in the early afternoon of May 26, 1945.

Shortly after lunch, this canny operator got word on the voice frequency from the pilot of a two-engined Navy bomber that he was in trouble. What with only one of his two engines running, he had to land, and soon. But the pilot did not know where or how to locate the nearest submarine.

After a brief conference with his navigator, Hiram asked the flier—Lieutenant Commander Vernon J. Coley—if he were within sight of land. The answer was: "No." Commander Cassedy then asked him to change his course to the westward until he was within sight of the coast.

A little while later the sub skipper learned that land had been sighted by the bomber. A few minutes more, and Commander Coley was able to describe the contours of the shores of Honshu beneath him.

On the basis of this description, Commander Cassedy and his navigator were able, from their charts, to determine the bomber's position, and it was a-b-c stuff to give the plane a beeline course to the Tigrone. The call for help came at 1223.

At 1315 lookouts on the submarine sighted a Navy bomber limping toward it on one sputtering motor.

With mock formality, that gave all hands a welcome laugh, Commander Coley asked permission of the sub to enter the latter's landing pattern and inquired for "instructions."

Skipper Hiram told him to ditch upwind and close ahead on the starboard hand. At 1325—dragging his left wing low enough to make a furrow—Coley made a beautiful landing on the choppy sea. At 1326 the bomber sank—so fast that there was no time to release rafts. So, one by one, Coley and his crew were picked out of the ocean. They were: Ensign Richard W. Rehrig, and crewmen Irving Adler, John Paul Kolars, and Thomas M. Schroeder, all of Bombing Squadron 133.

"What's all the shooting about?" asked Pilot Coley as he climbed aboard the Tigrone and noticed that the 20-mm and 40-mm guns were fully manned.

"Well," chuckled Hiram in reply, "in this Lifeguard League you've got to be ready to pitch at any moment and, frankly, until we got the cut of your jib, we had you in our sights with trigger fingers at the ready."

"So-o-o-o," murmured Coley.

"Yes," grinned Hiram, "in this business we take a lot of chances, but we also take nothing for granted."

As rescue operations go, this incident was decidedly on the easy side. And so, for that matter, was the rescue four days later of the seven-man crew of an Army Rescue PBY which was damaged while taking off after having saved the crew of a B-29 that had to ditch. Thus, in one swoop, the Tigrone increased its zoomie population by sixteen.

Pilot of the lost Army PBY was Lieutenant Royal A. Stratton, who was barely alive at the time of pickup as the result of deep head injuries inflicted by the port propeller of his plane. The prop tore through the pilot's cockpit when the plane nosed into a wave while attempting to take off.

The PBY men were: Lieutenants Ralph Collier Zalkan and Walter Daniel Icheuch and Sergeants Edgar Eugene Holliday,

John Frances Logan, Viterbo Atanasio Vargas, and Samuel R. Xuck, all from the Army's Fourth Emergency Rescue Squadron.

Members of the B-29 crew were: Captain Clyde Allen West; Lieutenants Charles Edward Gibbs, Walter David Lloyd, Roderick Gale Wilcoxon, and Anthony Louis Verdeschi; and Sergeants Arthur L. Cody, Samuel James, Edwin Alden Weaver, and Alfred Tangret. Sergeant Weaver was pretty badly hurt and, according to the plane commander, three other members had gone down with the ship.

Cassedy destroyed the wrecked Army PBY by gunfire as soon as he recovered its battered personnel and immediately thereafter—at 1514—headed for a new position where one of his SCAP planes reported that it was circling a lifeboat.

From that time on, difficulties and death stepped into the picture. First off, both his covering planes had to return to base to refuel before he was able to locate the lifeboat. Next, the weather turned bad as night came on. The wind howled like a flock of banshees on a bat, and the seas worked themselves up to a towering thirty feet from trough to crest.

Tough weather for any poor devil in a life raft that night!

Cassedy had requested that a "bird dog" destroyer with a doctor be sent to take aboard the badly wounded Lieutenant Stratton.

How such a transfer was to be made in a raging sea was another of Hiram's worries, but the sad answer to that problem arrived at 2120 when First Lieutenant Royal Arthur Stratton died.

As if this were not enough, night-flying enemy planes' radar beams began playing hide-and-seek on the Tigrone's PPI (Position Plan Indicator) scope. Commander Cassedy decided this was too much—no raft could ever be located under existing conditions anyhow—so he sought the peace and seclusion of one hundred feet of the Kuro Shiro ['current'] and had a bit of rest till daylight.

Somewhere in between, he got off a message turning back the onrushing "bird dog" destroyer with the news that the patient had died.

With twenty-one zoomies aboard—a near-record catch—and people trying to sleep in every nook and cranny, including the empty torpedo racks, the Tigrone more closely resembled a flop house on skid row than one of Uncle Sam's proudest submarines, but Hiram with his infallible sense of humor and unsinkable determination did not let the situation get him down. Conditions inside the Tigrone might be bad, but at least her people were dry and safe... Still, he could not help worrying over those poor devils in their raft.

"0445—Surfaced in heavy sea," wrote Cassedy in his log, "and commenced search. Conducted simple burial ceremony and committed the remains of Lieutenant Stratton to the deep. A sad duty."

Many hours after that solemn and stormy dawning—at 1705, to be exact—the sub was informed by a PBY that it was circling survivors at a position which the submarine reached half an hour later. The wind had died down, but the surface of the sea was still wildly turbulent. The rescue was made doubly difficult because of the generally helpless condition of the men.

Three parachutes leading off the raft's port beam tended to act as a sea anchor and made it next to impossible for the sub to hold the raft alongside. Not being seafarers, the fliers did not know how to handle lines, and they were too exhausted to cast loose the parachutes.

Finally, Lieutenant H. D. Ragge jumped aboard from the sub. He cast off the chutes, rigged the lines properly, and helped the survivors aboard when the Tigrone once more came alongside.

Part of the crew of an Army plane of the 39th Bomber Group, the rescued men were: Lieutenants Arland F. Christ-Janer, Edward Barry Gear, Howard Lewis Howes, and Ralph Vernon Hayenga; and Sergeants Richard Frank Wilcox, Frank Eddie Williams, and Elias Tobias Schutzman.

They were an exhausted and bedraggled lot, more dead than alive after the protracted punishment they had taken from buffeting wind and seas. When the plane ditched, four men had been unable to reach the raft. They were carried away on the gigantic seas and were never seen again.

Plane Commander Gear painted a conservative but grim word-picture of how the survivors, some of them quite helpless, had been washed overboard a number of times during the night. But, miraculously, they had always managed to grab the handropes that were looped along the side and muster strength to climb back into the boat.

Knowing the condition of the storm-driven sea during the night and seeing how the raft had been held beam-on to the sea by the parachutes, it was a wonder that any of the men survived.

It should be noted that this outstanding Lifeguard patrol set a new record for recovery of aviators which stood through the war. Before the Tigrone returned to base on July 3, she had picked up a total of thirty aviators. The very excellent navigation and bulldog determination displayed by the Tigrone in effecting these rescues were most commendable. A lot of families back in the States had reason to be very grateful to the old Tigrone.

The crowding of the officers and men of a submarine that carries twenty-nine hands and mouths beyond its regular complement can easily be imagined. However, at this stage of the war, the problem of accommodations had been eased by reducing the number of torpedoes carried. The empty torpedo skids served well as bunks.

One of the most valuable talents aboard a sub on patrol is that of being able to get along with other people—to adjust under all conditions. And, fortunately, those aboard the Tigrone possessed a full measure of that highly desirable quality.

Deep in the heart of the Pacific stands a wave-pounded rock, the tip of a long-submerged mountain. Once it might have had ambitions to become an island, but the mountain mass beneath it lost its push, with the result that what might have been a fair-sized island some 180 miles north of the Bonin Islands remained a small, completely useless, and highly dangerous upthrust of rock.

The name of this rock is Sofu Gan. But for reasons best known to the early navigators—possibly because centuries of tenancy by sea birds have given it a whitish appearance—its English name is Lot's Wife, the pillar of salt of the Bible.

Whatever may have been the origin of its name, Lot's Wife, standing on the sea lanes from Midway to the China Coast and from the Marianas to Tokyo, became well known to submariners and aviators alike during World War II, appearing in scores of Patrol Reports.

No one would have been surprised to see billboards blossom on its rugged sides—or fingerposts to the ports of the world, such as one found on every American-occupied island in the Pacific.

Bleak, wet, and storm-ravaged as it is, Lieutenant Arthur A. Burry of the 45th Fighter Group of the USAF would have given quite a lot if the falling engine of his fighter plane could have carried him those few score miles that separated him from the forbidding shores of Sofu Gan. His craft was disabled during a raid on Japan on June 1, 1945.

As days went by and searching subs and planes found no trace of Burry and his raft, the flier was given up for lost. In fact, his chances of recovery were considered so slim that he had not been reported to the submarine Trutta as a potential client of the Lifeguard League.

This vessel, on its Second War Patrol, had departed its refit base on June 2, 1945, and was bound for Lifeguard duty in the East China and Yellow Sea areas. Even if it had been told to keep watch for Lieutenant Burry, the chances are that all hands aboard the Trutta would have concluded that the one-man rubber raft, on which the flier might have climbed after he ditched his plane, would not have survived the typhoon which swept the war-torn waters of the western Pacific during the first week of June.

From June to November, typhoons breed in the vicinity of Yap, Ulithi, and Guam, sweeping with destructive force up through the Philippines, curving along the coasts of China and Japan, and finally blowing themselves out between Japan and the Midway Islands.

The typhoon of June 4, 5, and 6, 1945, was indeed one to remember. Not only did it raise the devil with numerous island and shore establishments, but it wreaked terrific damage on the Third Fleet. The flight decks of two large carriers were broken down at the bow; the forward section of the cruiser Pittsburgh broke off 125 feet from her stern; and the bow of her sister ship, the Duluth, cracked at the same point. ... In short, 'twas no weather for life-rafting.

At midnight on the night of June 5-6, the navigator aboard the Trutta reported to his Skipper, Lieutenant Commander F. P. Hoskins—one of the eleven Reserve Officers who rose to the responsible rank of Submarine Commander—that the barometer had taken a nosedive of twenty-two points during the last hour.

Skipper Hoskins, who was up to his ears in unavoidable paperwork on the table in the wardroom, ran into the control room to take a look for himself and, sure enough, the barometer had done a major tumble. It checked with the glass in the conning tower.

In a submarine, securing for bad weather is a rather simple procedure. Few are the things that are not always secured for considerable angles of roll and pitch.

However, the Skipper sent the Executive on a tour of inspection to check the torpedo racks and tail stops, loose equipment, locker doors, and galley gear.

There was every evidence that the Trutta was in for a real blow. It would have been easier if the ship could have submerged to more peaceful levels, but time was precious.

According to orders, the Trutta was to be in position for a special "en route" assignment to serve as Lifeguard during a bombing attack on Kobe on June 7.

This precluded her diving under the rapidly rising storm.

Hour by hour, the typhoon grew in intensity. At 0100 the glass read 28.90, an additional drop of eleven points; at 0200 it read 28.61, a fall of 29 points; at 0300 there was a decline of 27 points to 28.44.

By now the seas were mountainous and the main engine induction and ventilation trunks had been secured. All air for the laboring main engine—only one was in use and that at slow speed—was taken in through the conning tower hatch.

On the bridge the quartermaster's chief job was to try and predict when a "big one" was coming over and slam the hatch so as to prevent flooding the conning tower. Frequently his guess was not good enough and the crash of water down over the struggling helmsman and into the control room below added to the discomfort of the night.

"God pity those poor wights [spirits] ashore on a night like this," once said an old Cape Horn sailor, "trembling in their beds for fear their chimney pots will fall down on them."

Hoskins' thoughts probably echoed that sentiment, for there is little about bad weather to dismay a submarine sailor. These little ships ride well and pitch easily. They do roll considerably, but no matter how far they heel over, the great weight of batteries and machinery concentrated low down toward the keel will always bring them back. Three destroyers did capsize in the great typhoon of December 1944. But no subs.

The Trutta's lookouts had long since been sent below because of the danger of losing them overboard, so that the only two men in the ship who really had to take the storm on the chin were the OOD and the Quartermaster.

At 0400, daylight was near, but the barometer was still falling and stood momentarily at 28.16 inches—a new low.

The Trutta was still riding it out with the seas on her quarter. When it came time to change the bridge watch at eight bells, there was no standing on petty formalities. The men released vanished down the conning tower hatch and headed for the warm chow and hot coffee that waited for them in the galley. Having been buffeted, tossed, and punched by wind and wave, their bodies were bruised, and their muscles weary from bracing themselves and hanging on.

"The Trutta rides surprisingly well," noted Skipper Hoskins. "Of course, we ship water down the upper conning tower hatch occasionally when a big one comes over. Also, we are opening out to eastward to keep clear of the storm's center—if such is possible."

At 0500 the barometer trembled at 28.02—a drop of 14 points in the last hour.

"The seas are mountainous," recorded the Captain. "The waves tower at heights of from forty to fifty feet."

The scene from the bridge was terrific. It was also tinged with considerable peril to the men on watch there when the great green, roaring combers swept aboard.

In the trough, the ship had no vision, for the waves towered high above the bridge; and, naturally, a periscope could not be raised while the ship was tossing so wildly.

But from the crests, the seascape was grim, terrifying, and beautiful. The wind shrieked at a breathtaking 100 knots; the salt spray stung eyes and found its way down necks and up sleeves.

I have witnessed such scenes many times and have wished for the talent to paint them; and I have never ceased to be awed and humbled by the thought of the tiny, fragile cockle shells—as compared with modern ships of steel and steam—in which our forebears penetrated every ocean of the earth... They indeed were men!

As gray daylight slowly stole upon this tremendous scene, Skipper Hoskins' eyes swept the madly churning oceanic world that surrounded him. With a shudder, he wondered whether any poor devils in rubber rafts had been caught by the storm. He was certain no raft or raftee could survive such an onslaught.

With the coming of full day at 0550, Hoskins decided that it was time to save his ship and his men from an unnecessary beating. All indications were that the center of the storm was about to pass over them.

Wrote he: "With the barometer at 27.91 and still falling, I decided to take the ship down. So, we submerged to two hundred feet. Even at that depth, the Trutta rolled ten degrees. We settled down to cleaning up the water-soaked conning tower and control room. Another objective was to let the crew get a good and well-deserved eight-hour rest."

When, at 1330, the submarine rose from two hundred feet to periscope depth, the Skipper was amazed to find a moderate sea with little wind! How the picture had changed! As the Trutta surfaced, Hoskins noted that the barometer had risen to 29.26 and that it was still rising slowly. The storm had gone as swiftly as it had come. The ship must have been within twenty-five miles of its center, Hoskins thought, as he set course for his Lifeguard station.

The following forenoon, while on Lifeguard station, lookouts sighted dead ahead, a life raft with a survivor in it. A quarter of an hour later, a rescue party picked up Lieutenant Arthur A. Burry. He had been in a small rubber boat since June 1.

During this time, a matter of a solid six days and nights in still and storm, he had survived the typhoon of June 6. The Skipper noted that Burry was physically numbed and slightly incoherent as a result of his terrible ordeal. However, the sub's Chief Pharmacist's Mate took him below and gave him careful and competent treatment for long exposure.

"That boy," remarked a radioman, "sure had his J-Factor working for him."

"You can say that again," murmured the Chief of the boat.

19 - AAF Pays a Tribute

During the closing months of World War II—May, June, and July 1945—General LeMay's heavy bombers operated practically around the clock against the home islands of the Empire. Results were cataclysmic for Japan, but American losses in planes and men were heavy. Official USAAF figures show that during those three months alone, 530 airmen are known to have ditched, crashed, or parachuted into the sea.

Of this number, 358 were rescued—an overall percentage of 67.5. During the peak month of May the rescues reached a phenomenal 80 percent. The Army Air Force understood the blood and sweat and danger which were integrated into those figures.

"The statistics, unhappily, do not show," says the official record—Army Air Force, World War II, Volume 5—"the human side of the story—the long hours of frustrating search in the patrol planes, or the long hours of anxious waiting in the rubber rafts, or the patient and hazardous vigil in the submarines.

"No column of percentages can do justice to the skill and daring of the men who made the pickups off the very shores of Japan and from the Inland Sea itself, but the record is there to read in the logbooks of the submarines and in the circumstantial interrogation reports of survivors. There is no war literature that assays more richly in tales of derring-do."

My thanks too to the AAF historians for this graceful tribute to all the life-saving services. The statistics of rescues are cheering and inspiring, but no statistics can ever show the heartbreaking circumstances which attended failure to find the men who were missing—or finding them too late.

To understand more fully just what triumphs and tragedies entered into the making of these statistics, let us have a quick look into the Fifth War Patrol of the Pipefish. Commander Wm. N. Deragon of New York was her skipper. Her Lifeguard station was south of Tokyo Bay in the string of islands called the Nanpo Shoto.

The day—the twenty-sixth of May 1945—began as any other patrol day aboard a small and very crowded submarine surfacing on a large and very empty ocean. According to the Pipefish's log, the vessel arrived at 0015 on Lifeguard station for the day's bomber raid on Tokyo.

During the next few hours, those concerned aboard the sub checked the procedure setup for the rescue operations. The "Boxkites," "Dumbos," and other aerial watchdogs reported present and on their respective stations. Hell could pop loose on its hinges—the gang was all there.

In a few hours, long before daybreak, came a flash from "Boxkite" Number One that a B-29 was down twenty miles, bearing 128° true, from Hachijo Shima, a dot on the ocean's surface sixty miles south of Tokyo Bay.

At flank speed, the Pipefish headed for the spot, when "Boxkite" Number Two reported it was circling survivors of a bomber crash at a different but nearer location.

Two ditchings at once. What to do? Deragon decided that the nearest zoomie was the best zoomie; so he reversed course and headed toward the location given by "Boxkite" Number Two.

At 0705 the sub was where the ditching should have taken place. But no survivors. At full speed the skipper held to his base course because the wind was blowing in that direction.

He concluded that the way the wind blew was the way the survivors would have drifted. An hour later the gamble paid off. Lookouts sighted a large life raft from which the sub rescued Sergeants William F. Linki, Robert W. Riherd, and Herman C. Knight. All were hale, happy, and unhurt.

These successful rescues, the first of the Fifth Patrol, spread a feeling of cheer and satisfaction throughout the ship. This mood was, however, to be of short duration. Twenty-six minutes later three more fliers were brought aboard—all of them dead from drowning or exposure, probably the latter. The bodies had been in the water from six to seven hours. According to their dog-tags, these men who paid the full, tragic price of their devotion to country and to duty were Lieutenant Elby W. Huelson, Jr., and Sergeants George W. Shaw and Oakley A. Simon.

One by one, at half-hour intervals, the bodies, held afloat by their yellow life jackets, came into view and were reverently taken aboard. The Pharmacist's Mate checked each man carefully for any remaining spark of life, but in vain.

Throughout the morning and early afternoon hours the craft came upon other discouraging proof that zoomies thrown upon their own resources on the surface of the sea did not always survive. Empty rafts and empty life jackets. Empty hopes at the end of frustrating furrows plowed through the ocean in search of living men.

On one occasion the Pipefish approached a raft. At first it appeared empty. Then one of the lookouts sang out: "There's a body—I mean a man—anyway, something under a rubber sheet!"

The sub pushed silently and slowly toward the yellow raft. "There's a guy there. Holy-gee!" And there was real awe in the sailor's voice as he continued, "The guy is asleep! Dead to the world in a place like that!"

Loud and clear came the shout from another lookout to the sleeper on the raft: "Hey, Mac! What you doing?" When "Mac" awoke and looked upon his laughing liberators through sleepy eyes, he was too amazed for words. He turned out to be Lieutenant Robert M. Calridge of the Army Air Force. Less than an hour later Lieutenant Abram Grossman, very weak and barely conscious, was rescued.

Throughout the day—since shortly after the body of Oakley Simon was taken aboard at 1040—Captain Deragon had had a gnawing feeling of uncertainty. It began when he realized that while Sergeant Simon's body was being taken aboard, the Number One main ballast tank had been flooded to bring the forward deck down closer to the surface to ease the work of the rescue detail. While all hands were engaged, the aviator's parachute and half-inflated rubber boat had disappeared, evidently under the ship.

Deragon was worried over what had become of these two items especially the parachute. If they were merely wrapped around the TDM (Torpedo Detector) head, that was not so serious, even though it left the Pipefish vulnerable to ambush by lurking enemy submarines.

However, if that chute had been sucked up into the Number One ballast tank and drawn into the vent risers, that was a horse of another color—a very dark color, indeed. In that dangerous situation, the ballast tank could not be flooded and the submarine—clawing desperately to get under in order to evade death-dealing Zekes or Zeros—would be left floundering on the surface with futile, thrashing propellers, a wide-open target for enemy bombs and bullets.

Not a pretty picture. To have the end come that way would not be inspiring. "Damn that chute," muttered Deragon.

Doing his best to hide the waves of alarm that swept through him, the Skipper headed casually for his stateroom and told his Executive to come along. Once in the tiny cubicle, barely large enough to hold a bunk, Deragon closed the curtain that serves as door and whispered: "Keep this under your hat. No use scaring hell out of all hands, but we may be in one helluva fix!"

"Yes?" answered the unruffled second in command. "What's up, sir?"

"I am not sure that we can dive!"

"What!" exploded the no longer unruffled S.I.C.

Hastily, the skipper unfolded the story of the rubber raft and the parachute that had vanished.

"The stuff is either up in the Number One ballast tank or, if we are lucky (provided my theory is correct), it is wrapped around the TDM head. If the worst happened, I can imagine how the chute will look in the vent risers." Before the subject passed beyond this point, word reached the Captain that another drifting airman had been sighted. He was Lieutenant Harvey L. Swensen, and he was dead.

Soon after, another empty life jacket was sighted. Deciding that he and all hands had had enough of this steady dose of gruesome reminders of men who had joined the Ghost Parade, the Skipper gave orders to head south. He did not give his reason, but it was governed by several important factors. The most important of these was that the Pipefish needed waters far removed from enemy bombers until all doubt about her being able to dive had been settled.

"We'll have to put a diver over the side tonight," explained Captain Deragon to his Executive, "to find out if we can dive, and I do not believe that our Lifeguard station is a good area for that kind of an operation. Too many chances of Japs sticking their noses in."

The Skipper made this decision and acted on it at 1700. However, the operation was not destined to be quite so simple. At 1731 the SD radar picked up a plane contact at thirty-three miles, but it came no closer.

"That's luck," said Deragon.

As darkness came on, the Skipper's hopes mounted, but at 2000 another contact was made. This time the operator reported one plane at seventeen miles and another at twenty-four.

"Well," thought Deragon, "we'll never find out any sooner," and quietly he gave orders to clear the bridge and stand by to dive.

By 2003 the unseen enemies had closed in to ten and seventeen miles, respectively. With great calm he watched the lookouts and bridge watch hastening below. Waving at the OOD to precede him, Deragon was last to leave the bridge and, therefore, the man who pulled the diving klaxon. He scrambled down the ladder into the conning tower.

Around him he heard the briskly spoken orders and saw the well-drilled action that changed propulsion from engines to batteries, shifted the ventilation supply, and prepared the ship for submerged running. Slowly, smoothly, the slant of the deck under his feet changed as the good old Pipefish nosed downward into her beloved deep. The dials told their stories as the sub slid deeper into its element.

"Hold her at periscope depth," said Deragon to the Diving Officer. "Thank you, thank you very much, Sir," said Deragon silently to God.

Later investigation revealed that the missing parachute had wrapped itself around the TDM head, a fairly harmless position as contrasted with the flooding intakes or vents.

2300—In the piping times of peace, this would have called for six smart strokes on the ship's bell, and personnel on watch would have reflected pleasantly that the bunk would feel mighty good in another hour.

This night, with bells removed for the duration, 2300 meant to the Pipefish's crew that the long and tiring hours of May 26 were drawing to their close. In another hour, there would be a new day and, please God, one filled with less sorrow. Too, it was the hour set for the burial of their dead.

There are nights on the ocean when it seems as if sea and sky—starshine in the heavens and moonbeams on the white-laced waves—unite to clothe the universe with a special sense of spiritual sanctuary—the kind of sanctuary that one finds only beneath the vaulted domes of old cathedrals.

That night, with its gentle wind, starry sky, and silvery moon path, was such a night. And it furnished a soul-stirring setting for the simple services Captain Deragon conducted before the remains of Lieutenants Elby W. Hudson, Jr., and Harvey L. Swensen and Sergeants George W. Shaw and Oakley A. Simon.

With bared heads, men of the air and men of the sea joined in the Lord's Prayer, and presently the deck space where four canvas-clad flag-draped forms had rested was empty.

Slowly all the men, except those who had business there, left the deck and the bridge. Today had almost run its course—tomorrow was another day.

In many Lifeguarding situations, submarines had to operate within the Ten Fathom Curve—in waters that would float a submarine but would not permit of diving to escape attack.

A case in point is the Lifeguard duty performed during the Seventh War Patrol of the Ray, skippered by Commander Wm. I. Kinsella, another Pennsylvania lad, in the muddy waters of the Yellow Sea.

Two rescues, one made under most adverse weather conditions in shoal enemy waters, resulted in twenty friendly aviators being picked up and returned to port. In addition, a total of twenty-one well-planned and expertly conducted gun attacks were made on miscellaneous small power boats and sailing vessels that were engaged in hauling rice from Korea to the Empire. All were sent to the bottom.

Long after sunset of the evening of May 15, 1945, the Ray, just south of Saishu To, a rock-ribbed island south of the toe of Korea, started to submerge because of a rapidly closing plane. On the sub's way down, the aircraft was identified as friendly. It reported survivors in the water twenty-five miles to the southwest of the vessel.

Returning to the surface, Skipper Kinsella asked the plane to stand by him. This the pilot agreed to do. To expedite discovery, another plane would circle the raft and mark it with flares from time to time.

It was the sort of a night at sea that landlubbers love to describe, but sailors love to escape—a howling storm with spray and spume flying from mountainous seas. Solid water socked the bridge with brutal impact. The wind force was about 30 knots.

The Ray was making turns for about 15 knots and getting about 8 by the pitometer log.

"This is going to be tough," shouted the OOD over the howling of the wind.

"Yes," agreed Commander Kinsella, "and to make it even tougher, the reported position is four thousand yards north of Shiro Se Light and there's a nice ragged reef smack between the light tower and the raft."

The rescue message arrived at 2031. At 2318, after almost three hours of severe pounding, the Ray sighted a rocket fired from a raft at a distance of about one mile.

It took steady nerves, perfect navigation, and seamanship of a superior order to proceed from this point on. It also took more lights than any warship—even a battleship—would normally dare to use close under an enemy coast.

"Turn on the searchlight and keep it on the rafts," yelled Kinsella. "We've got to work fast, make our pickup snappily, and then get to hell out of here."

"Chief," he called to the Chief of the Boat (Senior Petty Officer of the ship), "get plenty of men on deck with ring buoys and heaving lines—and all with life jackets on!"

Overhead the two planes swung in circles. Their landing lights cast weird patterns of light and shadow on the rising and falling mountains of foam-crested water. At 2341 the sub began the tricky task of maneuvering to recover the ten men who huddled in two tight clusters aboard the rafts trying to escape the pounding of the storm. Close at hand, right and left, were deadly shoals. Beyond the rafts, three miles to the west, were enemy shores.

"With all this display of planes, flares, and searchlights," wrote Kinsella, "the Japs ashore now probably thought they were about to be invaded. A nearby island began sweeping us with searchlights."

"All we need now," muttered the Executive as he watched the Skipper desperately trying to get the submarine alongside the wildly pitching rafts, "is a few Jap planes. That would make it perfect!"

Shore based radar began to saturate the Ray's radar detecting receiver (APR), and Kinsella braced his nerves for the shock of large-caliber shells screaming overhead. The tension of waiting for the dreaded barrage was almost worse than the bombardment in reality could have been.

"Go on and shoot, you so-and-so's," cursed the Skipper.

At long last, five minutes past midnight on the morning of May 16, line contact was made to the rafts. Five minutes later, the Ray began taking the exhausted airmen aboard. After twelve hours in cold, rough waters, they were hardly able to move.

"For a time, it seemed as if the sea was worsening," explained the skipper. "We found it almost impossible to keep a lee [position sheltered from wind] for the rafts. Several zoomies and at least two of our own men were washed over the side. But, thank God, they were quickly recovered. One survivor was so exhausted that he was almost lost as the exploding seas overturned the first raft.

"In the midst of handling these problems—and they really called for cool heads in hot corners—one of our planes told us that the Ray was in immediate danger of being blown on two rocks a mile away. A quick radar check, however, told us they were three thousand yards away; close enough but not too close if that is what the game calls for.

"All survivors were aboard at 0023. We recovered ten; three were lost with the plane. The pilot said that a second plane (both PBM's) was shot down in flames with no survivors. The job done, we notified the air-cover planes to put out all lights and commenced clearing the area. Condition of the survivors was excellent considering their ordeal."

Another submarine that dangerously exposed herself to coastal artillery fire in the course of rescue operations was the Jallao, skippered by Commander Joseph B. Icenhower of Parkersburg, West Virginia. The Jallao, on her Third War Patrol, was a new ship but had won her spurs by sinking the Japanese light cruiser Tama on the night of October 25, 1944, as the latter was trying to escape the bombs and aerial torpedoes of Admiral Marc Mitscher's carrier aircraft after our splendid naval victory off Cape Engano.

Commander Icenhower's handling of that midnight attack showed no lack of skill or experience, and it proved that determination was one of his strongest characteristics.

On the morning of May 9, 1945, Icenhower was assigned a Lifeguard station off Marcus Island, some one thousand miles southeast of Tokyo Bay. Marcus, which was the scene of the very first Lifeguard effort in September 1943, proved to be what is sometimes called a "sleeper," for it had been worked-over earlier in the war and supposedly had been pretty well reduced to impotence. However, such was not the case. The strike for which the Jallao was Lifeguarding was more or less a routine raid by naval aircraft based at Tinian just to ensure that no air strength was allowed to build up there.

Icenhower had made contact with his Privateer air-cover when, at 0930, he received word that four rafts had been sighted about five miles off the northern shore of Marcus. After five hours of searching, the submarine came upon one raft from which it rescued Lieutenant Maurice R. Wallace, Ensign Jerome Palma, and crewmen Elthus J. Lassite, Jr., Harrison J. Henders, and Robert L. Livesay. All these men were wounded, two of them quite seriously.

For that reason, the rescue operation was rather protracted. Two men had been taken aboard—but the most seriously injured were still to be transferred—when a heavy-caliber, probably eight-inch, shell from Marcus Island landed fifty' yards away on the port bow. Four more landed about thirty seconds apart—some seventy-five yards away; others within twenty-five feet.

It was up to Icenhower to decide if the Jallao was to stick it out or if she was to dive for safety, keep an eye on the remaining three airmen through the periscope, and complete the rescue at a more propitious moment. After a hasty' look at the three men on the raft, the Skipper was convinced that their condition was so serious that to leave them a moment longer than necessary would be tantamount to signing their death warrants.

The three wounded men were in pain but not unconscious. It was going to be extremely difficult to get the helpless men down narrow hatches and vertical ladders and through slit-like passageways into the interior. They would have to help and have to suffer. But it was that—or death.

"Although seriously wounded," wrote Icenhower with great admiration, "and suffering from shock, no more than suppressed groans were heard from those three men while they were being assisted aboard and down the hatch. With their desperate courage and help, we were able to get all three below."

Meanwhile the shells were landing around them at half minute intervals. Some were much too close.

"But," continued the Skipper with a wonderful sense of humor, "at 1443:30 we dived to a previously prepared line of defense at one hundred feet."

Obviously, Marcus Island needed further attention from our air and surface forces. ... It was not neglected.

20 - Gabilan Target of U.S. Guns

To Lifeguards—and, of course, to all submarines—every type of anti-submarine attack was full of dread possibilities. Some were merely more dangerous than others. But if one kind of attack was hated, by submariners and zoomies alike, more than any other, it was gunfire directed at them by air- or water-borne compatriots by reason of mistaken identity.

When the word was "Dive! Dive!" because an American fighter or bomber put the enemy label on their particular sub, anger ran red among submariners. Lord, how their trigger fingers itched to return the fire.

As I have noted elsewhere in these pages, nine out of twenty-eight such attacks resulted in serious damage to submarines and one, the Dorado (although not a Lifeguard), was lost with all hands. But when ships of their own Navy, manned by former shipmates or classmates, loosed gunfire or depth charges at our submarines, then the verbal pyrotechnics really rose to stratospheric heights. One such mistaken attack undoubtedly cost us the life of the Seawolf and all on board her.

Lifeguard subs were forced to dive for safety from American Army, Navy, and Marine fliers all too frequently. But for subs standing guard to serve as targets for U.S. naval vessels—well, that happened less often; but it did happen.

To relive such a spine-tingling episode and gain an insight into its rage-rousing features, let us turn back the pages of history to the evening of July 18, 1945, when the Gabilan, commanded by Commander William B. Parham, a hot-blooded youngster from Alabama, was on Lifeguard station in the waters off the entrance to Tokyo Bay. So far during this Sixth War Patrol the sub had picked up no less than fifteen aviators.

Three of the fliers were snatched from under the noses of the Nips in the very entrance to Tokyo Bay. Bill Parham's comment after this rescue was typical of the spirit of the Gabilan: "We have now concluded that we can recover pilots from the Imperial Palace moat if we have enough fighter cover."

The Gabilan's guests were Navy carrier pilots, Army fliers of Mustangs or B-29's, and Marine fliers. All of these men had faced death in planes crisscrossed by enemy fire, but probably none of them thought he would live to see the day when he would be a target for the weapons of his own countrymen... But they did!

The curtain rose on the Gabilan's unhappy experience at 2049 on July 18 when the sub was cruising slowly in ocean waters just cast of O Shima, the volcanic island which sits twenty miles southwest of Tokyo Bay entrance.

It had been a successful, exciting, and rewarding day, and this was the first time the Skipper had been able to relax.

Suddenly, the radio messenger burst into the wardroom with a red-hot, urgent dispatch from Comsubpac to clear the area at top speed and remain north of 350 15' until daylight in order to avoid a cruiser-destroyer Task Force of the rampaging Third Fleet which was coming in on a sweep for coastal shipping.

It was a futile gesture, as everyone must have known, for there just was not any coastal shipping bigger than a *sampan* [small boat with oars] left to destroy. Submarines had seen to that.

But, after the day's successful carrier strike, one of Uncle Bill's hot-shot Task group commanders had no doubt badgered him into permitting this nonsense, just as SCAP planes pestered submarine captains into permitting them to execute private strafing runs.

When the news of this forthcoming strike hit my headquarters on Guam late that afternoon, I protested to Admiral Nimitz and sent a desperate dispatch to Admiral Halsey, giving the positions of the Lifeguards involved, which, of course, he already knew. My dispatch to the Gabilan could best be described as frantic. I knew she could not get out of the way and I had grave fears that some so-and-so would not "get the word."

Even the news that the Gabilan had rescued fifteen aviators could not raise my spirits that evening, and my Operations Officer, Captain John Corbus, and I sat around our offices with our chins on our chests. And, as it developed, we had good reason to be glum.

Aboard the Gabilan, Bill Parham's quick glance ran through my warning message. As one man, he and his Executive leaped to their feet and dashed for the control room plotting chart.

"All ahead flank," yelled the Captain up the conning tower hatch. "Bring her around to course zero nine zero... Radar, get me a round of bearings... Great Gawd and General Jackson," drawled Bill, "how are we going to get out of this trap? That's a seventy-five-mile run—four hours in a head sea—and those trigger-happy tincan [destroyer; so-called because the hulls of early versions were said to be as thin as tin] sailors are on their way here right now!"

The ship heeled as the rudder was put hard over, and the vibration of the hull gave assurance that the lads in the engine room were "pouring on the coal."

As the Gabilan came to her new course, a crash of water down the conning tower hatch spoke eloquently of the kind of sea she was bucking.

Parham remembered what had happened to the Nautilus at Tarawa in a similar mix-up—a hole through her main engine induction pipe and a destroyer's unexploded five-inch shell rattling around in her conning tower fairwater.

Unless the Gabilan "shook a leg," these might be her last few hours, for Bill had no illusions about the shoot-'n-be-damned attitude of "the cavalry of the sea," just spoiling for action and hungry for any kind of a target. The Gabilan would have to be on her toes.

The big danger lay in the fact that our own submarines, early in the war, had mined the shallower waters along that part of the Honshu coast. Hence the submarine could not skirt it too closely and would undoubtedly come within radar range of the screening destroyers as they swept in toward the Tokyo Bay entrance.

By this time the Skipper was buttoned into his wet-weather clothing and sprinting up the ladder with the speed of a courting squirrel ascending to his honeymoon treetop. Only there was no joyous anticipation in Parham's heart. This would be a wet ride and a dangerous one.

"Bring her to course northeast as soon as we are clear of the minefields and Nojima Saki," he flung over his shoulder as he parted from the Executive.

"Aye, aye, sir," came the acknowledgement. "Should be able to change course in half an hour."

2100: and on the bridge Parham found whatever shelter he could against the sharp wind that keened out of the steel-gray night. The sub plunged, yawed, and vibrated as the invisible horses of its four powerful diesels drummed invisible hooves over the sea's invisible highway. Below, some submariners swore; some zoomies prayed.

2145: still pounding north-northeast; the Gabilan was still many miles below the safety zone that began north of 350 15'. The cheerful, quiet atmosphere that usually dominates a submarine during long surface runs was wholly absent. There was tension throughout the ship. In the conning tower, the control room, the navigation room, and the engine rooms, grim-faced men looked older than their years. Their watches were stood in apprehensive and almost total silence.

In the forward and after torpedo rooms and along the passageways, submariners off duty and zoomies who could only stand and wait, braced themselves against the wild bucking of the ship as they gathered in small clusters and exchanged whispered opinions. The opinions, usually about tincans and their ancestors, were not flattering.

2215: Bad news! To the bridge from below came word for Parham that the radar operator has 10 centimeter interference on the radar screen, undoubtedly from U.S. men-of-war.

This was indeed bad news. A quick check on her position showed that the Gabilan was as close to the coast as she dared to go. Only luck could now keep her from being picked up by the Task Force's radar—and after that—?

In the Gabilan's pounding forward torpedo room a Torpedoman explained to an Army Air Force gunner: "These boys," he said with a perverse kind of pride, "will shoot first and won't even bother to ask questions."

In the wardroom: "But why don't we dive, if we can't make it?" asked an Air Force pilot.

"Because they'll catch us on sonar or echo-ranging if we do!" answered the Communications Officer. "We lost the Seawolf with all hands in just that kind of a deal. She was trying to make sonar recognition signals when they hit her with a hedgehog projectile."

On the bridge: "Now the fat will soon start frying," observed Parham. "We've picked up their U.S. air search radar on our APR radar detection gear."

2240: The Gabilan turned on her ABK self-identification signal for sixty seconds.

No acknowledgement from the approaching but invisible Task Force.

2300: The Gabilan picked up pips that indicated units of a Task Force—several cruisers and two destroyers.

"Give them the ABK again for another sixty seconds," ordered Parham. "No, never mind the sixty seconds, keep it running and let's hope it rings somebody's bell!"

His voice was calm, and his bearing was steady, but underneath his mind was seething with worry. Should he dive and try to evade? Diving would certainly look suspicious to the destroyers. He could not forget that the Seawolf was lost that way... Better save that for a last resort... "Damn them," he muttered, "why don't they answer?"

Well, it would not be long now. Below, in the conning tower, Parham could hear his Talker repeat his comment so that everyone aboard would know what the score was.

2304: "We have pips, sir," said the Chief Radar Operator who had taken over at the radar controls, "from 16,000 to 28,000 yards. Looks as if two smaller units—probably destroyers—are starting to close us."

Time, immeasurable time, went by in quick spurts and dragging starts. Too fast. Too slowly.

2330: Now, two light units, destroyers according to expert radar readings, are at 13,000 yards on parallel course. The Gabilan is still streaking northeastward at the rate of her utmost 19 knots. Again, Parham asked for his position. Again, he learned that he could not turn more to northward and that he still had a long stretch to go before he reached 350 15'.

Suddenly, off to the east, the darkness of the night was ripped by the angry orange spurt of gunfire. One, two—half a dozen shots, rapid fire at a range of 12,800 yards.

"Fire a green star rocket," ordered Parham just as water spouts from rumbling shells rose out of the sea, "and give them the recognition signal."

This was done. But instead of answering it, the watchdogs of the Task Force continued to rain shells all around the sub. The situation seemed so utterly unreal to Parham that, were it not for the shell splashes that spouted all around them dangerously close, he might have thought it all part of a nightmare.

The horror of it, the pity of it—one American ship with ninety-some fighting men aboard being savagely attacked by another American man-of-war just because someone was too negligent or too careless to inform himself of the situation and the correct procedure.

What price Lifeguard duty, performed at the cost of your own life? Or should downed aviators be left to fend for themselves?

Whatever the answer, this was no time to soliloquize. With radar-controlled shooting much too good, it was time to pull the plug.

"Take her down!" ordered Parham.

But it was not quite as simple as that. Parham gave the proper orders, but the Gabilan was heading into a heavy sea (always a detriment to quick diving) and the bow planes chose this moment to refuse to function.

"Commence firing the submerged signal gun," cried Parham, desperately hoping to halt this hail of death. A single one of those shells might be fatal to the submarine. "Keep firing until we get under!"

The next two and a half minutes were the longest Parham or anyone in the Gabilan had ever lived through. The submarine's bow pumped with the seas and, without the pull of the bow planes to drag it down, stubbornly refused to take a down angle.

In the forward torpedo room and in the control room men were frantically trying to clear the bow plane jam, spurred on by the now continuous slam of five-inch shells smacking the sea and screaming away into the night.

Finally, at 2336, the bow planes bit into the water and took the ship down. "Thank Gods" were on everyone's lips. A ragged cheer went through the ship, but it was not too lusty. The danger had not yet passed.

Still on her 045 course, the Gabilan ran at her best submerged speed.

2345: Sonar reported: "Two sets of fast screws coming in on starboard bow."

"Take her to three hundred feet. Rig for depth charge; rig for silent running," came the Skipper's order.

"Rig for Hell and Hereafter," said a small voice.

From his position near the Number One Periscope just back of the helmsman, Parham settled down to the submariner's ancient game—evasive action. One factor in his favor was that the cold sea water gave the sub a favorable temperature gradient which should give the antisubmarine detecting devices of the destroyers a bit of trouble.

Throughout the Gabilan the human and mechanical noises came to a sudden stop. Men spoke in whispers or not at all. Some even took off their shoes. All over the ship, men froze into whatever positions they had held at the moment the order was issued.

What thoughts raced soundlessly through the minds of these men is not difficult to guess. Especially of the airmen. Here they had survived bitter warfare against the enemy in the air and now it looked as if they were about to be consigned to Davy Jones's locker by the weapons of their own compatriots.

At 2358 the sonar operator reported fast screws passing down the starboard side. In the hushed stillness of the submarine, the menacing drumming of destroyer propellers was plainly audible to everyone.

"Don't send any sonar recognition signal," said the Captain, "but keep your ears trimmed for one from the destroyers." Turning to the Executive, he said, "I'm not going to give them another chance to blast us. We'll slip away under this cold layer of the Japan Current—if the Good Lord lets us."

And so—by the grace of God and smart maneuvering—that is just what the Gabilan did. Under its Skipper's able direction, the sub was able to sneak away and leave the over-zealous destroyers empty-handed to report that they had sunk an enemy patrol boat!

Later, in his log, Parham wrote: "I estimate that we were straddled by salvos of shells about ten times before the boat was completely submerged. It is an act of God that we are still here. If we had been holed by shell fire and had to surface, those boys would have eliminated all trace of the Gabilan. The narrative in this log of the above incident might sound as if we were calm and collected, but such was far from the case at the time."

Parham was willing to call the Gabilan's shelling by "friendly" forces just one of those things. By the time his patrol report was turned in, the Armistice had been signed. We were about to forgive our enemies—why should we not forgive our friends?

21 - WHALE PROVIDES CURB SERVICE

"ON THE RAFT THERE—STAND BY FOR A MOMENT and you can paddle right aboard," megaphoned Lieutenant Commander Freeland A. Carde, Jr., a Rocky Mountain lad from Colorado, to the two Mae West-jacketed aviators whose yellow life raft bobbed gently on the ground swells as the Whale's dark hull eased to a stop close alongside. Bending toward the IMC mike on the bridge, Skipper Carde continued, "Control. Flood after group."

"Flood after group, sir," came the reply and, true to her name, the ship's after vents popped and two whale-sized spouts of spray issued from below the deck plating as the designated tanks flooded. The stern settled rapidly into the sea until waves lapped at the after end of her conning tower fair-water.

With wide grins the zoomies paddled aboard forward of the after-gun mount and were met by two men of the rescue squad and the smiling Executive Officer. "This is what we call our curb service," he explained. "You gentlemen are a bit late for lunch but I'm sure the cook can whip you up a snack. Please go below and let our Pharmacist's Mate look you over. I'll join you as soon as we pick up the next zoomie. We just had a report that another airman is down in our area."

"Blow after group," ordered the Captain. The high whining note of the low-pressure blower, responding to his command, almost drowned his words of welcome to the new shipmates, Lieutenant (jg) Dennis L. Herron and his radioman, Omar D. Kerouack, as they struggled down the hatch.

"All ahead flank. Course two seven zero," shouted the Skipper and the Whale was off on another lifesaving mission.

Humming a snatch of a popular song, the Captain scanned the waters ahead as he leaned on the breast-high railing of the bridge. It was a nice day; Lifeguarding was good business; and those whom the Gods loved, they put aboard submarines. The Whale had a big bone in her teeth as her stubby snout piled up a huge bow-wave.

"Left full rudder," yelled the port forward lookout. There was a note of terror in the pitch of his voice. Instantly all eyes trained forward to a black sphere awash in the cresting seas a scant fifty yards ahead.

Hardly had his cry been repeated and executed before the Captain sang out: "Right full rudder!"

No questions were asked among the men of the bridge watch. They had all seen that near brush with death—the mine that, thanks to the sharp eyes and quick thinking of the lookout and the Skipper, missed the Whale by a mere five feet. A quick S turn such as the Whale executed saved many a submarine at that stage of the war.

Later, in his log, Skipper Carde, in recording this incident, wrote: "Many stomachs sank to the deck."

In wartime, hostile seas are apt to sprout a sinister crop of mines. While drifting mines are, according to the Geneva Convention, supposed to be harmless, no sane sailor would want to risk finding out if a floating mine is really a safe toy to play with.

In this particular location it behooved the Whale to maintain a most careful lookout. Her Lifeguard area was in Bungo Suido ['channel'], the middle entrance to the beautiful and shallow Inland Sea.

Down its length often drifted dangerous samples from the long-established minefields that guarded Japan's vital inland ports. The older such fields are, the larger the number of runaway mines that have broken their anchor cables. On this patrol the sub counted fifty-five drifting mines. She sank four by gunfire.

The incidents just related took place on July 24, 1945. On that day, Carrier Task Force 38 of Admiral Bill Halsey's Third Fleet delivered its first strike against the shattered remnants of the once powerful Imperial Navy holed up at Kure in the Inland Sea.

The summer of 1945 was just one long tragedy for the Japanese. Death and destruction were everywhere. Their cities and munitions-producing areas were hammered day and night by Army Air Force Superforts. Their ports and coasts were scourged by the crusading Third Fleet.

To the already overwhelming strength of Admiral Halsey's forces had been added the most powerful battleships and carriers of the British Royal Navy. Thus, was created the most formidable armada the world has ever seen. And, unlike the Spanish

Armada of Elizabethan days, it was not to be turned back. Japan had no Sir Francis Drake. The Third Fleet struck at heat lightning speed around a summer horizon. No one—not even Uncle Bill Halsey, I sometimes suspected—knew where the next blow would fall.

Naval bases, munition plants, airfields—all suffered death and disintegration from its guns and airborne bombs.

The Whale, which up to the time of this first strike on Kure had spent five profitless weeks in the Bungo Suido area, was put into the zoomie-saving business with a rush.

Like all other Lifeguard missions during this particular stage of the war, the Whale's days and nights were crowded with rescue calls. Some were bona fide reports of downed aviators, well-founded and with correct geographical coordinates. Others were faked by the enemy, designed to confuse the Lifeguarders, to wear out their nerves, to cause the loss of downed aviators, and to force the needless depletion of the submarines' fuel tanks by high-speed chasing.

More and more, airmen complied with instructions regarding the reporting of downed planes, pilots, and aircrews. This meant quicker rescues and more certain identification by subs of approaching aircraft and a reduction in the time and energy spent in making sudden dives to avoid a plane that could be an enemy but might be a friend.

The morning of July 24 began auspiciously. Commander Carde observed: "The two planes that are flying air-cover today made the most gentlemanly approach we have experienced. Amazingly, to properly identify themselves they did everything the rules demanded. First, they called by VHF voice telephone long before we sighted them. I believe we sighted them before they sighted us, but even though we reported them in sight, they did not come closer than seven miles, where they informed us of the maneuvers they intended to make. We were positive of their identity when they finally closed in. And that was certainly comforting.

"Some three hours later, our SCAP planes were relieved by two more fighters. Without a second's delay, the relieved pilots zoomed over toward Honshu looking for coast-wise shipping; but, as we suspected, there was none. They ended up by strafing a lighthouse."

At 1045 came a flash report that a plane was down at fifteen miles from the Whale. Half an hour later, as the vessel sped toward the location, voice radio brought news that a "sick" TBM was coming in to ditch alongside the sub. Carde had just alerted his bridge watch and lookouts to try to locate the disabled plane when he was advised to be ready for a "sick" fighter who would be dropping in to ditch. This was crowding things a bit.

The skies overhead were literally black with planes—hundreds of them thundering in from the south headed for the Inland Sea. The weather was ideal, and the blue sea sparkled in the sun. One could almost feel a physical impact from the ear-dinning roar of their wide-open throttles. It was an awe-inspiring and sobering sight.

"I hope to God," murmured one of the older Chief P.O.'s, "that my family back home never has to see an enemy flight roaring in like that."

To which we can all say, Amen.

Now from the south came a solitary black dot. It grew larger, took on the familiar form of a TBM, and plunged into the sea about three hundred yards on the Whale's starboard bow.

Turning to the Junior Officer of the Deck, Carde told him to keep all eyes open for the "sick" fighter pilot while the rescue detail concentrated on hauling the PBM crew out of the marrow-chilling sea.

While Ensign William A. Steenberg and crewmen Robert N. Craft and Howard F. Gray were brought aboard the submarine, the JOOD [Junior Officer On Deck] saw the "sick" fighter plane make a fairly healthy water landing.

In fact, the pilot ditched his plane perfectly and climbed out on the wing. Then he seemed to slip and fall into the water. As the Whale approached, it was seen that the flier's rubber boat had been opened but not inflated; it had probably been ripped or punctured. The belly tank showed holes from flak which had pierced the plane from bottom to top on a line which might have gone up through the cockpit.

On the approach to the scene, the Whale's bow planes had been rigged out to serve as a rescue platform. This proved to be a mistake. The sea was too rough to put a man on them, and with the planes rigged out it was impossible to place the boat close alongside the man. The first heave of the life ring was a bit short but well within the pilot's reach.

However, he made no effort to reach for it. He was floating with his head underwater most of the time; his Mae West, flapping in the waves, was not inflated. Before a swimmer could dive for him, the pilot went under and did not come up again.

"This was a heart-rending experience," wrote Commander Carde in recording the ditching in his log. "A black moment that few of us will ever forget. In spite of all our efforts to relocate him, he never reappeared."

None of our lads were ever able to take the tragedies of Lifeguarding in stride. Saving lives never became a "business" or cold-heartedly "wholesale." Each loss of a downed flier was a very personal thing to our skippers. They undertook as much risk and trouble to save one life as they did to save many lives. The sadness over the loss of this young man, who was never identified, hung like a pall over the men of the Whale, and the spell was only broken when the raft holding Herron and Kerouack was paddled aboard the slightly flooded vessel.

Not content with the havoc his bombers and fighters had wrought at Kure on the twenty-fourth, Uncle Bill struck again on July 28. This time the death blow and last rites were administered to the Japanese Navy.

The fury and destruction unleashed on the battleships Ise, Hyuga, and Haruna; the carrier Amagi; and the cruisers Tone, Oyodo, Hoba Iwate, and Setten made the score more than even for the Pearl Harbor "day of infamy."

However, the Japanese ack-ack was good. The Inland Sea and coastal waters were littered with the wreckage of American aircraft and with fliers awaiting rescue. Many were beyond all need of rescue.

Again, the Whale swung into action. The following excerpt from her log of July 29, covering an extensive and concentrated period of zoomie hunting, is inserted here to show the effort and ingenuity employed by sub skippers and cover planes in rescuing downed fliers.

"1600: Lookout spotted life raft. This was the first time we had sighted a survivor without the help of a plane, and it restored faith that if there had been survivors within the radius of our former searches, we would have seen them.

"1602: Another life raft.

"1615: Picked up Second Lieutenant James Cloud Brechtbill, USAAF.

"1617: Second raft was empty. This was one which had been dropped by a B-29.

"1637: Sighted what seemed to be a man in a Mae West in the water but a thorough investigation revealed nothing.

"1640: Sighted red flag being waved from another raft. Headed for him. The red flag was a great help to a searching submarine.

"1655: Sighted another life raft. The DRT (Dead Reckoning Tracer) was excellent for plotting these positions.

"1657: Sighted a B-29 and contacted him on VHF. He joined the search.

"1715: Brought Second Lieutenant George Sylvemus Lomas, USAAF, aboard. He had a dislocated shoulder and was in pretty bad shape. 'Super Dumbo' assisted on this man by dropping smoke bombs and zooming. After we had the survivor in sight, the 'Super Dumbo' started looking for another raft. The 'Dumbo' was very helpful.

"1719: Sighted another raft. The man in this raft jumped up and down to attract our attention.

"1725: Picked up Staff Sergeant Kirk Narvel Icenhower, USAAF.

"1727: Headed for raft which plane was circling. He also dropped flares.

"1751: Brought Corporal Warren Eugene Bartlett, USAAF, and Sergeant Harold Leslie Windberg, USAAF, aboard. Plane had departed to look for more survivors.

"1759: Sighted mine.

"1800: Learned from rescued fliers that they were members of a B-29 crew had lost a propeller returning from the raid of two nights ago. The propeller had flown off into an adjacent engine and fuel tank which started a fire along the side of the plane. It went into a flat spin. They had all jumped with the exception of three who probably couldn't get out.

"That left a probable three in the water. By keeping a DRT record of where the men were picked up and determining in what order they had jumped from the plane it was possible to make a fair estimate of the course of the plane and the probable position of the remaining survivors.

The 'Super Dumbo' cooperated by searching in the sectors we suggested.

"1824: 'Super Dumbo' located another raft and dropped a smoke bomb.

"1847: Rescued First Lieutenant Raymond Edward Shumway, USAAF, plane commander, and Sergeant Sam Clark Kidd, USAAF. The latter in very bad condition, suffering from shock, sunburn, and water immersion. These two men had been in a one-man raft for two days.

"One more possible survivor; so, planned to search until 2300, when plane promised to escort us from the area.

"Picking up these fliers, particularly the last ones, proved to us that flooding down aft was the most practical way to bring people aboard. We also found that it was much easier to spot men who waved red flags from their rafts than those who did not.

"1850: Commenced search plan to locate eighth crew member.

"2035: No luck yet; so fired rockets, hoping he had one with which to answer. Had already requested Dragonet to take our Lifeguard station for the night.

"2300: Flank speed on four engines to clear the area with our excellent 'Super Dumbo' for an escort.

"2400: Released plane as we were clear of the restricted area. Explained that we would make arrangements to return if he located the last man."

In the course of his operations, Captain Carde found that in rough seas it was occasionally hard for a plane to sight his submarine. He found that by running at full speed with full rudder he could churn up a white circle of water which helped the pilots considerably. Also, after completing the circle several times, the seas were generally calmer in the center of the circle. This valuable tip, well known to our "destroyer Navy" cousins, was passed along to other submarine commanders.

In order to give the reader a gull's-eye view of a day's range and coverage by a Lifeguard submarine, I quote what Commander Carde modestly calls "an estimate of the results of the day" in his log of July 24, 1945:

"We received reports of the positions of about twelve downed planes, and of these five were so far into Bungo Suido they were beyond our reach. We contacted three of the remaining seven. All three of these were kept in sight by us or planes from the time they ditched until rescue was attempted.

"The diameter of the dispersal area was about sixty miles, and we were unable to get to some of the points before the covering planes had to depart due to fuel shortage. We searched around one reported point for six hours with help from two to seven planes with no results.

"Our own search had covered about fifty square miles. This does not include the search area of the planes. With a reference point only twenty-five miles away, the reported position and our search position should not have been too greatly in error. Two reported points were not investigated except that our CAP must have passed over the one close to the point of our afternoon search. The other point was a bit uncertain.

"Unless it was a Jap on the air he must have tried to ditch near our originally assigned station. Since he was the most uncertain and away from the area where we spent the day within sight range of the Jap coast, we planned to search for him by moonlight. One other survivor, only a few miles up into the Bungo Suido, should be able to paddle out by tomorrow. Asked for cover and the assistance of the Dragonet for the next day. Also asked for a complete recapitulation of survivors unaccounted for and gave the positions of the ones we picked up.

"Our air-cover planes were very cooperative, but even with the help of some of our rescued aviators, we found it was difficult to get them to understand what we wanted. They were used to flying in pairs and it was impossible to get them to break apart in order to double their search area. We finally left their search to their own discretion. Some were very systematic, but others were haphazard. Possibly that was because they considered their prime duty was to protect us. Wish we could have gotten them to spread out."

The Whale made no surface ship contacts on this patrol—a disappointment to her skipper and crew. That they were used to stronger meat and the thunder of torpedo warheads is attested by the Whale's official record of nine enemy ships, including one aircraft ferry, for 57,716 tons sent to Davy Jones's Locker. However, her record of fifteen rescued aviators on this Bungo Suido patrol puts her name high on the list of those to whom zoomies are thankful.

During this same series of strikes by the rampaging Third Fleet the Peto was on her Tenth War Patrol along the south and east coasts of Honshu from mid-July 1945, to the cessation of hostilities. The series of rescues performed by her rank high among outstanding, heads-up feats. Her Skipper, Commander Robert H. Caldwell, Jr., from the deep south of Georgia, had starred his ship's record with three cargo vessel kills.

His performance in saving from death or imprisonment twelve downed zoomies, some of whom could almost have waded ashore to Japan, shows that his hot southern blood was backed by a fine, cool nerve and excellent judgment.

On the particular day with which this episode starts, July 24, the Peto had not been assigned to a Lifeguard station, but she was in excellent position to assist; so, her Skipper just grabbed the ball and ran with it—true submarine spirit.

It was a lovely summer day and swarms of Lexington Corsairs had just bombed and burned Hamamatsu, a seaport on the east coast of Honshu. It was a nice show, but Caldwell and his lads would have been happier if they had not been compelled to spend most of the afternoon without air-cover. There was no way of knowing if Japs were among the scores of planes that buzzed under the blue cupola of the skies like angry bees over a flaming hive.

At 1552 five carrier fighters circled the sub and waggled their wings while one peeled off and ditched near the Peto. The pilot, suffering gunshot wounds in both legs, was hauled aboard. He was Lieutenant T. A. Sinclair of the Lexington.

Before he would let the rescue team take him below for treatment, he insisted on reporting that another pilot was down and, he thought, much closer to the shore than he was. However, the word "shore" does not fit too well in this instance. It builds a picture of a more or less uninhabited region populated mainly by sea and cliffs.

In this case, "beach" was a better word, because bathing beaches, highways, railroads, docks, and houses ran along the waterfront of Hamamatsu. There were boats in the harbor and from all over the place anti-aircraft batteries stuck their lean snouts toward the sky as they sprayed shells.

There were other kinds of artillery to be reckoned with, for it was inevitable that a fine beach, so suitable for invasion forces, should be backed by heavy guns and innumerable pillboxes.

Somewhere in the waters closer to this hot spot of combat was a pilot afloat on a raft and completely helpless. He might be dead if cruel enemies had used him for a target. He might be a prisoner if Japs had discovered him and decided to take him in alive. There was no pattern to go by. It might be a merciful end brought by a bullet; or it might be prison and torment—inhuman, unbearable torture—to wring military secrets out of men who knew no secrets of any real value to the enemy.

There was but one way for the Peto to get the low-down on the downed flier, and that was to go and look for him. Luckily at this time two Hellcats winged in and flew cover for the sub as she approached land at full speed. At this time, too, came word that still another pilot had been sighted clinging to something that might be a channel buoy and quite close to land. That made the potential zoomie score ahead a total of two. Good work if he could get them, thought Caldwell.

The Peto made top knots heading into a dangerous area. As the coast drew near, Caldwell sent all bridge personnel below. Only the OOD and the Skipper remained on the bridge. A rescue team stood by beneath the conning tower hatch. Gunners were at their belowdecks stations ready to emerge if defensive fire was needed.

But for the quick, thrumming beat of the engines, all was quiet on the Peto. Still and steady was the word. All but the fathometer—it had the galloping heebie-jeebies as it registered less and less water between the sub's full, round bottom and the ocean floor.

But if the Peto looked deserted, such was not the case ashore. The terrific working-over which Hamamatsu was receiving had driven everyone who could walk, ride, row, or find gas for a jalopy, out of the city. Hence, the roads and beaches were crowded and a railway train was plainly visible standing on a trestle outside the town—and no doubt trying to look as small as possible. Trains were favorite moving targets for our sharpshooting zoomies.

Now the Peto, with her roaring air-cover escort, drew the attention of the crowd and, unfortunately, of the beach defenders. Shells began screaming over the submarine, which was in thirty-five fathoms of water and four miles from shore when—as Caldwell phrased it—the sub "made a lightning rescue of Ensign H. F. Donneley."

"People along the shore had ringside seats," he continued, "to see the sight. But since we were not there to sightsee, we commenced retiring at flank speed. Lieutenant Laboon did a heroic job by jumping into the sea with a lifeline to grab the exhausted pilot. He dragged him aboard before all the way was off the sub. Laboon was barely aboard when the air-cover planes waggled their wings and left us alone and absolutely barefaced. I was just about to tell the wide-open spaces what I thought about that kind of treatment when they were replaced by two Corsairs.

Strangely enough, no more pot shots were taken at us, although we must have been within range for another fifteen minutes. While we picked Laboon up, we saw a black can-buoy about a mile and a half further in. That may have been the buoy the other survivor had been clinging to. But there was no one on it now and our air-cover could not see anything that looked like a downed airman in need of rescue."

On the morning of August 9, the day after the world's second atom bomb exploded at Nagasaki, the Peto was the target of a do-or-die air attack. It was staged by a pilot of the kamikaze type. On its first pass, the plane dropped a bomb two hundred yards from the Peto. On its second try, it was within a hundred yards of the sub when the timely arrival of four friendly fighters ended the pilot's career as an avenging angel.

Six days later, the day the "Cease Fire" became effective, there was but this single entry on a Peto log sheet: "Thank God, it is all over!"

"Japan had no Sir Francis Drake."

22 - RAF Fliers Take Sub Ride

During the months of July and August 1945, the Third Fleet's carrier strikes and battleship bombardments fell thick and fast upon the doomed homeland of Dai Nippon. Admiral "Uncle Bill" Halsey moved so rapidly from launching position to bombardment position and back to launching position again that the enemy never knew where to expect him.

Likewise, these rapid shifts added a most unwelcome element of insecurity to the operations of our Lifeguard submarines. For, as that veteran submariner Admiral R. S. "Dickey" Edwards often said: "There's always some so-and-so who doesn't get the word."

During this terrifically exciting period, the submarine Scabbardfish on its Fifth War Patrol, skippered by Commander Frederick A. Gunn, occupied Lifeguard stations along the south and east coasts of Honshu. There, with a fine display of a big supply of the stuff from which heroic history is made, she recovered seven downed aviators, including two Royal Navy pilots.

Three of these rescues were made close inshore on an enemy-controlled coast. They showed far less concern for the lives and safety of the submariners than for the lives and safety of the zoomies that they sought to save. It was obvious, as the war progressed, that Lifeguarders and aviators alike were becoming disdainful of the enemy's offensive and defensive power—an attitude of overconfidence which too often led to disaster and death. More and more frequently one heard the "Old Gray Mare" song with a popular new line: "The U.S. flag will fly over Tokyo—less than a year from now."

The dice in one of the most dare-devilish of these games against death and destruction began rolling at 0743 on July 28, 1945, when the Scabbardfish received word that two pilots were down in Owase Wan, a small body of water some sixty miles southeast of Kobe.

It was important because of the fishing fleet and the antisubmarine patrol craft based at Owase town. The prime targets that day for Halsey's fighters and bombers were the well-camouflaged remnants of the once mighty Imperial Japanese Navy then hiding in their great naval base at Kure in southwestern Honshu.

The right flank of the carrier formation was held by Vice Admiral Sir Philip Vian's Royal Navy carriers, whose targets were the shipyards and steel mills of Kobe and Osaka.

No sooner had the report of these crashes come in over the VHF than Commander Gunn called: "All ahead flank," and the exhaust of all four main diesels poured into the morning air.

"How's the water in there?" was Gunn's next question to the Executive at the conning tower plotting board.

"Plenty of water, if we don't get too far in, Cap'n, but there is a mean-looking island which might mount some heavy guns."

The Captain sent his lookouts below in the event that an extra-fast dive became necessary and ordered the Talker to caution all hands to be on their toes. He was determined to make the pick-up on surface, if possible, and resort to the well-known periscope sleigh-ride only if forced down. British pilots might not have been fully briefed on this rather rough technique.

Now it so happened that although the Scabbardfish's regular Hellcat air-cover was flown by U. S. pilots, the flier who guided Gunn and his sub toward the downed airmen was a true product of Britain. Even to this day, Dunn recalls that his voice—coming over the VHF—had a very clipped, "veddy, veddy English accent."

But, as Captain Gunn wrote me in a recent letter dealing with this particular zoomie adventure, "he did augment our air-cover going into the inner bay. In fact, he and my Hellcats strafed the very hell out of the beach and a small island in the center of the Wan [bay] as we went in."

Skipper Gunn's Executive Officer on this and other famous Scabbardfish patrols was Lieutenant Commander Clifford Myer "Trigger" Esler, who hails from the little Texas town of Dennison, birthplace also of President Eisenhower. Gunn himself is a native of Kansas City, Kansas, boyhood home of another noted sub-skipper—Roy Davenport, with whom Gunn used to play trombone in the Wyandotte High School band.

In re-living the spine-tingling adventure of this outstanding rescue, after the lapse of a solid decade, "Pop" Gunn did a truly wonderful job. His account is so full of realism and detail that I reproduce it here, virtually word for word:

When we first had word, Trigger and I both assumed that the fliers had ditched off the coast in the open ocean. However, as we approached the mainland, we could not make out the yellow life rafts so blithely described by our British "guide" as being "just a short distance ahead."

In answer to our repeated "Where?" he would give the above form answer and then zoom a spot some distance ahead. I really think he was afraid we would refuse to go into the Bay after his men and was trying his best to lure us in by these tactics. The outer bay is a long, shallow indentation, and following our guide's lead toward the coastline, we were actually in the bay before we realized it.

I demanded to know where the downed fliers actually were, and our guide finally admitted they were both just inside the narrow entrance to the inner bay which was guarded by a nice little rocky island in the center of the channel. It looked like an ideal gun-emplacement to me.

We asked the guide if there were any ships inside and he said only a small gunboat tied up to the village pier, which was a short distance to the left after passing the island going in.

The two fliers had landed on the far side of the inner bay and, as I remember, they said they got their paddles out and were making good headway toward the outer bay when the small ship opened up with a small-caliber gun.

Later, after they had been picked up by us and identified themselves as Lieutenant H. Keith Quilter of Loughton, Essex, England, and Lieutenant T. F. Stirling of New Zealand, the two pilots told me that each time they stopped paddling, the Jappy's would stop shooting. However, the enemy at no time made an attempt to intercept and capture them.

So, in between volleys, they continued to paddle across the inner bay toward the entrance to the outer bay. When we finally reached them, they were about 1,500-2,500 yards on the inboard side of the island.

After a short discussion with "Trigger," I told the guide and the remainder of his flight (I think there were two other British planes) to strafe the beach and particularly the island and we would get his men.

He replied: "Think nothing more about the island."

And, sure enough, the planes proceeded to really raise the dust in both spots.

We never did see Quilter and Stirling until we got even with the island. "Trigger" got a few men on deck to yank them aboard when we got them alongside, and I made a wide turn so as to be heading back out toward the outer bay when we came alongside the rafts, which were separated about one hundred yards.

At this point, I could see the small craft at the dock. It looked like a small coast guard cutter of some sort, but I was too busy maneuvering to notice details. Lieutenant Quilter, our first pick-up, came aboard with no strain. However, Lieutenant Stirling tried to outguess my twisting approach and paddle toward the sub. I finally told him that if he didn't stop paddling and throwing me off, I would leave him. He threw the paddle overboard and we had him aboard in a jiffy and were on our way out to open ocean.

As soon as the men were on board our British guides said "Thanks much" and took off for their carrier. I had ordered our four Hellcat CAP to remain in covering position all the way in and out. All four were griping as usual about CAP duty being no fun. I decided that if we had seen the Jappy, he had undoubtedly seen us and might give trouble later on Lifeguard station. So I ordered the air-cover in to sink the ship with their rockets. Shortly thereafter we heard a nice explosion and soon our CAP returned and very happily announced: "Mission accomplished."

Actually, except for a few gray hairs I got while passing that small island at about one hundred yards range, the whole affair was not much to talk about. Frankly, I was worried about the island because I remembered a luncheon date with you in your Makalapa Quarters at which your guest, Colonel Vandegrift, USMC, described the elaborate concealed gun positions on the cliffs at Iwo Jima.

I was also worried over whether our British guide would make the grade. He had told me at the outset that he was low on gas but would not, as leader of the flight, leave his men in the lurch. I might end up having him on my hands on a raft. But, fortunately, his gas held out.

After we were well out of the Wan, over chow and coffee, my two zoomies told me they had zoomed down to shoot up a nice innocent-looking bridge near Owase Wan when the Japs opened up on them with "Beaucoup de AA" and damaged them both so badly they could do nothing but ditch in the nearest water, which was Owase Wan.

Shortly after this incident our station was shifted to the eastern point of Sagami Nada where we had three P-51 (Mustang) pilots from Iwo bail out almost simultaneously. I remember telling the second and third planes to hang on as long as possible to give me a little time between pick-ups. The second pilot's answer was: "Sorry, Skipper, no can do! Here I come!"

Almost immediately the third said: "Me, too!"

And then there were three parachutes in the air at the same time.

The Scabbardfish was really busy in the midst of that "airdrop." To us, it looked like the graduating class at Ft. Bragg. We got all three in good shape. The first one alongside did not have his silk umbrella, and when we told him he had to give us his parachute before he could come aboard, he really looked worried—and well he might, because it was about fifty yards distant and some twenty feet underwater and sinking rapidly.

The next pilot was an old hand, having been picked up twice before by submarines during the fighting around the islands west of Guadalcanal. He had his parachute neatly folded, and as he came aboard he calmly stated that he was qualified to operate the head and wanted to know what we had for chow.

Next, we shifted station to a point about twenty miles off the mainland and slightly north of a latitude line through Tokyo to cover daylight raids of a Carrier Task Group. About 1000 we received a report that a pilot had ditched about 0700 that morning. The position given put him just inboard of the offshore minefields indicated on our charts. The sea was calm and it was very foggy.

At this stage of our Lifeguarding we were getting a little brazen about charging through a minefield which might or might not exist, so off we went after our man. Because of the fog our aircover could not locate the flier, and we were worried for fear we might miss him in the fog. Also, there was a good chance that the current had drifted him into the beach since his ditching.

Thank God, the fog finally lifted and the covering planes located him very close off the beach, frantically paddling toward open ocean and steadily losing his battle against the current.

When we got him aboard, he was all in and said he had been paddling steadily since the time he ditched because he knew the war was going to be over very soon and that it griped his soul to think of being captured so very near the end. Our chests swelled just a little with pride when he later told us that he knew that a submarine was in the area and that as long as he kept paddling and kept off the beach he was sure we would get to him, minefield or no minefield.

Thus ran the account of Captain Gunn of the Scabbardfish's venture into dangerous Japanese waters. It may be added here that Captain Gunn's chest swelled once more with well-deserved pride when, shortly after the war, he received a "mentioned in dispatches" award from England signed by [Albert Victor] Alexander, First Lord of the Admiralty.

"Gosh," observed modest Captain Gunn, "I felt like Horatio Hornblower getting orders to his first ship."

And who would not under similar circumstances? An award well earned.

First Lord of the Admiralty Alexander

23 - Aspro in Hirohito's Front Yard

"0930: Held divine services."

The custom of prayer before battle is as old as battle itself. Kings, generals, private soldiers—Christian or barbarian—have bowed their heads to petition their gods for strength in battle and for the defeat of their enemies. From such humble, heartfelt communions often have come the comfort, confidence, and courage that win victories.

The submarine Aspro, from whose log of August 3, 1945, this brief entry is taken, was to have plenty of need for divine assistance before that day was ended. Under command of Commander James H. Ashley, Jr., of Clinton, Indiana, she was on Lifeguard station off the east coast of Honshu. The date marked the beginning of the second week of her Seventh War Patrol in a section of Japanese waters sanctified by the heroic blood of hundreds of American fighting men—airmen and submariners.

Those who follow the inspiring patterns of human courage and brilliant achievements in man's efforts to ensure survival of his friends and bring destruction to his enemies will find in that patrol a monument to the truth of the ancient biblical injunction which demands that man shall be his brother's keeper.

Like the mounted, armor-clad Crusaders of old, who practiced the creed of brotherhood, Ashley was a two-fisted Christian with a two-handed, twin-edged sword. Jim's protective armor was embodied in the fighting power of swift-winged combat planes that swung overhead, and his twin-edged sword was a vessel that could fight on the surface of the sea or below it.

The deep, wide, and fog-shrouded area that adjoins the outer reaches of Tokyo Bay is divided into two portions for purposes of identification. The southernmost portion, which meets the waters of the Pacific abreast the volcanic island of O Shima, is known on the charts as Sagami Nada or Sea. The northern, which skirts the gently curving shores of Honshu Island, is called Sagami Wan or Bay. Together they unite to form the outline, inside view, of a human head facing to the west—a rough study by an impatient sculptor of a plug-ugly, broken-nosed, double-chinned thug.

Just about where the Adam's apple of this head would be, lies O Shima Island, mentioned above. Going north in a straight line from this craggy island to the mainland, at the top of the study's skull, is a distance of about one hundred miles. The water in this area is deep, averaging from five hundred to six hundred fathoms—the kind of sailing submariners like.

During the summer of 1945, increasingly large numbers of American combat planes—speedy fighters and heavy bombers—cast their fast-moving shadows on the waters of Sagami Wan. And while Japan's sea power and land forces abroad had crumpled under the weight of Allied arms, the enemy still had enough planes left in the homeland to put up a fairly good defense against Allied airstrikes on Tokyo and other vital war industrial centers that were slated for destruction.

As our island-hopping Army, Navy, Marines, and Air Force moved their front-line bases closer and closer to Kyushu and Honshu, the industrial keystones of Hirohito's shrinking empire, the force and frequency of short-range air strikes and carrier sweeps increased. In line with this activity, the business of Lifeguarding expanded from what one might call a retail sideline to a wholesale main activity.

The job of training our crews and equipping our submarines for Lifeguard duty, now concentrated almost wholly on the coasts of the Japanese home islands, became the principal function of Comsubpac at Guam and other submarine bases in the Pacific. And I am proud to say that the closer our growing numbers of combat planes came to their well-protected priority targets, the closer our Lifeguard subs came to the critical areas where downed airmen, exposed to enemy revenge fire, depended upon them for their last chance of survival.

It was more than a duty to try to bring the zoomies home alive. It was a matter of pride which was shared by all hands. "We'll pick you up in Tokyo Bay!" was the boast. Hell—if their subs had been amphibious, those lads whom I was honored to call "mine" would have rolled up the slopes of Fujiyama to rescue survivors above the snowline—and thought nothing of it!

Tokyo Bay? But for a cautious Force Commander—meaning myself—who knew of its shallow water and the thickly dotted minefields and nets which guarded its dooryard, things might have been different. It might even have become a legendary doormat on which daredevil submarine Lifeguarders would write the word "Welcome" in large heartwarming letters for the benefit of airmen whose disabled planes could not defeat the force of gravity. But that would have been tempting Fate too far; therefore by orders, Tokyo Bay was "off limits" to submarines.

One of the finest pieces Ernie Pyle ever wrote about war, men, and courage was the story of Ensign R. L. Buchanan, a pilot from the carrier Cabot, who was fished out of the lower edge of Sagami Wan by the Pomfret and its stout-hearted crew under the leadership of its cool-headed skipper, Lieutenant Commander John Borden Hess.

Ernie Pyle passed away long before his time. Had he lived until that August day in 1945 when the Aspro pulled Captain E. H. Mikes off a rescue boat deep in the confines of Sagami Wan, he would, beyond any shadow of a doubt, have put that story on the Page One—Must spindle and called it the top-lead in the realm of stories that deal with self-sacrificing courage that is as beautiful and inspiring as it is daring and pulse-stirring.

The third of August began aboard the Aspro much as any other day had begun on this, its Seventh War Patrol. The rising sun found her surfaced east of O Shima Island, the Adam's apple of the crude head sketched by the east coast of Honshu.

At 0538 a starboard lookout saw a speck in the air toward the mainland. "Looks like a Zero," he observed to his partner on the port side and pointed with a well-gloved thumb.

"That's no Zero," sneered the other and older lookout. "It's a Pete... Betcha two bits."

"Whatever he is," said Jim Ashley, "he ain't ours. Clear the bridge."

Pete or no Pete, there was no percentage in letting him get a good fix on the sub's position. Besides, it was just about time for the Aspro's morning trim dive to check her buoyancy after the long night run.

"Take her down," called Ashley as the lookouts, still arguing about their two-bit bet disappeared down the hatch.

"How about that two bits?" whispered Bill Port.

"You're on," replied Johnny Starboard.

Three hours later, breakfast, change of watch, and other morning chores disposed of, the Aspro surfaced again and proceeded toward her assigned Lifeguard position for the day's Mustang strike on Tokyo.

At 0955, almost simultaneously the radar man and the after lookouts on the periscope shears reported plane contacts astern.

"Nice work, you lookouts," called Ashley. "Keep your eyes peeled. We'll need plenty sharp sky-watching today."

"Those look like our 'Dumbo' planes, Cap'n," said the OOD.

"Radio—call our 'Dumbos' on VHF."

"We have them, sir," came back the reply; "they hear us loud and clear."

A good augury for the day's performance.

This brace of B-17's—each with a large, parachute-equipped, and well-provisioned lifeboat slung under its belly—was on hand to search the seas for zoomies beyond the sub's visual range.

At a quarter past ten o'clock, mere minutes ahead of the thundering parade of bomb-carrying Tokyo-bound Mustang formations, came four playful Mustangs. After proper identification, they zoomed the Aspro's deck and soared into the sky to take up their positions as air-cover for the submarine.

"Looks like those boys had beans for breakfast," chuckled the OOD.

"Yes," agreed the Skipper, "and they will probably need 'em on a day like this."

And now, for all practical purposes, the Aspro was in business. All she needed was a customer or two. The strike was running its course. Soon the distant thunder of bombs told of Tokyo's agony. Hardened in the fires of war though they might be, I doubt that anyone ever heard this rumble of death without a twinge of pity in his heart... And some of those deaths would be among our own lads.

"God, what hell that must be," murmured the Quartermaster.

Now some of the Mustangs that had been among the early birds could be seen winging southward with empty bomb racks, bound for the home base.

A curly-haired radioman with a pair of outsized earphones clamped over his ears stuck his head up the hatch.

"Sir," he reported, "I just picked up a message over the VHF that a pilot has parachuted into Sagami Nada."

Sliding down the ladder from the bridge to the control tower, Ashley hastened to the plot table where his tracking team was already on the job with parallel rulers, pencils, and speed tables on a large-scale chart of Sagami Nada and Sagami Wan. Learning that the downed pilot's position was thought to be just inside the bay, the Skipper sent one of his "Dumbos" to investigate.

The report reached the Aspro at 1104. Only eleven minutes elapsed before the B-17 pilot reported that he had located the downed flier. "I dropped my boat. It landed near him right side up and the airman climbed aboard it—looks as if he is okay. His position, as I make it, is 35-11 north and 139-20 east."

"Roger," acknowledged Ashley, "and a nice job, 'Dumbo' One. Keep circling and we will go ahead full power. The position you have given us puts him much deeper into the bay than the first estimate placed him. Even if we can get that far in without being bombed all to hell, it will take us at least two hours to reach him."

Now came the long, tense run to the scene of the chuting. The Aspro ran at its highest possible speed while still retaining ballast water enough to permit an extra-fast crash dive. To blow all tanks dry in order to gain a knot or so of speed while practically running past the front gate of the Emperor's summer palace would have been too foolhardy—but how those minutes dragged!

On the bridge, eyes strained toward the horizon ahead and the skies above, the lookouts and bridge watch were pretty tense. Ashley, smiling inwardly, wondered what would happen if someone dropped a monkey wrench on the steel deck. "We'd probably all jump overboard," he decided.

To add to the Skipper's worries was the question of how far in he dared go. Were the inner waters mined against an invasion fleet? . . . Also, as the Aspro went deeper into the bay, she entered areas swept by shore radars of all descriptions—even civil-defense observation posts could pick her up. How long would it be before someone called out the home guard or the territorials?

It did not require a soothsayer to predict that it would not be long now—nor was it.

Shortly before noon, two B-24 Privateers took the places of the two B-17's. Not knowing how long the rescue operation would take, Ashley asked his new "Dumbos" to jettison their bombs in order to save gas. This was barely done when the air-cover fighters reported that they were low on fuel and would have to return to their base in a couple of hours.

"Hells bells," exploded Ashley to his Executive, "fuel, fuel, fuel. Nobody ever has enough gas. That's what gets me down on these missions. Even the 'Dumbos!' They are supposed to be able to fly to Hell and back—and yet even they never have more than a few hours of gas when they are on Lifeguard duty."

At noon the Aspro crossed the invisible line that divides Sagami Nada from Sagami Wan. Checking the chart, just to take his mind off his other troubles, Ashley saw that the depth beneath him was 579 fathoms. Anyway, if he had to duck and do it fast, he need not worry about hitting bottom.

When the Navigator gave him his noon position, Ashley gave voice to a low whistle. "Holy smoke, boy!" he ejaculated, "35-03 north and 139-27 east. Even Commodore Perry didn't get much deeper into Japanese water than we are going. And he didn't have to worry about Zeros or Zekes. Why, they even rolled out a red carpet for him."

To himself, Ashley carefully estimated the situation—and it did not look good. The Aspro was in a mighty vulnerable position and something was bound to happen soon. But I will wager that never for an instant did he wonder if it was not time to reverse course.

Somewhere in the dim distance to the northwest, the "Dumbos" stood guard and guide duty over a lone flier in a lifeboat. That lad, Ashley was determined, was not going to wind up in a Jap prison camp or dead from strafing bullets—not if the Aspro could prevent it.

High overhead, the Mustang air-cover followed the Aspro's course by flying in large and lazy circles. Between gritted teeth and speaking largely to himself, Ashley observed: "Here we are, sticking our necks out longer than a snapping turtle, and we've still got a mighty long way to go. But you know what they say about a turtle: he never gets anywhere until he sticks his neck out!"

As if some far-off force had been activated by Ashley's grim forebodings, several Rising Sun fighter planes stormed out of a cloud cover and attempted a surprise sweep upon the Mustangs. The latter, however, were not to be caught napping. With blazing guns, they rose to meet the enemy. The Aspro watched, hardly daring to breathe.

"Geez, pipe them Petes," whispered Mr. Starboard.

"Nuts," hissed Mr. Port. "They are Zeros! Betcha four bits!"

"You're on," answered Mr. Starboard.

Captain Ashley edged toward the diving alarm as the battle overhead developed into a full-fledged dogfight. It was almost like a blow to Jim's solar plexus when a Mustang tumbled screaming out of the sky, hit the water with an explosive crash, and vanished—pilot and all—in a column of smoke and flame about two thousand yards on the Aspro's starboard beam. No use looking for a survivor there.

Not a word was spoken in the group of six men that was crowded into the small space within the protection of the sub's tiny bridge. The moment the Zeros came into view, Ashley had ordered the four lookouts into the forward part of the bridge and had sent the OOD down into the conning tower. Thus he was in a position to make a lightning-fast dive if the Zeros attacked the sub.

Fortunately, the firepower of the two B-24's—which joined the battle as fast as their high-powered engines would let them—sent the Zeros into a hasty retreat. And none too soon. Had the dogfight lasted five minutes longer, the Mustangs might have been beyond the point of safe return. Nothing then to do but ditch—and the Aspro would have had three more mouths to feed. Luckily, the Zeros broke off the attack in time to let the Mustangs go home.

During the battle the sub stuck to its base course, and just before the fight ended, the straining eyes of the men on the bridge were rewarded by the sight of the survivor's boat on the northern horizon.

At 1256 the Mustangs winged homeward. At 1303 the "Dumbos" revved their fastest revs toward the zoomie who had now become the target of Zero bullets.

"Hey," shouted Ashley to his radioman, "tell those Privateers to chase those flies away from our zoomie. We haven't come this far just to lose him."

No sooner said than done. The B-24's, their forward guns clacking like giant castanets, dashed toward the Zeros who made knots for safer territory the moment the bombers were within range.

The degree of respect entertained by the Zeros toward the heavier firepower of the B-24's was obviously high. They pulled off into the distance as the Aspro crowded on every bit of power her engines could produce. The day was warm. The sun shone brightly and yet the brows and bodies of the men on the bridge were wet with cold sweat.

A starboard lookout cried: "Pete on starboard beam! He's heading our way."

"Tell the 'Dumbos' to drive him off," ordered the Skipper. "It'll take more than a threat to drive us down now. I want two men of our rescue team to stand by in the conning tower, ready on an instant's notice to get on deck and pull that zoomie in."

"Aye, aye, sir," answered the Executive. "They're there now and ready."

By now the two "Dumbos" had returned from chasing the Pete out of bombing position. They flew as if fixed on a merry-go-round with the Aspro in the center of the circle. Tilted high and almost standing on their left wingtips to prevent skidding, they roared past the sub at a height of less than one hundred feet above the deck.

It seemed as if a big blunt wingtip might wipe off a periscope at almost any moment. And the racket, the terrific roar of eight powerful motors swinging eight mighty props, produced an earsplitting mixture of howling, drumming, whining, and exploding sounds—a concert such as one might hear on Doomsday when the gates of Hell swing wide to admit the hordes of the damned.

But to the men on the Aspro whose ears, faces, bodies, and brains were being clouted by blasts of propeller-driven air, as well as the engine noises, it was supremely beautiful music. Wide grins spread over their grotesquely windblown faces.

At 1318 the Aspro approached the boat with the bridge 20-mm gun ready to discourage interference. "All engines, back full!" the Skipper shouted preliminary to coming to a dead stop alongside the boat. "Stop all engines!"

Quickly executed, the order brought the Aspro drifting gently toward the boat whose sole passenger—a badly sunburned young man in a torn and bloody shirt under his yellow life jacket—was standing, ready to jump aboard the sub, the sweetest looking ship he had ever seen.

The Pete selected that split second to start a new bombing run. Although the sub's 20-mm gun squirted long streams of bullets at him, the Pete kept coming. Tracers showed hits in the left wing... But still he came.

Although the B-24's were crowding the Jap off toward the sub's bow from its original position on the beam, the risk of remaining on the surface in the face of even one bomb was too great.

"Clear the bridge. Take her down!" shouted Ashley.

No one had to be told that this was urgent, even if the Skipper's voice was under good control. As they tumbled down the ladder, heads and shoulders of the men on the way down took a beating from the clumping feet of those trying to get below the lip of that conning tower hatch.

Because the Aspro was virtually dead in the water, all the Diving Officer could do was to open vents, scream for flank speed, flood negative, and pray for survival.

Clearing the bridge may have broken all records, but the dive itself, if anyone remembered to time it, was probably the slowest in the Aspro's log book—and God knows it seemed several slow-moving eternities before water gurgled over the deck and the depth gauges seemed to awake and show some interest.

The thoughts of that zoomie in the lifeboat, thus abandoned to the tender mercies of the Pete, defy my imagination. In fact, it is probably fortunate that they were not recorded.

The Aspro needed at least five hundred tons of sea water to fill her various ballast tanks. Only then would she have enough weight to do her aquatic vanishing act. Being under way helps a sub fill her tanks, and she also can take advantage of the planing effect of the deck and the bow planes. In a stationary dive, she sinks slowly, like a sponge absorbing water.

While the submarine completed its much too gradual dive, two loud, dear, close explosions bounced off the Aspro's hull. A rapid periscope peek revealed that the Pete, through ruse or bold speed, had broken through the B-24 defenses.

For that Jap to get through the combined opposition of the two "Dumbos" made him a contender for the Luckiest-Man-Alive Cup. But some Japs had plenty of luck, pluck, and skill. This one did—while it lasted.

Diving and dodging, he had dumped two bombs from an altitude of about eight hundred feet. They fell some one hundred feet short on the Aspro's starboard bow when the sub was at a depth of twenty-five feet.

1320! Only two minutes since this part of the show had begun. It seemed ages. "Up periscope," called Jim Ashley as he bent forward to catch the eye piece on its way up.

The ship's Talker, standing at his Skipper's side, leaned forward as if hoping to share the view. When Ashley spoke, the Talker repeated the words so that they could be heard throughout the silent ship.

"Tell all hands," said Ashley, "that I got the scope up just in time to see that Pete crash in a cloud of smoke and fire about a mile off to port."

A ragged cheer ran through the ship. Unless he was very hard of hearing, even the man on the lifeboat must have heard it.

A longer look through the periscope revealed the B-24's circling above the sub and the zoomie sitting quietly in his boat, watching the ocean as if wondering what might come next.

"Down periscope!"

Pausing briefly and rubbing his well-shaven chin with his right hand, Ashley was about to give order to surface when he reconsidered, took the ship's microphone, and spoke to all hands: "I need not tell you that we are in a very tight corner. Even if we rescue this downed aviator, we still have a tough row to hoe in getting out of this bay into open water. Everything—our lives and the safety of the ship—depends on every man being on his toes—knowing and doing his job instantly.

"We have been seen and reported by Zeros and Petes and there's bound to be more where they came from. We have lost our fighter air-cover and pretty soon we will be minus even our 'Dumbos.' Not too good. But that's the way the cards lie and that's the way we'll play them. Stand by to surface again, and when we are surfaced, I'll be the only man to go on the bridge. Lookouts and bridge watch stand by for orders in the control room and conning tower."

He took a reflective pull on his cigarette and continued: "On that last dive we were caught with our diapers dangling and that could really have been our last one. I do not want us to be caught again under the same circumstances. It could be fatal! . . . Sound three blasts."

The Chief of the Boat stood at Ashley's side as the vessel surfaced. The moment the depth gauge showed twenty-five feet, thus indicating the conning tower hatch was out of water, the Chief spun the wheel that released the dogs of the hatch. Up it popped like a manhole cover in a seagoing sewer pipe, a deluge of water poured down, and up through it went the Skipper.

At first glance all looked serene. The "Dumbos" were circling. The zoomie waved a hand in friendly greeting as he paddled toward the sub. All quiet... Then suddenly the serenity was shattered by the screaming howl of a Pete coming toward the sub in a steep dive from high altitude.

"All ahead full! Take her down!" yelled Ashley as he headed for the hatch. He needed forward momentum to get into a quick dive.

The sub's motors hummed and she surged forward.

The Aspro's log records that all this action, from the time the Skipper hit the bridge until he hit the conning tower deck going down, took exactly one second! Even allowing for someone's stopwatch being wrong, that should be a birdie for the course.

Down through the hatch he went. The Chief pulled the lanyard, twirled the wheel, and dogged the hatch cover above Ashley.

"Up scope," the latter whispered as he knelt in front of the Number One periscope with its high-magnification attack lens.

1327-01: The Aspro dove.

1327-40: Two bombs exploded as the Aspro passed forty-five feet.

Things looked pretty grim aboard the sub at this point. That was one solid fact the Talker did not need to impress upon his captive audience. They knew it. But the news Ashley handed out from his position before the periscope was more encouraging. "Tell all hands that the 'Dumbos' are splashing the Pete that just bombed us. And they are doing a magnificent job of returning that pilot to his honorable ancestors."

A grim chuckle followed by silence. Ashley was trying to decide what to do. He was tempted to continue his submerged run toward the open sea—let the Japs pick the zoomie up.

This business was too big a gamble. Hazarding a whole ship and her crew for the sake of one man was too much to expect... But could he do that? Could he face his crew afterward? Could he hand out a death sentence to that young flier in the lifeboat? Could he forever after live in peace with himself?

Then decision came in a flash—and he had known all the time what it must be!

"Down periscope!"

He knew that, for the mere sake of safety, he could not let his ship and his shipmates down—nor that poor devil up in the lifeboat.

"Right full rudder. Reverse course," he ordered firmly.

When the ship was headed back for the lifeboat, the zoomie could be seen paddling toward the periscope. That helped considerably. That boy was keen to get aboard.

"When we surface—if all is clear as it is now—a rescue party of two men will follow me on deck."

After a careful search of sea and sky from a depth of forty feet, Ashley asked the B-24's by VHF if it was safe to surface.

The reply, a little hesitant, was: "We believe so—at this moment, anyway. We just splashed another Jap and no other Pete has come out to take his place—as yet."

At 1344 the Aspro surfaced. At 1345 Captain E. H. Mikes, USAF, was aboard—and averred that he was "Glad to be aboard" in traditional seagoing fashion.

This done, Ashley told the "Dumbos" that they could go home. The jubilant bomber boys really started reaching for altitude. Sea level is no place for heavy bombers.

Down in the conning tower the sub's radar screen showed clear. So Ashley went ahead full speed. He hoped to get at least a few miles behind him before he was driven down by a fresh string of enemy planes. If the Aspro submerged now, she would still be in the bay when she surfaced at dark.

1348: Radar contact at six and one-half miles and closing.

1348-02: Crash dived to one hundred feet. No bombs. No bullets. Their new shipmate, Captain Mikes, was in good condition. His left arm had been grazed by a strafing bullet and his boat and both life rings had been riddled. It is a miracle how they missed him.

Five uneventful hours slipped by when the Aspro, back on the surface and making good time, saw a patrol boat astern. She escaped it through evasive action. After dark, she sighted searchlights sweeping the surface, but they were far astern, far to the north of the Aspro.

"Well," said Mr. Starboard to Mr. Port over a cup of Java in the crew's mess room, "from now on I'll remember a Pete when I see it."

"Yeah," replied Mr. Port, "but don't forget the six bits you owe me for being wrong."

Six bits for being wrong on the subject of Petes and Zeros—a very low cost indeed. Men have died because of such ignorance.

0525: Dived.

0930: Held divine services.

1036: Surfaced on Lifeguard station for Mustang strike today. So begins the log of August 5, 1945, of the Aspro at the start of its last week on Lifeguard duty during its Seventh War Patrol in Japanese waters.

To those of my readers who may be surprised at the mention of divine service aboard a submarine, may I say that this was not unusual at all. All Navy vessels carry the standard Navy Prayer Book; hence they are equipped for spiritual emergencies—including the burial of the dead. The captain usually officiated at church service, but in some submarines others led the devotions.

I made a trip on one submarine whose chaplain—so-called—was a Torpedoman. This trip from Pearl Harbor to Midway Island, according to my wartime diary, began on July 20, 1944, aboard the Paddle, commanded by Lieutenant Commander R. H. (Bob) Rice.

The Paddle was on her way to the East China Sea and I was merely a relaxing passenger as far as Midway. When I learned about their "Padre" and had talked to him, I looked forward to Sunday with special interest. Sunday came, and after breakfast, services were held in the forward torpedo room.

There was a well-arranged program of hymns, prayers, and sermon—all conducted by a tall, rather gangling twenty-one-year-old, a highly intelligent and devout Negro who hailed from Mississippi. Although not ordained, he had, he told me, been the minister of a congregation in his home town before he enlisted in the Navy.

To the crew of the Paddle he was known as "Padre." He was extremely well liked and his services were usually attended by all hands from Captain down, except those who were on duty.

On some submarines, such as the Paddle, a crew member looked after religious services week after week during patrols. On other subs, various individual submariners would volunteer to prepare and conduct services from week to week. None of the services was denominational and their make-up was usually quite simple. As a rule, the singing was highly inspiring. On boats that carried men who were musically inclined the singing would be accompanied by instruments ranging from harmonicas to accordions.

On the Haddock, for instance, the Captain, Commander Roy Davenport, a very devout and sincere Christian, conducted divine services and led the music with his well-known and justly famous trombone.

On other vessels the atmosphere of solemnity would be set by the playing of appropriate music on the record player. Speaking for myself, I have always found it particularly stirring to attend divine services aboard a submarine. They are usually held in the forward torpedo room. Here all hands make themselves as comfortable as they can, sitting on or leaning against the reserve torpedoes, and if the ship is submerged as the men are gathered in prayer, the solemn silence that prevails throughout a submerged submarine lends added spiritual impact to the occasion.

Through this spectacularly inspiring demonstration of courage and seamanship, the Aspro takes her place high among the ships that won undying fame by service along the gun-studded coast, under the plane-infested skies of the sinister maritime portals to Tokyo Bay. Why our Lifeguards were attacked by so few enemy torpedoes, I will never understand. At that particular time, Japan had scores and scores of midget submarines designed for coast defense.

So far, in this history, we have mentioned a few of the submarines that ventured into Sagami Nada. There were others; and because of the highly dangerous character of their work, their valor deserves attention here.

As evidence of how deadly the waters of this area could be, there is the experience that befell the Perch on its Seventh War Patrol. Commanded by Lieutenant Commander Charles I. McCall, a native of New York, she was on Lifeguard duty along the east coast of Honshu in the close vicinity of Tokyo Bay entrance. The date was August 13, 1945, just the day before Admiral Nimitz signaled "Cease fire."

In the afternoon, on learning that three men were adrift on a raft in Tokyo's inner bay, the Perch turned her own two covering fighters over to a PBY amphibious rescue plane so that it could perform a hit-and-run, in-and-out mission that a submarine could not stage. The planes left at 1350 and returned at 1530, when the PBY reported that this almost unprecedented and terribly dangerous mission had been accomplished.

The lives of three American fighting men were saved. These heaven-blessed lads were Ensign Brega with two crewmen, Proudfit and Warehime. Hardly had this been accomplished before news came that two additional fliers were in a life raft inside Tokyo Bay. Again a PBY was hurried to the rescue, and fighter planes of the Perch's air-cover were again dispatched to accompany it. When they arrived at the reported position of the downed fliers, no life raft was in sight. The flying boat remained to circle the position while the fighters circled the bay in search of the missing raft. Suddenly the fighters received a frantic message for help from the PBY. The pilot said he was being attacked by Jap fighters... Then silence.

When, a few minutes later, the fighters reached the rescue plane's position, they found mute proof of tragedy in the form of airplane wreckage on the sea. There were no survivors. Not even empty rafts.

Said the log of the Perch: "Words cannot express the sadness we all felt that this brave crew had met disaster."

God knows that that brief entry is far too laconic to describe the tragedy which had taken place and the heroism of this unnamed PBY crew who entered heavily guarded Tokyo Bay in a lightly armed plane in an attempt to save the lives of their fellow men... May God rest their gallant souls.

PROPAGANDA POSTER FOR PLANNED INVASION OF JAPAN

24 - A-BOMB CHANGES WAR PLANS

THERE WAS BUT ONE TOPIC OF CONVERSATION, only one subject on which solitary ponderings centered, among members of my staff at Comsubpac Headquarters on the verdant island of Guam during those sun-burnished and moon-beamed dog-days of early August 1945. That was the combined Army, Navy, Marine, and Air Corps assaults in which General MacArthur and Fleet Admiral Nimitz were to weld their respective commands into a massive invasion force. The mightiest armada of men, ships, and machines ever mustered in the Pacific, it was designed to pommel, invade, and conquer the Japanese home islands.

The opening gambits had been made in the huge Pacific chess game: pawns (such as Guadalcanal, New Guinea, and the Malay Barrier) and the much more valuable court-pieces (such as the Philippines, Saipan, Guam, Iwo Jima, and Okinawa) had been swept off the board. Now had come the time for battle to the death among castles, queens, and kings.

The first of these mighty blows, coded as "Operation Olympic," called for severing the southernmost island, Kyushu, from its two northern sisters by a terrific attack from both coasts on Nov. 1, 1945. Going ashore in the landing craft that day would be thirteen American divisions of the Army and Marines, and a grim percentage of those men would never come back, never again see that Golden Gate through which most of them had sailed westward—their symbol of home and beloved faces.

The second and final crushing blow—coded as "Operation Coronet"—demanded no less than twenty-five divisions. This avalanche of man and firepower was to fall on the Tokyo plain in March 1946.

Already the opening presentation of American planning had been made in the closely guarded, king-sized Quonset hut theatre atop Cincpac (Commander-in-Chief Pacific) Hill on the island of Guam by Lieutenant General Southerland, Chief of Staff for General MacArthur, and by Rear Admiral Forrest Sherman, Chief of Plans for Admiral Nimitz. Huge charts showed assembly ports, supporting airfields, and landing beaches. Tasks were delegated to Fleet and Force Commanders.

To the Submarine Force was assigned the job of charting all minefields in invasion areas, as well as equipping and providing submarines to serve as radar pickets to protect against enemy air strikes and kamikazes. These, as the world will never forget, had produced terrific tolls of death and destruction among our destroyers and surface patrol vessels at Okinawa.

Last, but not least, submarines were to provide an almost unlimited number of ships for the Lifeguard League. This last phase—rescue plans to save downed aviators—was my onerous but not unwelcome responsibility.

To ensure optimum co-ordination, we had placed liaison officers—ex-submarine skippers—with the Army and Navy Air Forces in the Philippines, at Iwo Jima, and at Okinawa.

Almost all submarines then at sea were on stations where their primary duty was Lifeguarding.

The about-face of submarines from killers and destroyers to rescuers and good Samaritans had been taking place progressively since the Skate put on her star performance at Wake in October 1943. As enemy ships—men-of-war or cargo carriers—were scuttled by American submarine torpedoes and aircraft bombs, the submarine changed from an instrument of death to an implement of life.

Therefore, aboard the Holland—which was my home, headquarters, and flagship—Topic One during those August days and nights of 1945 was Operation Olympic and, within its frame, our increased Lifeguarding responsibilities. We worked on the problem singly or in groups around the clock, and we took it with us to table when mess calls were sounded for breakfast, lunch, and dinner.

When we sat down to dinner in the cabin of the Holland in the quiet evening twilight of August 5, 1945, Captain C. Q. Wright, skipper of the flagship, sat opposite me.

He had cut his eye teeth in the early "pig boats" and, in World War One, had had a misadventure with a British transport, which in a fog mistook his O-class submarine for a Hun U-Boat and ventilated C.Q.'s conning tower with two quick twelve-pounder hits before the sub could dive.

Other occupants of the white-covered chairs around the table that night were Captain Bill Irvin and Commanders John Corbus, Barney Sieglaff, Walter Griffith, and Bub Ward.

Commander Bob Kaufmann, the Flag Lieutenant, was our most junior member; a fine pinch-hitter in any department. We sat in companionable silence as the steward and mess boys filled water glasses and deftly set plates before us. All my staff members were combat-tested submariners whose combined bag of sunken enemy ships mounted high in our records. Usually our spirits were high with wisecracks and banter from the irrepressible Bill Irvin and his cohorts.

Frequently, with lamentable lack of respect for my three stars and gray hair, I was on the receiving end of their jokes. But during that period of high-pressure planning, all hands were preoccupied by the demanding problems of our heavy responsibilities. It was neither the time nor the atmosphere for wisecracks.

True, it looked as if the end of the war was in sight. But the road to victory might be a long and heartbreaking trail, and many a good man, perhaps some of those seated around our table that very night, might never live to see that end. Nor even live to see the fruit of the planning they tackled with such effective vigor.

No one could predict whether final conquest of the home islands would force the surrender of large Japanese forces in Korea and Manchuria. Mopping up might take a long time...

And so, as we sat down to dinner that night, our thoughts were a bit on the nostalgic, questioning side in spite of the many cheering factors in our problems.

These 1945 August days I speak about were days devoted to expanding our fleet of FM Sonar-equipped submarines—the electronic Hellsbells which had enabled our nine Hellcats to penetrate the minefields of Tsushima Strait in June of that year—an electronic discovery which Admiral Halsey regarded as a made-to-order item for reconnoitering and charting the minefields along the Pacific coastlines of the Japanese home islands.

Such charts would enable American troops to invade Japan after Nippon's shore defenses had been bombed and shelled to ruins. They were days devoted to studying the distribution of submarines to cut whatever the Hellcats had left dangling of Japanese lifelines from Korea; days devoted to speeding up the installation of new SV radar for aircraft detection on submarines selected as pickets; days devoted to planning the new and elaborate set-up of submarines assigned to the Lifeguard League.

However, this particular date of August 5 was of considerable importance to us at Subpac HQ because, on the morrow, the aircraft carriers, Task Force 38, under Vice Admiral J. S. McCain, were scheduled to strike Kyushu for the first of a series of softening-up bombings which could be expected to continue until the troops hit the beaches in Operation Olympic.

In support of that strike we had stationed four submarines close in along the target shorelines to rescue aviators, some of whom would inevitably be shot down or forced to bail out in enemy waters.

I had just turned to John Corbus—my Operations Officer—to ask if all Lifeguard submarines had reported that they were on assigned stations, when my attention was attracted to one of our young communications officers. He was standing in the doorway of the cabin holding out a message board. There was nothing remarkable in this procedure. Top Secret communications, hot off the decoding machines, arrived at all hours of the day or night.

My orders were that they must be delivered to me or to the next senior officer on board before the ink had dried. The thing that struck me most forcibly about the officer's appearance was the expression on the youngster's face.

It was a portrait of complete bewilderment, intense curiosity, and deep concern—so compelling that I halted my question to John in mid-passage, replaced untasted a forkful of the cabin steward's best spam-hash, and braced myself for the crisis which I felt the message must contain.

Incidentally, our communication officers were a remarkable group of ensigns and junior grade lieutenants who stood watch round the clock in the oven-hot communication center of the old Holland amidst the chatter of radio keys, electric coding machines, and teletypes.

No matter how stifling the air or how many urgent priority messages were stacked up, I had never seen one of them lose his aplomb or the precision of his diction. They were a corps delete, and so security-conscious had the Navy become that each of them—and my staff and myself as well—had been required to take an oath never to reveal Top Secret material or any of the devious means by which we gained vital bits of intelligence. They carried their responsibility most seriously, and normally no

Grenadier Guard at Buckingham Palace gates could have been more imperturbable.

Hence, when the young lieutenant hurried to my place fairly stammering, "Admiral, this is urgent!" I was prepared for anything from a major naval disaster to the entry of Russia into the Pacific war on the side of Japan.

Heads went up all around the table. The mess boys stopped in their tracks while Irvin, Corbus, Sieglaff, and Ward, on whose capable shoulders would fall the job of taking instant steps to meet any crisis, converged quickly at my end of the table.

I stared at the message and then wonderingly read it aloud:

"From Commander-in-Chief, Pacific, to Commander Third Fleet and Commander Submarines: Scheduled carrier air strike cancelled. Retire all ships and lifeguard submarines one hundred miles from the coasts of Kyushu and southern Honshu prior 2400 (midnight) this date."

I am sure that when I looked up from reading this dispatch, my face was just a blank and just as puzzled as were those around the table. It was not unusual to have an air strike cancelled—usually because of predicted bad weather conditions in the target area.

But why pull our ships back one hundred miles from the strike area? Had Hirohito surrendered? Had the enemy produced some fabulous secret weapon—a death ray—against which we had no defense? Had Cincpac's Headquarters staff suddenly gone off its rocker?

"What the—?" asked Barney, of no one in particular.

"Well, I'll be—" muttered mystified Bub Ward. "And we have two boats in those waters charting minefields."

Always practical, and right on the ball, as befitted the top-notch Communications Officer that he was, Bill Irvin brought us back from our puzzled gropings: "Whatever it means, sir, it will take fast work to pull those ships back a hundred miles!"

"Right you are, Bill," I answered. "We will execute the order first and hold our guessing bee afterward. Let's have a look at the Operations chart." Turning to Ward, I continued, "And, Bub, after dinner call away the barge and get up to Cincpac H.Q. fast. This new play, whatever it is, may require considerable rearrangement of stations in a day or so. Find out what it's all about and, also, when we can put the subs back on the job."

"Aye, aye, sir," replied Bub who, instead of continuing with the meal, asked the Officer of the Deck to call away the staff speedboat. "It's faster than the Admiral's barge," he explained.

"I'll get dinner later!" he added with a cherubic grin at me—and was gone.

"Hot, straight, and normal," said Barney Sieglaff, referring to the true torpedoman's dream of a "fish" making a beeline for its target, "that's Bub Ward."

With a nod, I led the way to the Operations Room—guarded by a sentry and the painted warning on its door denying entrance to all except Operations Staff—where a huge chart of the home islands of Japan and their surrounding submarine patrol areas covered the entire starboard side of the bulkhead.

Dotting its steel-backed surface were some dozens of tiny magnetized silhouettes, each marking the position of an American submarine. Some of these guarded the flyways of the Army B-29's from Guam to the Empire. Other subs were charting minefields along the coasts of Kyushu and Honshu and some were spotted at the most likely points where aviators from McCain's carriers might be picked up on the morrow.

A quick glance at the chart showed which submarines we would have to pull back in compliance with the mystery order. In no time at all, Captain Bill Irvin began dictating messages to the electric coding machine operator; Commander Barney Sieglaff reset the picture on the chart; and presently we had the necessary urgent dispatches on their way.

I tried to picture the bewilderment of their recipients—but failed. As we stood back from the chart to view the new setup, it certainly looked curious—actually as if our submarines were fleeing from the coasts of Kyushu and southern Honshu; as though the Devil himself, or the plague, were behind them! Plague? Was it possible the enemy was initiating some sort of gas or germ warfare?

Could be. But anyway, Bub Ward was a good scouter and he would soon be back with all the news. So, we waited, more or less impatiently.

With the messages underway, Bub Ward at Admiral Nimitz's office, and everything done that we could do to carry out the strange set of orders, I went out on the Holland's boat-deck, which stretched dark and silent along the length of the ship. Only the stars, twinkling through an overcast sky, lit the scene as I stood at the venerable old submarine tender's rail and let my thoughts drift out past the breakwater that protects Apra's harbor—and up along Guam's rugged coastline that stretches north-northeast from where I stood puffing on my pipe.

Dinner? . . . Oh, dinner could wait! My mind was crowded by a jumbled traffic of stray thoughts struggling for attention. Confusion . . . speculation . . . guesswork caused by this peculiar order to pull back. Reflections. . . ponderings . . . recollections dealing with this new business of lifesaving in submarine operations.

The startling fact that during the few short weeks of May, June, and July 1945, submarines, dozens of them—and often under heroic circumstances—had saved the lives of some 247 aviators who otherwise would almost certainly have met death by drowning, exposure, enemy strafing, or sharks. Through the Lifeguard League, the submarine had indeed entered upon a new kind of business—and big business, at that!

As they acquired "night vision," my eyes subconsciously strove to pick up the hazy outlines of rugged Orote Point at the harbor entrance and the rising foothills that framed the surf-beaten coast. And presently, even before I was aware of it, my thoughts had jumped the short gap—less than a dozen miles—to Agana Bay where but one year previously a young American carrier pilot was rescued by a submarine while under enemy fire.

In those early island-hopping days the technique of Lifeguarding by submarines was relatively new. Yet it had progressed to a point where the bomb-pitted, shell-blasted beaches of Agana Bay witnessed one of the few periscope rescues on record—a spectacular exhibition of superior seamanship. This was the stage on which the Stingray played the thrilling part which we have already described.

My reverie was interrupted by one of the younger officers who hurried up to where I stood at the rail of the Holland's boat-deck, saluted, and said: "Admiral, Commander Ward has returned from Cincpac Hill and is looking for you. He's in the Operations Room."

I strode quickly back to my hot and humid headquarters office. There I found Commander Ward. As expected, he was back from the headquarters of Admiral Nimitz within the hour. But, contrary to our expectations, he had no information whatever.

"Sorry, sir," and there was genuine regret in Bub's voice, "but I could not get a line on anything. They wouldn't explain why our subs had to be pulled back a hundred miles. In fact, they wouldn't even talk to me. Mum is the word and I would have to be at least a three-star admiral tonight before that gang would even give me the time of day. Sorry, sir!"

"Oh, well," I replied, "we've done all we can. Sufficient unto the day is the evil thereof."

For a moment I toyed with the idea of telephoning Admiral Nimitz but dismissed it. I would ask him in the morning at our regular nine o'clock conference. However, I did not have to wait that long to receive the much-sought answer. It came on the morning of August 6, just before the conference hour, in a message that read: "The Commander-in-Chief, Pacific, informs all forces, ships, and stations that an atom bomb has been dropped on Hiroshima!"

A new era in warfare had begun. We had lived to see the opening of the atomic age... Will the limitless power thus brought into the world be used for good or for evil?

The blasted Genbaku Dome, Hiroshima

25 - Lifeguard Earns Hearty Well Done!"

THE CURTAIN FELL ON THE LAST SCENE of the last act of World War 2 at a time when the great forces of American military strength of land, sea, and air were being marshalled to deal the final crushing blows to our enemies through Operations Olympic and Coronet.

At 2304 of August 14, Fleet Admiral Chester W. Nimitz, Commander-in-Chief, Pacific Fleet and Pacific Ocean Areas, issued the following cease fire order: "Cease offensive operations against Japanese forces. Continue searches and patrols. Maintain defensive and internal security measures at highest level and beware of treachery or last-moment attacks by enemy forces or individuals."

American bases all over the Pacific Ocean areas, which had hardly noted the arrival and passing of VE Day, pulled out all the stops for the celebration of Armistice Day in the Pacific. Whistles and sirens blew themselves hoarse, ships' bells rang till they threatened to crack, fire hoses spurted joyful fountains into the air. Very pistol stars, signal rockets, and even five-inch star shells added their color and din to the riot of sound that enveloped ships and bases.

The Armistice came as a surprise to most of us. Japan's sudden collapse was not anticipated, even in the higher command echelons. But to each of us who knew of the plans for the final assault on the Japanese homeland and of the thousands of American fighting men who would lose their lives therein, came only one grateful and reverent thought: "Thank God, it's all over."

And with that prayer of thankfulness came memories, faces of friends, shipmates, gallant men of gallant ships, who would never come sailing home again, for whom all wars were over forever.

Fifty-two submarines with 374 officers and 3,131 enlisted men were the price which the submarines had paid for victory. That, for a war which, except for the insane desire for power and aggrandizement of the enemy High Command, would, never have been fought at all, was a high price indeed.

It was in this spirit of thankfulness and sorrow that I sent out my own Victory Message:

"The long-awaited day has come and cease firing has been sounded. As Force Commander I desire to congratulate each and every officer and man of the Allied Submarine Forces upon a job superbly well done. My admiration for your daring, skill, initiative, determination, and loyalty cannot be adequately expressed. Whether you fought in enemy waters or sweated at bases or in tenders, you have contributed to the end which has this day been achieved. You deserve the lasting peace which we all hope has been won for future generations. May God rest the gallant souls of those missing and presumed lost."

With the coming of peace came the end of all combat activities, including plans for a greatly enlarged program for the Lifeguard League.

Twenty-two submarines were on Lifeguard stations on the last day of the war. Except for those in the Sea of Japan which had run through the enemy minefields in Tsushima Strait to cut the last remaining supply lines to the Empire, submarines had practically no duties other than Lifeguarding. The seas had been swept clean and submarines formed a tight blockading ring completely around the Empire.

True, we were preparing twenty-four subs to act as radar pickets for the Fleet in the forthcoming invasions, and others were charting enemy minefields along the coasts of Japan to assist those same operations, but those activities were in effect an extension of Lifeguarding. Submarines had been almost completely metamorphosed from killers to lifesavers, and, for the first time in military or naval history, a combat team of tremendous power and competence had been assigned to missions that were entirely designed to save the lives of comrades in arms.

From its very inception, the Lifeguard League—unique and unparalleled in the annals of war—built a framework for cooperation between submarines and fighting aircraft which not only saved hundreds of lives and boosted morale but is available for infinite variations and far greater exploration in operations of the future. It was never a perfect machine, but with the improved communication facilities of today, its potential value is high indeed.

From the time regularly organized Lifeguarding began, until Lifeguarding ended, eighty-six submarines performed a total of 504 rescues. A few submarines were lucky enough to bring in fairly large numbers of fly-fly boys, but the vast majority of them counted themselves fortunate to bring home one, two, or three zoomies.

A remarkable and gratifying thing which came out of the Lifeguard League is the knowledge that most of the perhaps ten thousand submariners who took part in rescues of airmen considered this duty, despite its obvious dangers, as a privilege and an honor. Many friendships, born of these meetings under desperate circumstances, between pigboat sailors and zoomies will endure throughout their lifetimes.

After the war ended, I requested Admiral Nimitz' permission to send a tender and twelve of the nearest submarines into Tokyo Bay, as representatives of the Submarine Forces, to witness a surrender ceremony which some 3,500 of our lads had given their lives to help bring about. The Admiral agreed that we had had a large stake in this game, and it was so ordered.

Lifeguard duty brought personnel reactions that varied with the type of Lifeguarding performed. Universally the submariners enjoyed Lifeguarding for carrier strikes. These strikes, which lasted two or three days at the maximum, were jam-packed with thrills for the submariners.

They had ringside seats for real heavyweight slugging matches. They saw the bombs drop and the explosions; they watched dogfights in the air; they listened in on the attack frequencies and heard the pilots discussing their attacks and reporting their results, and they rightfully felt that they were playing an important part in the work in progress.

On the other hand, sitting around on an empty ocean under empty skies waiting for the land-based bombers was thoroughly disliked. That was boredom with a capital B. Eternal communications difficulties between Comsubpac and the air commands concerned put obstacles in the way of smooth operation. Invariably, important information on last-minute cancellations of strikes would not reach the Lifeguard League until several hours after a strike was scheduled to take place. Consequently, submarines spent many a long hour sitting on the surface in enemy waters Lifeguarding for strikes that never occurred.

The importance of accurate weather reports was emphasized by the fact that often Lifeguard submarines, enjoying beautiful sunshine and clear skies, would receive word that a certain strike had been cancelled because of bad terminal weather. Beginning early in the phase of the war when bomber strikes were plastering the Empire, submarines added periodical weather reports to their other daily chores.

As in the British Navy, so the submariners in Uncle Sam's fleet have had to win their way to acceptance and understanding. In the olden days of naval battles, Death was an honorable fellow who approached his victims in the open with cannons roaring, sails set, banners spanking the breeze, and bright-colored signal flags fluttering from yardarms. With the introduction of submarines, Death changed not only his appearance but his manners. He became an invisible hit-and-run opponent who skulked in the deep, sneaked in under cover of night, sank vessels with torpedoes that ran as silently as sharks—and finally ran from the fight and hid in the deep, dark womb of the sea.

Being, as I was for many years, a submariner of fairly ancient vintage serving in a branch of the service that is relatively new, I know from first-hand experience the difficulties we have had in convincing our own seniors and brother officers not only of the great striking power and utility of submarines, but also of their legality as weapons of war. True, they do not exercise the time-honored formality of visit and search of ships at sea, but neither does a moored or floating mine. True, they may take the lives of non-combatants, but so do bombs dropped on cities by aircraft.

We must face the fact that modern war is total war and, once declared, the aim is to destroy your enemy as quickly as possible with the least possible loss of your own personnel and property. Thousands of non-combatant men, women, and children will be destroyed, but that is a calculated risk which governments must compute before declaring war.

After convincing our own Service, the next job was to convince the Army, Marines, Air Forces, and civilians that we did not, in the sense of moral values, live on the wrong side of the tracks.

Even as late as the start of World War Two, submarines were a thing apart to a lot of people who should have known better—

mean and sinister weapons, a necessary branch of the service that had to be tolerated.

Not that they failed to appreciate the sinking of enemy tonnage and warships by the subs. It was nice to have vessels around who could do the dirty work swiftly and well. But it was not until submarines made themselves felt as vessels of mercy and up-builders of morale that the attitude of our sister-services became one of friendly and warmhearted respect.

As the Lifeguard League grew in numbers and increased its operational scope, fraternal roots were put down. They grew between rescuees and rescuers and then, by word of mouth as time went by, these roots spread throughout the entire military structure. If there was any one thing that made the dangers and sacrifices of Lifeguarding worthwhile—a complete payoff for all the costly individual contributions made by submariners, high and low—it was the warm and sincere gratitude that sprang from those it benefited, directly as well as indirectly.

In the files of Comsubpac were many letters of appreciation and other testimonials of gratitude. Some of these messages referred to deeds of daring performed by Rear Admiral Jimmy Fife's submarines of the Seventh Fleet—sometimes called General MacArthur's Navy. Messages from carriers regarding the work of the Skate and the Tang have been quoted elsewhere in these pages.

From Admirals Halsey and McCain, following the two weeks spent by the Third Fleet in bombarding the home islands of the Empire, came this welcome message: "Following received from Comtask Force 38 (Vice Admiral McCain). Quote. Once more convey the heartfelt thanks of Task Force 38 to Comsubpac submarines. Unquote. To which I wish to add my appreciation for the excellent services of the Lifeguard League—Halsey."

Other dispatches typical of the favorable reactions within different commands on the subject of Lifeguarding include:

A message from General MacArthur regarding the rescue staged by Commander Paul C. Stimson and his men aboard the Sea Robin: "I wish to extend my sincere appreciation for your efforts in effecting the rescue of Lieutenant Alfred N. Royal. The presence of submarines adds materially to the morale of the Far East Air Forces combat crews, and has resulted in increased effectiveness of our operations."

A gratifying signal from the Commander of Task Force 93 and the Deputy Commander of the 20th Army Air Force: "The courage, cooperation, and untiring efforts of the officers and men in submarines on Lifeguard duty has contributed immeasurably to the morale of combat crews and to the success of our superfortress and Mustang operations over the Empire. To all a well-done. Good luck in our continued operations."

Another "To all submariners" was issued by the Commander of the Carrier Force of Task Force 58: "Again TF 58 is indebted to submarines for wholehearted support. Your efforts enabled us to do extensive damage. Your daring rescues earn our deepest gratitude. Thanks."

And the Kingfish received this tribute from the Commander of the Task Force 57: "Your highly efficient rescue work recently carried out in behalf of our downed aviators is greatly appreciated. We are very grateful for the excellent care they received subsequent to their rescue."

And, of course, never to be forgotten is Admiral Marc A. Mitscher's typically laconic comment on the occasion when the submarine Sea Devil, commanded by Commander R. E. Styles, quietly and as a matter of routine reported the rescue of three Marine fliers from the Essex: "Maybe it is routine for you fellows, but your rescue of our Marines is considered quite extraordinary in this force. Many thanks."

I could cover several more pages with testimonials of this kind. Suppose I close the flow of grateful and deeply appreciated messages by quoting the following letter from General Nathan F. Twining, until recently Chief of Air Force but, when he wrote the letter in 1945, Commanding General of the Twentieth Air Force:

"I wish to take this opportunity to express personal and official appreciation to you and your command for the splendid air-sea rescue job you did for the Twenty-First Bomber Command and the Twentieth Air Force. From the beginning of operations, we were impressed with the interest and enthusiasm you put into your Lifeguard work, and the persistent efforts you made to improve the operational procedures and equipment involved. In my opinion your efforts went beyond any routine assumption of an assigned responsibility.

"I am told that your submarines picked up 131 of our B-29 aircrewmen from twenty-two aircraft, and that you manned for us 490 separate Lifeguard stations. I feel sure that these rescues will furnish some of the most inspiring history of this war. But even this impressive total of men saved does not tell the whole story. There is no way to evaluate the boost in morale that came to our aircrews from the knowledge that your submarines guarded the routes to and from their targets.

"Your staff has always reflected your own personal interest in air-sea rescue, and I wish to convey my appreciation to them. I would particularly like to commend Captain R. G. Voge, Captain W. D. Irvin, Commander N. G. Ward, Commander R. W. Laing, Commander H. Cassedy, and Commander J. A. Adkins. These men, from the beginning of our operations from Saipan on November 24, 1944, to our final mission on August 14, 1945, gave unstintingly of their time and energies, and showed the utmost of cooperation in working out common problems."

These words of high praise from the men who count were most welcome to me and to all submarine Lifeguards because they showed that coordination can be achieved between the several services—something that must be done if unification is to work in any future war.

Likewise, these messages gave the lie to the oft-repeated cynicism that aviators are expendable. The commanders who wrote those communications held the lives of their airmen very close to their hearts and left no stone unturned to ensure that they had not only the best weapons to fight with but also the best chance of coming back alive.

I experienced only two cases wherein hard-boiled Air Generals were lukewarm or refused to cooperate. Perhaps I did not present the case well enough. Their names are of no importance now.

And so comes to a close this too brief and too incomplete saga of the lifesaving submarines. In writing these chapters from the book of their experiences, it was impossible to include accounts of all the vessels that performed so valiantly. The job was, primarily, to select instances that were representative in forming an overall picture of the Lifeguard League so that in time to come it will be remembered that the men of the Silent Service of the sea were faithful to that keynote of the Old Testament, namely that every man is his brother's keeper.

This tenet was held high and true by the men of our ships of mercy for, in extending the hands that snatched doomed men from death, they saved both friends and foes.

An entire decade has passed since the last lookout on the last Lifeguard mission sang out: "Zoomie bearing three-five-one. Distance 1500 yards." Followed by the Skipper's command: "All ahead flank; course three-five-one." And how often this was succeeded almost instantly by the shout: "Plane coming in low. Bearing 185. Range six miles."

What would it be? Friend or foe? And, if a friend, would it recognize the sub as American or line up for a bombing run?

That was always a most vital question during those exciting, blood stirring days of Zoomies, Subs, and Zeros.

THE END

Made in the USA
San Bernardino, CA
05 May 2019